Figures of Memory

Figures of Memory

Poetry, Space, and the Past

Charles I. Armstrong

palgrave
macmillan

First published 2009 by
PALGRAVE MACMILLAN

Palgrave Macmillan in the UK is an imprint of Macmillan Publishers Limited, registered in England, company number 785998, of Houndmills, Basingstoke, Hampshire RG21 6XS.

Palgrave Macmillan in the US is a division of St Martin's Press LLC, 175 Fifth Avenue, New York, NY 10010.

Palgrave Macmillan is the global academic imprint of the above companies and has companies and representatives throughout the world.

Palgrave® and Macmillan® are registered trademarks in the United States, the United Kingdom, Europe and other countries.

ISBN-13: 978-0-230-22353-0 hardback
ISBN-10: 0-230-22353-2 hardback

This book is printed on paper suitable for recycling and made from fully managed and sustained forest sources. Logging, pulping and manufacturing processes are expected to conform to the environmental regulations of the country of origin.

A catalogue record for this book is available from the British Library.

A catalog record of this book is available from the Library of Congress

10 9 8 7 6 5 4 3 2 1
18 17 16 15 14 13 12 11 10 09

Printed and bound in Great Britain by
CPI Antony Rowe, Chippenham and Eastbourne

To my parents, Richard and Hazel

Contents

Acknowledgements

Thanks are due to the Department of Foreign Languages, at the University of Bergen, for financial support. Part of this text was written while I was a post-doctoral fellow, financed by the Faculty of the Humanities (Historisk-Filosofisk fakultet) at the University of Bergen. Other sections were written while I was a visiting scholar at the Centre for Irish Studies at the National University of Ireland, Galway. During an early phase of this work, I spent a year at Wolfson College, University of Cambridge, as a research fellow.

I am very grateful to my colleague Stuart Sillars, who – apart from unceasingly encouraging and assisting me along the way – read a draft of the manuscript, giving invaluable feedback. In addition, I would like to give special thanks to two valued colleagues, both scholars of English-language poetry, namely Ruben Moi and Janne Stigen Drangsholt. I'm indebted to both colleagues and students working at what until recently was known as the English department of the University of Bergen for providing the everyday environment that made this study possible: Randi Koppen, Anne Holden Rønning, Zeljka Svrljuga, and Orm Øverland have been particularly helpful with detailed feedback. Nessa Cronin, Sean Crosson, Tadhg Foley, Anne Karhio, and Maureen O'Connor all helped make my stay at NUI-Galway both inspiring and productive, while Charles Moseley and Clive Wilmer were of gracious assistance during my sabbatical in Cambridge. Irene Gilsenan Nordin and other members of the Nordic Irish Studies Network have provided me with a forum that has been of steadily increasing importance for my work. For various acts of kindness and criticism, I also extend warm thanks to Morten Auklend, Peter Fjågesund, Gunilla Florby, Asbjørn Grønstad, Margaret Mills Harper, Jeremy Hawthorne, Kari Jegerstedt, Robert McFarlane, Anthony Mellors, Ellen Mortensen, Ingrid Nielsen, Gisle Selnes, and Jill Walker. Thanks are due to staff at Palgrave Macmillan, most notably the editors Paula Kennedy and Steven Hall. Last but not least, my sincere thanks go to friends and family for their unfailing support. I'm deeply grateful to my beloved wife, Inger M. Stoveland, who has given me far more than can be expressed here. This book is dedicated to my parents, two Irish emigrants whose ability to share their personal and collective pasts with my siblings and me has never excluded a firm commitment to the present and a solicitous eye to the future.

An early version of the third section of chapter 2 has appeared as ' "This Wide Whisper Round My Head": *In Memoriam* and the Complexity of Memory,' in *Nordic Journal of English Studies*, 2004, vol. 3(3), 241–262.

The author and publishers are grateful to the following for permission to reproduce copyright material:

Carcanet for extracts from *New Collected Poems* by Eavan Boland (2005) and extracts from *Domestic Violence* by Eavan Boland (2007). Faber and Faber for extracts from *The English Auden: Poems, Essays and Dramatic Writings 1927–1939*, edited by Edward Mendelson, by W. H. Auden; extracts from *The Complete Poems and Plays* by T. S. Eliot; extracts from *Death of a Naturalist, North, Station Island, Seeing Things, The Spirit Level, Electric Light,* and *District and Circle* by Seamus Heaney; and extracts from *The Thing in The Gap-Stone Stile, Dart,* and *Woods etc.* by Alice Oswald. An excerpt from 'September 1, 1939' by W. H. Auden is reproduced electronically by permission of Curtis Brown Ltd. Excerpts from 'Ash Wednesday' in *Collected Poems 1909–1962* by T. S. Eliot, copyright 1936 by Harcourt, Inc. and renewed 1964 by T. S. Eliot, reprinted by permission of Houghton Mifflin Harcourt Publishing Company. Excerpts from 'Burnt Norton' in *Four Quartets* by T. S. Eliot, copyright 1936 by Harcourt, Inc. and renewed 1964 by T. S. Eliot, reprinted by permission of the publisher. Excerpts from 'East Coker' in *Four Quartets*, copyright 1940 by T. S. Eliot and renewed 1968 by Esme Valerie Eliot, reprinted by permission of Houghton Mifflin Harcourt Publishing Company. Excerpts from 'The Dry Salvages' in *Four Quartets*, copyright 1941 by T. S. Eliot and renewed 1969 by Esme Valerie Eliot, reprinted by permission of Houghton Mifflin Harcourt Publishing Company. Excerpts from 'Little Gidding' in *Four Quartets*, copyright 1942 by T. S. Eliot and renewed 1970 by Esme Valerie Eliot, reprinted by permission of Houghton Mifflin Harcourt Publishing Company. Excerpts from 'The Naming of Cats' in *Old Possum's Book of Practical Cats*, copyright 1939 by T. S. Eliot and renewed 1967 by Esme Valerie Eliot, reprinted by permission of Houghton Mifflin Harcourt Publishing Company. Excerpts from *The Thing in the Gap-Stone Stile, Dart,* and *Woods etc.* are reprinted by permission of United Agents on behalf of Alice Oswald ©, as printed in the original volumes. J. H. Prynne for extracts from *Poems* (2nd enl. ed, Freemantle (WA): Freemantle Arts Centre Press, Tarset (Northumbria, UK): Bloodaxe Books, 2005). Copyright © J. H. Prynne 2005.

Every effort has been made to trace the copyright holders but if any have been inadvertently overlooked the publishers will be pleased to make the necessary arrangement at the first opportunity.

1
Introduction:
The Returns of the Past

Memory has a tendency to harass us, reminding us of things we'd like to forget. When we do yield to the pleasures of the past, suspicion arises about our being overly self-indulgent – nostalgic, in short. Alternatively, we only really think of memory when it fails: especially in light of the vast archives available in print and in virtual form, forgetting is today so much more conspicuous a phenomenon than the routinely successful acts of recollection on which we base our everyday lives. Little wonder, then, that memory is often derided and belittled. Not only does it have a reputation for being a simple faculty, copying rather than imaginatively enhancing experience, but also its link to the past is often unfashionable in light of modernity's cult of the future and demand for constant innovation.

A poetry of the memory would seem to be, at best, something tame and ultimately self-contradictory – for is not *poiesis* an act of creation? At worst, it might seem an imposition blocking the way for more fruitful engagements with time or space. Given such assumptions, it is perhaps not surprising that almost all of the poetry addressed in this book will be shown to be fleeing from some or another conception of memory. Even central poets such as Thomas Hardy and Alfred, Lord Tennyson – who not only are figures of memory in the sense of being canonical figures of our literary tradition, but also understood themselves as essentially concerned with the past – were trying to escape from the stranglehold of memory.

Yet even if such poets turn away from recollection and the weight of the past, they almost invariably return to it soon after. This will be shown, in this study, in readings of ten English and Irish poets of the two last centuries. In various eras, poets will be demonstrated as rejecting one conception of memory, only to embrace another. Their itineraries

1

can thus be said to trace, in general terms, a similar departure from, and return to, memory – even if the site or conception with which they end up is subtly different from where they started. While nineteenth century poets such as William Wordsworth and Christina Rossetti will be seen to distance themselves from ideas of memory as a simple act of copying the past, they will do so in order to expand and complicate our idea of what memory can be. Other poets will be subsequently shown as resisting Victorian schemas of memory that were conceived of as being overly nostalgic, only to insist upon forms of remembering that involve a firm – if unsettling – sense of situating oneself in a specific place. With literary modernism, poetry's link to a personal past becomes a *bête noire* to be avoided and derided, yet modernist poets still return to a notion of personal memory that is bolstered by the underlying system of a particularly elaborate form of spatial structure. Finally, it will be demonstrated that contemporary poets are not finished with the business of ridding themselves of the past. Either through escaping memory altogether through immersion into forms of spatiality linked with the present or future, or through politically motivated revisions of existing traditions, the poets of today also have a problem with memory – and yet they cannot avoid embracing a revised sense of memory in their attempts to diversify and challenge our understanding of poetry.

A majority of the poets covered in this study are central figures in any account of poetry's history over the last two hundred years, and are therefore already part of a more or less established canon. Yet this will not be a simple affirmation or solidifying of that canon: although central continuities will be noted, important individual differences between the poets, as well as more large-scale changes, will be scrutinized. Both breakdowns of memory and discontinuities in tradition will be traced, in this study, as they become apparent against a backdrop of forceful attempts to unify and control temporal assemblages. Rather than affirming memory's transparency or naturalness, I will address the mystery and multiplicity of poetry's dealings with the past. In doing so, I will confront what Richard Terdiman has termed the 'memory crisis' of modernity, which shows itself in a pervasive anxiety about the value and efficacy of memory.[1] Yet where Terdiman intentionally and explicitly neglects what he terms 'the moment of stabilization' in favour of 'the moment of contingency',[2] generally privileging symptoms over responses to crisis, I will seek to give an extensive account of the exploratory and affirmative responses poets have made to this problem. Memory's challenge does not necessarily find its final issue in a state of anxiety or impasse. Crisis frequently leads to critique, as many of the poets addressed here will be seen to develop their own conceptions of memory via critical acts whereby reigning or clearly insufficient models are contested or revised. Problematical issues concerning recollection may also provoke a productive state of wonder at the mysteriousness of the workings of memory, and in some cases new configurations issue out of this wonder. A key mystery concerns the question: how are present and past capable of being meaningfully linked together? David Farrell Krell has presented the problem in the following manner:

> If memory's objects are not of the present, what is it that becomes present, comes to presence, or presents itself when we remember? ... Remembrance thus poses an ontological paradox and even 'impasse' as it allows what is past to become present *as* past, transposing us – sometimes faithfully, sometimes not – to what is no longer that which is.[3]

It was a version of this ontological paradox or aporia (addressed via the difficult coexistence of remembering and forgetting) that led Saint Augustine to exclaim: 'I do not understand the power of memory that is in myself, although without it I could not even speak of myself.'[4]

If we do not really know what memory is, then not only the metaphors stemming from philosophers such as Augustine, but also those of poets, can aid our understanding of this phenomenon. A major interest will therefore be the scrutiny of particular metaphors used by the poets studied, in order to bring out their heuristic value – or how figurative language is employed in a way that avoids ignoring the irreducible qualities of memory. This will be one of the ways in which this book pursues 'figures of memory', strongly at odds with how Paul de Man's version of deconstruction led to a long-term severance of tropology and epistemology.[5] Prevailing accounts of memory are challenged, and in some cases enriched, due to the figural inventiveness with which poets formulate our encounters with the past. William Wordsworth's comparison of memory to a dim abode of distant winds; Alfred, Lord Tennyson's organizing of his memories of Hallam according to the structure of a graveyard; T. S. Eliot's understanding of withheld personal memories as constituting something like an underground; J. H. Prynne's linking of memory to the metonymical structure of a never-ending song: all of these tropological manoeuvres, and many more, will be interpreted in the pages that follow in terms of what they tell us about the workings of recollection. If memory turns in different directions during the process of literary history, it is to a large part due to the constantly renewed twists and turns it is subjected to by the tropology (from the Greek *tropos*, meaning 'a turn') of poetry.

An important and recurring figure will be that of the organically unified body: from Wordsworth and onwards, memory is consistently grasped by poets of the British Isles as a construction that attempts to unify a group of disparate elements into a larger, dynamic whole. By comparing memory to organic unities, these poets find a way of articulating a desired sense of coherence and permanence. But organicism is not a model without its flaws and internal problems: multiplicity constantly tends to derail or obstruct poetic attempts at organic cohesion, as the latter neither stills the anxiety nor fully satisfies the wonderment awakened by memory's mysterious status. Frequently, this shows itself through figurings of memory in terms of metonymic rather than metaphoric relations. Furthermore, there are different models at work: the organic metaphor will be differently deployed in, say, Wordsworth's comparison of the self to organic unity than in the case when Eliot compares literary tradition to a similar structure. A more radical encounter with difference is announced towards the end of this study: if Seamus Heaney uses organicism to construct unitary accounts of memory, contemporaries of his such as Alice Oswald and Prynne have been more willing to explore broken or fragmented models – in some cases even attempting to eschew temporality in favour of a purely spatial form of writing.

Being attuned to the multiple models and uses of memory helps us bring in a wider reach of concerns than, say, a genre study of the poetic elegy. A key thesis of this book will be that poetry's use of the past takes place in the intersection between different kinds of memory. As Nicholas Dames has pointed out, 'the methodologies involved in a pursuit of human remembrance remain opaque, unsystematized, and persistently (if productively) chaotic. No strong consensus yet exists about the boundaries, forms, and contents of a study of memory.'[6] Scholarly work on nineteenth century memory has unearthed conflicts between mentalistic approaches and more objectifying ones based on the methods of the natural sciences. Yet today, as has been demonstrated by Paul Ricoeur's *Memory, History, Forgetting*, the field embraces an even greater diversity of types of memory.[7] Only by detailing the interaction and conflicts between these various forms of dealing with the past can a truly nuanced account of the vicissitudes of poetic memory be brought to view. One important distinction has already been briefly touched upon: i.e., that between the individual memory of Wordsworth (famous, say, from the 'Intimations' ode) and the collective memory of

Eliot's 'Tradition and the Individual Talent'. In modern poetry, an act of memory is often presented as something undertaken by a solitary being. Frequently, that being will be identified with the poet, and there will be some (implicit or explicit) distance between the poet's written identity and the autobiographical background of that individual's private life. Both autobiographical and more exclusively 'aesthetic' memories will be interpreted in this book, and some of the problems concerning their interaction and distinction will be addressed.

Both of these kinds of memory – aesthetic and autobiographical – can be differentiated from collective acts of memory, where either an individual primarily remembers on behalf of a group or a group's shared past is understood as having a virtual existence that can be summoned through particular symbols or monuments. Recent accounts of collective memory, though, have typically understood it as being particularly closely linked to space. Particularly the recent French *lieux de memoire* project has alerted us to the fact that collective memory is spatially articulated. According to Pierre Nora's provocative dichotomy, 'Memory fastens upon sites, whereas history fastens upon events.'[8] Tradition typically consecrates places, making them mediating symbols where the present can come in touch with the past. Ideally, this is not a static process: 'It is also clear that *lieux de mémoire* thrive only because of their capacity for change, their ability to resurrect old meanings and generate new ones along with new and unforeseeable connections (that is what makes them exciting).'[9] Many of my readings will fasten onto sites of memory: this is most decisively the case in Chapter 3, which looks at the importance of place in poems by Tennyson, Hardy, and Yeats.

Although places in many cases supply an important setting for the use of poetic memory, place itself can be deployed less as a concrete site and more as a figural resource – more, one might say, in terms of an abstract space than a specific place. Often, though, the difference between these poetical strategies can be marginal. While the focus on organicism as a meta-metaphor involves a more abstract notion of space (memory compared to the spatial articulation of a living body) than the focus on memory sites such as Ben Bulben in Yeats's poetry or the river Dart for Alice Oswald, in both of these latter two cases we have a fundamental imbrication of spatiality and temporality. Thus figurality becomes, fundamentally, a meeting place for memory and spatial extension. Despite Henri Bergson's philosophical strictures on all spatializing of time, this study will show that poets have been making a virtue of this connection over the last two centuries.

The following chapters present a roughly chronological series of readings, all focusing on the role of memory for important poets and poems from England and Ireland. Chapter 2 raises fundamental issues that will recur later on, including the question of how poets seek to circumscribe or control the multiplicity of finitude through acts of mourning. While Wordsworth stresses memory's role in the constitution of personal identity, an opening towards the other occurs in his poetry, which challenges solely 'self-centred' accounts of memory. Wordsworth's open-ended questioning also leads to a fundamental vacillation regarding memory's relationship to language and perceptual images: both the word and the eye are shown to provide relevant, though not sufficient, figures for memory. In the same chapter, Christina Rossetti's 'Song ("When I Am Dead My Dearest")' and Tennyson's *In Memoriam* are read in terms of their complicated negotiations of mourning. Rossetti's renunciation of mourning and the rituals of death is shown to be a contradictory affair, both inviting and resisting remembrance. In his elegy, Tennyson musters up organicism's disciplining and assimilating power to prevent being overwhelmed by grief and the riches of memory, but this gesture is shown to be at least partially undermined by the semi-autonomous nature of the poem's personal memories, as well as other textual evidence of what Tennyson called the 'indigestions of the brain'.[10]

Chapter 3 explores three uses of western regions of England and Ireland as privileged sites of memory, each reading questioning Victorian nostalgia or its heritage in a different manner. The reading of Tennyson's *Idylls of the King* addresses the ontology of the memory-image, and shows how the innerness of memory is supplemented in ambivalent ways by the apparent solidity of external space and collective recollection. Next, Hardy's 'Poems of 1912–13' is interpreted in light of the Cornwall setting of the sequence, as I argue that the area's associations with Arthurian romance provide Hardy with an apposite context for his affirmation of loss and the impossibility of re-experiencing the past as fully present. The third and final reading of Chapter 3 teases out some of the heritages hovering around the margins of William Butler Yeats's grand act of self-commemoration in 'Under Ben Bulben', making use of biographical and contextual evidence to contradict the monological and transcendental tenor of Yeats's postcolonial linking of place, self, and recollection.

In Chapter 4, I address two instances of how modernism's attempts to leave personal memory behind are subsequently abandoned. The first section provides a reading of perhaps the most influential of all statements on the role of tradition in the poetry of the British Isles, namely

T. S. Eliot's essay 'Tradition and the Individual Talent'. Countering reductive readings of this text with an account of the richness of its use of organic resources, I nevertheless show – by tracing the development of Eliot's structural thought on to *Four Quartets* – how Eliot's early dismissal of a Wordsworthian form of personal memory was overly emphatic. Subsequently, my reading of Seamus Heaney takes its bearings in his expression, during the 1980s, of a desire for a new modernism. Heaney's attempt to break out of the mainstream of twentieth century poetry on the British Isles is shown to be self-contradictory and lacking radicalness, even while evincing a rich and rewarding deployment of mnemonic resources.

Chapter 5 contains a trio of readings that confront challenges to memory in contemporary poetry. Eavan Boland is read in terms of a feminist critique of literary tradition, which also brings with it an attempted revision of the link between figurality (primarily addressed through the emblem) and poetic memory. The contemporary avant-garde is approached via the poetry and poetics of J. H. Prynne, who – despite showing leanings towards a spatial aesthetics primarily directed towards the future – formulates an alternative account of an open-ended, metonymical form of memory. Finally, Alice Oswald is interpreted as a representative of ecopoetry. While her short lyrics embrace an isolated present as a way of circumventing the technical rationality blamed for the environmental crisis, her longer poem *Dart* shows that memory and history can be of use in articulating the temporality of a limited, mortal form of subjectivity emphatically situated in a natural environment.

The latter, concluding interpretations of contemporary poets all involve a questioning of subjectivity in one form or another – but in this particular respect they comply (if in a radicalized manner) with the main gist of this study. If memory is indeed an irritating and disquieting topic for us today, insofar as we do not give in to the wistful pleasure of nostalgia, this is perhaps also one of its main virtues. Like an underestimated insect or threatened species, it is certainly far more valuable than we might want to think. The poetry addressed in this book will show that memory may bolster and support the self in various and frequently enlightening ways, but it is also a factor that tends to repeatedly upset the complacent bulwarks we build around ourselves. Through engaging fruitfully – but also often despairingly – with the challenges of recollection, we are not only reminded of the limitations and blindnesses of human subjectivity, but also encouraged to engage less reservedly in the great ocean of signs, objects, and places into which memory constantly thrusts us. Indeed, it also leads us to return to our very understanding of the past in a ceaseless process of reinterpretation and recalibration, which further enables us to face, once more, that which is to come. It is, in short, not the least of memory's gifts that it returns us, again and again, to the future.

2
Multiplicity and Mourning: Wordsworth, Christina Rossetti, Tennyson

Can there be anything more immediate, more direct than memory, save perhaps perception itself? Memory, for some, conjures up a relation of plenitude and referential straightforwardness. Through giving us access to the past, it restores us to that which is given, the concrete data of perceptual experience as they are yielded up by the world. Artists who paint or draw from memory give us respite from the abstraction and conceptual obscurity of modern art. Similarly, poets of memory avoid the complications and inventive waywardness of the imagination, returning us to the thing itself. Penetrating to the heart of a time period or place, they are the conscience, or purveyor of truth, that is the *desideratum* of every community. In times to come, it is implicitly or explicitly claimed, such remembering poets will be able to tell future readers how it really was.

Such a naïve understanding of poetical memory will be contradicted throughout this study. Memory's figures quite simply present a more complex, more demanding, challenge than the straightforwardly mimetic account lets on. In this chapter, three poets – William Wordsworth, Christina Rossetti, and Alfred, Lord Tennyson – will be read in terms of the obstacles with which their poetical uses of memory grapple, and in terms of the challenges they hand down to their readers. In each case, multiplicity rather than unity will be the result of acts of poetic memory. In my reading of Wordsworth, which will primarily focus on *The Prelude*, having recourse to the past will be shown to expose identity to otherness and language to a manifold of figural concretions. Although apparently a refusal of memory – specifically, of mourning – Rossetti's 'Song ("When I Am Dead, My Dearest")' opens itself up to a conflicting diversity of critical reconstructions of its relation to recollection, due to its lack of a single, unequivocal framing context. Differing autonomous, feminist, and Christian interpretations are enabled by the poem's ambivalent stance with regard to memory. Lastly, Tennyson's *In Memoriam* will be shown to seek, with limited success, to control the burden of commemoration through fetishism (the text as a substitute object) as well as the abstract spatiality of a scheme of organic maturation.

A 'dim abode in distant winds': Wordsworth's precedent

Since Wordsworth is one of the most celebrated figures in the history of English literature, every year sees the arrival of a spate of academic books, articles, and other dealings with his memory; a mass increasing with an effortless ease that seems to suggest that recollection, in this case at least, is automatic and painless. Yet the opposite is arguably just as true: Wordsworth is subject to so much scrutiny precisely because he is hard to assimilate into any collective or institutionalized memory. Remembering Wordsworth is a complex and challenging endeavour, and, if we ever tend to forget the resistance inherent in this challenge, we need only consult the poet's own writings: for remembering, he tells us, is a mysterious thing. This is paradoxical, since Wordsworth's poetry takes its point of departure in what broadly speaking is a demythologized world. With the Enlightenment questioning of traditional religious truths, a momentous shift of paradigms occurs in which the self is thrust into the very centre of the realms of discourse and epistemology. Wordsworth's poetical self takes this position as its starting point, and fortifies it against flux and mutability through the cohesiveness of personal memory. The resulting sense of identity brings with it a radical sense of being mortal, but also the desire for a transcendence of that finitude. Sceptical readings – particularly those made by Paul de Man – have argued the impossibility of such transcendence, returning Wordsworth to the ironies of an inescapable finitude that is linguistic in its essence.

Whether one adheres to this scepticism, or on the contrary follows Harold Bloom in stressing the potency of the Wordsworthian self, this poet becomes an exemplary inaugurator of the modern, even as he tries to escape from its quandaries. Yet such a historical canonization of his poetry is fraught with perils and unanswered questions. Recent historicist readings have reframed the study of Wordsworth in terms of an intensely and irreducibly personal context, transforming his position from that of exemplarity to eccentricity. Such an approach entails questioning the general sweep of overzealous history writing with the specificities of lived life and materiality, in a particularizing gesture which understands itself as working against the grain of Wordsworth's texts. The poet's attempts to fortify the transcendental and the spiritual in an age of increasing materialism and mechanization has to be reduced to an ideological smokescreen diverting attention from Wordsworth's own parochialism, political opportunism, and professional and personal anxiety.

Remembering Wordsworth in such a fashion is to reveal the repressed of his poetry, bringing forward the 'political unconscious' (as Fredric Jameson's influential precedent would have it) of history underlying the text.[1] It is to return his memory to its original, pre-ideological data – whether those data are understood as atomic facts, class affiliations, or more dynamic and shifting social energies. To engage in this hermeneutics of suspicion is itself a practice of memory: this is memory as *mimesis* or reproduction, something which becomes especially blatant when the act of reproduction is made in the name of the kind of objective facts characteristic of neopositivistic biography. As an example of the latter, one might cite Kenneth Johnston's attempt to locate the 'hidden' Wordsworth which is uncovered once one 'shows how deeply Wordsworth's poetry and metaphors are grounded in his life'.[2]

Although Johnston has made some forays into political critique of Wordsworth, later work has been more apologetic, vaguely excusing the poet's more controversial political manoeuvres by appeals to common human fallibility. This tendency is shared by a number of recent critics – among whom David Bromwich is particularly prominent – who have reacted against the denunciatory excesses of New Historicists and Cultural materialists following in the footsteps of Jerome McGann's critique of the 'romantic ideology'.[3] Rather than demystifying Wordsworth from some exalted vantage point presumably removed from the errors of ideology, Johnston and his ilk declare the poet to be one of us: a talented, yet also essentially human and fallible being. With such a gesture, Wordsworth is returned to a common humanity more representative of Enlightenment ideals than any subsequent critical or historical questioning. As a consequence, recollection becomes a translucent and seamless activity, since Wordsworth and the past are understood to be essentially continuous with our own present. The alterity of history is elided into a night, or day, where all is luminously transparent. Such an approach to history and memory is, however, not that of Wordsworth himself. What happens when one returns to the texts, rather than reduces them to historical source material? The very question of a 'source' (and a 'material') becomes problematical. Memory is necessary yet endlessly problematical in Wordsworth: it is an elusive process that invites specification, yet endlessly skirts it.

Contrary to the mentioned approaches, then, I want to insist upon the inscrutability of the understanding of temporality opened up by Wordsworth. Memory is neither a matter simply of the self, of language, or of ideology: it is a complex and variegated figuration of time *within* time, which resists any single delimitation or specification. It is mysterious and multiple. It is not fortuitous that Wordsworth's career commences on the eve of a century that saw the apogee of empiricism. The empiricist dismissal of innate ideas and timeless truths grants the concept of experience new validity and urgency. Nothing is known apart from what is experienced. The liberating effect of this postulate is, however, coupled with more alarming consequences: if experience is all, what becomes of the self? The self itself is only accessible through experience, and in time. The notion of a timeless soul is debunked, and all that remains is a personal self that survives, or is dissolved, in time. Locke draws the important conclusion that this self is given cohesion through acts of memory: 'as far as this consciousness can be extended backwards to any past action or thought, so far reaches the identity of that person.'[4]

Wordsworth will inherit the empiricist notion of identity, but with important modifications. For it is not enough to relate the past to the present: a special form of link is needed for identity to be at all meaningful. Here a parallel can be drawn to Jorge Luis Borges's famous short story 'Funes the Memorious', which illustrates, among other things, how unstructured a mere cataloguing of personal memories would be. The final reflection of this story's narrator on the gift of Ireneo Funes, a character blessed with a prodigious and unerring memory, signals towards this risk:

> With no effort, he had learned English, French, Portuguese and Latin. I suspect, however, that he was not very capable of thought. To think is to forget differences, generalize, make abstractions. In the teeming world of Funes, there were only details, almost immediate in their presence.[5]

Unlike the hyperempiricism of Funes, Wordsworth wants to attain unities and generalities through his acts of memory. Unlike Locke,

Wordsworth does not just want to link the episodes of his life together in an accidental chain of contiguous events; he wants his 'days to be / Bound each to each by natural piety'.[6] A life has to be vitalized and centred – in short, it has to be an organic rather than mechanical unity, a meaningful narrative with 'invisible links' (I, 639),[7] rather than a mere assembly of disparate perceptions. Crucial texts such as 'Tintern Abbey' and the 'Intimations' ode are struggles to convey meaningful progression in the face of both the vacancies and ravages of time. Binding together experience in a unity circum-vents vacancy, while the ravages of temporality are to be dismissed through the establishment of the continuity of vitality and presence through time. This organic structuring of memory will prove to be an important precedent followed by most of the poets later discussed in this study.

The famous pronouncement on the vivifying 'spots of time' is a pro-grammatic statement of Wordsworth's tendency to orient his life struc-turally around a series of centres.[8] The rarefied experience of a spot of time is of course a secularization of the religious epiphany, but it is formulated via the idealist notion of self-consciousness (in the form of what Schelling and Fichte called an 'intellectual intuition') as providing an absolute basis. Self-consciousness is explicitly granted a central role in Wordsworth's myth of memory:

> Such minds are truly from the Deity,
> For they are powers; and hence the highest bliss
> That can be known is theirs – the consciousness
> Of whom they are, habitually infused
> Through every image, and through every thought,
> And all impressions.
>
> (XIII, 106–111)

Memory becomes a storehouse of such grounding experiences. Yet the metaphor should not deceive: this is not a static and unalterable store-house. Thus the past gradually loses its vividness over time: 'I see by glimpses now,' Wordsworth writes, 'when age comes on / May scarcely see at all' (XI, 337–338). New instances of self-consciousness through memory, or other compensatory glories, must continuously be recap-tured. Unlike many of his recent New Historicist readers, who have tended to focus on the French Revolution as the exclusive referent of his texts, Wordsworth's understanding of temporality is profoundly historical, i.e., it is essentially related to flux and ephemerality. There is no single, privileged moment that does not require supplementation. This is why there are *several* spots of time, rather than just one central event to be remembered. Through this need for repetition, the poet's version of revelatory experience differs significantly from religious experiences of epiphany or conversion. Yet another religious phenomenon comes close to what Wordsworth is after: namely, the ritual. The spots of time are related to ritual, in that these two phenomena share a recurring need for confirmation of the numinous harmony of existence.

Certainly the unity of life established through memory has its own idiosyncratic motivation in Wordsworth, a motivation that in some respects leads him to horizons and questions quite foreign to the empiricist heritage on which he bases himself. Partly, this difference stems from his sense of a poetical vocation. For not only does Wordsworth consider himself a poet, he also understands that poetical vocation to be uniquely tied to the workings of memory, as his much-cited comment in the preface to *Lyrical Ballads* makes clear:

> I have said that Poetry is the spontaneous overflow of powerful feelings: it takes its origin from emotion recollected in tranquillity: the emotion is contemplated till by a species of reaction the tranquillity gradually disappears, and an emotion, kindred to that which before was the subject of contemplation, is gradually produced, and does itself actually exist in the mind.[9]

Wordsworth's largest completed effort of autobiographically recollective verse, *The Prelude*, is ostensibly written in order to justify his undertaking the *Recluse* project: it is to prove that he is not only an individual called to be a poet, but a poet who is capable of an absolute undertaking.

Read this way, Wordsworth's early poems of memory transcend the confines of the limited question of personal memory and point toward the radical heteronomy of genius. He becomes a poet not primarily confronting time, but rather going beyond that toward what he on one occasion calls his 'unconscious intercourse / With the eternal beauty' (I, 589–590). Eternity, rather than a form of being in time, becomes the poet's concern. This tendency underlies the title of 'Intimations of Immortality', and the turn to Platonic *anamnesis* in the controversial fifth part of the ode. There, birth is presented as being an event entailing 'sleep and forgetting' (58), an occlusion of the eternity that precedes it. Yet 'Not in entire forgetfulness ... do we come' (lines 62 and 64), for worldly amnesia can be revoked by the recollections of genius, liberating us from the prison-house of our mortality. In a later and circuitous note to the poem, Wordsworth remonstrated against readings that over-emphasized this borrowing of what he called 'an ingredient' or 'notion' of 'Platonic philosophy'.[10] Can one borrow a thought from a philosopher as one borrows an ingredient from a recipe? Or does something of the whole dish survive in a garnish? Be that as it may, Wordsworth – if we take his note at its word, and do not opt to read the contradiction in terms of a change in opinion – wants us to remember *somewhat* like Plato, yet forgetting what Plato meant. Thus Robert Langbaum's comment about *The Prelude* is justified also with regard to the specific problem of memory: Wordsworth is indeed 'both Lockean and anti-Lockean at the same time'.[11]

Geoffrey Hartman has been important in directing attention to Wordsworth's implicit scepticism towards his own constructed life-narrative. Temporal continuity is fissured by breaks and obstacles that render any projected organic unity perilous at best. Hence the death of a young child in the 'Boy of Winander' episode of *The Prelude*, for instance, is read not as an idealized form of mourning, but rather as providing 'a sense of disjunction in personal development'.[12] Remembering becomes an ambivalent endeavour, which facilitates the establishment of a body of experience as well as the probing into the wounds and crevices of that body.

Although Hartman thus makes allowances for the tenuousness of Wordsworthian memory, he nevertheless accepts the poet's own story of it as primarily a matter of the self. What neither Hartman's phenomenological approach nor the linguistically oriented (yet still quasi-phenomenological) deconstruction of Paul de Man can countenance is that the self itself might in its origin be derailed and defined by an other.[13] Levinas's claim that time not only undermines the self's unity with itself, but in fact relates the very identity of that self with an other,[14] has not been assimilated by either of these influential readers of Wordsworth. Yet it is anticipated by the poet, and arguably plays an important role both in his conception of memory and in the more general development of his career.

The otherness of the self crops up very early in Wordsworth's writings on memory, and arguably accounts for his general drift away from what ostensibly is self-recollection, in the early verse, to overt mourning of others in his later texts. In a passage which stems from the early, two-book version of *The Prelude* that was begun in Germany in 1798, his recollection of elevated spots of time of his childhood is interrupted by a surprising admission:

> A tranquilizing spirit presses now
> On my corporeal frame, so wide appears
> The vacancy between me and those days,
> Which yet have such self-presence in my heart
> That sometimes when I think of them I seem
> Two consciousnesses – conscious of myself,
> And of some other being.
>
> (II, 27–33)

If Wordsworth, then, can change what was originally a self-description into an account of the death of the Boy of Winander, this does not necessarily entail – as Hartman and de Man presume – that we have evidence of the unlimited imaginative powers of the self. Quite to the contrary, it can be read as an admission of how subjectivity is other to itself, and how a form of sociality constitutes it from the very beginning. Even if the splitting of the self is metaphorical ('I seem / Two consciousnesses'), it nevertheless points toward a fundamental possibility: rather than being identical to the subject, the past self is as distant or as dead as the Boy of Winander. Even to remember oneself is to engage in a process of mourning or raising of the dead.

William Hazlitt's writings of the same period extrapolate the ethical consequences of this possibility: if self-centred action is on the behalf of myself in another time, and I at that time have a different identity from what I have today, then all action is fundamentally altruistic. Egotism is not erroneous, but it is not thought radically enough: I may act on my own behalf, but in so doing I actually act on behalf of someone else. This view is presented by Hazlitt in 1805 in *An Essay on the Principles of Human Action*, which tries to overturn what it calls 'one of the most deeply-rooted feelings of the human mind', namely the fundamental opposition believed to exist 'between the interest we have in promoting our own welfare' and the interest 'which we take in promoting the welfare of others'.[15] Hazlitt claims that this subversion of a common prejudice is possible due to a fissure dividing the present and future instances of the self:

> so long as there is an absolute separation, an insurmountable barrier fixed between the present, and the future, so that I neither am, nor

can possibly be affected at present by what I am to feel hereafter, I am not to any moral or practical purpose the *same* being.[16]

Wordsworth knew of Hazlitt's essay,[17] and it may have had an influence on some of his most remarkable insights.

Finding an opening beyond the autonomy of the self in Wordsworth's writings has long been an aim of psychoanalytical criticism, the first and primary aim of which has been to reverse the fundamentals of a narrative which claims to find 'love of nature leading to love of mankind' (as the title of book eight of *The Prelude* will have it). According to this criticism, the 'Blessed Babe' passage of *The Prelude* should replace the meditation on the 'gentle breeze' (which actually begins the poem, in the versions of both 1805 and 1850) as its point of origin:

> Blest the infant babe
> (For with my best conjectures I would trace
> The progress of our being), blest the babe
> Nursed in his mother's arms, the babe who sleeps
> Upon his mother's breast, who when his soul
> Claims manifest kindred with an earthly soul,
> Doth gather passion from his mother's eye!
> Such feelings pass into his torpid life
> Like an awakening breeze, and hence his mind,
> Even in the first trial of its powers,
> Is prompt and watchful, eager to combine
> In one appearance all the elements
> And parts of the same object, else detached
> And loth to coalesce.
>
> (II, 237–250)

Thus Wordsworth proffers an alternative beginning to the life history sketched in other contexts, now focused on personal, psychosexual origins rather than on nature or some timeless, Platonic realm. Michael H. Friedman sees the 'Blessed Babe' passage as showing how this primordial communication with the mother 'establishes the prototype for all subsequent experience of affective community' in Wordsworth.[18]

Yet it is at best a problematical prototype, as the acts of blessing are vague and potentially very variegated. Not only does the construction of this prototype only come about by ignoring Wordsworth's many insistences on the primacy of experiences of nature, but it also entails overlooking – or reducing – the ambivalence of passages which seem to straddle the social and the natural. The opening of the two-book *Prelude* is an important example of this, as it grants the river Derwent primordial influence by virtue of the way in which it early blended its 'murmurs with my nurse's song'.[19] Another complication lies in the fact that Wordsworth seems to hover between two different tales of psychosexual origin in the 'Blessed Babe' passage. Whereas one entails the babe 'gather[ing] passion from his mother's eye', and directing that passion outward in a first perception imitating the mother's gaze (which is directed either toward the self or the father of individual prehistory, one would presume), the other seems to evoke an even earlier stage of development. The latter explanation occurs soon after the cited passage, and is presented almost as a summation. Yet it avoids any ocular reference whatsoever, and presumably refers to an experience undergone by the unborn child while still within the mother's body: 'that first time / In which, a babe, by intercourse of touch / I held mute dialogues with my mother's heart' (II, 281–283). Here touch, rather than sight, is the original experience of sociality, and a paradoxical form of communication ('mute dialogues') is evoked.

Thus we are provided with different figures or images to describe a primary memory. The ambivalence between the tactile and the visual is not a minor issue, since it is tied to the struggle in Wordsworth between the unfinished and exploratory, on the one hand, and the monologically totalitarian (inherent in the unifying horizons of sight), on the other. The account of the 'spontaneous overflow of emotion' in the preface to *Lyrical Ballads* arguably raises the possibility of feelings which are dynamic proto-thoughts (rather than just irrational negations of thought) rooted in tactility. Yet this and Wordsworth's own critique of the exaggerated dominion of the eye in the picturesque (in *The Prelude*, XI, 138–222) cannot completely gainsay the common observation that this is an intensely *visual* poet. Even more importantly, the *medium* of memory – the underpinning and environment for acts of reminiscence – becomes ambivalent, if one reads the lines on the blessed babe as an originary (and therefore foundational) account of its workings. In an interpretation that concurs with his general tendency to radicalize the linguistic turn, Paul de Man has suggested that the passage in question shows the 'dependence on any perception or "eye" on the totalizing power of language'.[20] On the other hand, Geoffrey Hartman has been more sceptical over finding any latent and underlying rhetoric of temporality here: Wordsworth, he claims, gives no account of how 'language enter[s] the developmental process'.[21]

Hartman's reading of the passage suggests that the 'mute dialogues' of mother and child are not an originary language, but rather a prelinguistic occurrence. Here he goes contrary to the normal practice of deconstruction, which never hesitates to utilize linguistic metaphors to identify the workings of language (or 'arche-writing') even in what amounts to the purest and most spiritual realms of experience. With regard to memory, there is a long tradition – spanning from Plato's images of a wax tablet being imprinted with a seal, to Freud's speculations on a 'magical writing pad' – of allowing typological figures a special pride of place.[22] Thanks to efforts of Jacques Derrida in particular, it is hard to discount passages where Wordsworthian memory explicitly or implicitly is described in terms of a linguistic process. Here, for instance, is a fragment of one of those early spots of time, where the workings of language virtually thrust themselves into the reader's face:

> I would stand
> Beneath some rock, listening to sounds that are
> The ghostly language of the ancient earth,
> Or make their dim abode in distant winds.
> Thence did I drink the visionary power.
>   (II, 326–330)

When the poet remembers, he remembers something linguistic – a 'ghostly' language, but nevertheless a language. This might lead one to conclude that Wordsworth's memory overtly adopts a rhetorical guise, yet this is only one of several metaphors in this passage. Just as Wordsworth elsewhere resists granting the faculty of sight absolute dominion among the various senses, it seems reductive to insist that memory is an exclusively linguistic phenomenon, given the wealth of contending imagery in evidence here. For the sounds of the above passage are not only a language, they are also associated with a 'dim abode' and something one can 'drink'. These two metaphors are hardly unprecedented in Wordsworth's writings. Behind the visionary drink, one can glimpse not only a phenomenology of vision – compare, among many similar lines, the description in *The Prelude* of how the past becomes a 'visible scene' (I, 663) – but also the life-giving nourishment of the child's first contact with another human being. There are many references in Wordsworth to how memory gives sustenance of some kind. Apart from the reference to how our minds are 'nourished and invisibly repaired' (XI, 264) by memories of the spots of time, one of the most striking is the line in 'Tintern Abbey' stating that a privileged moment will give 'life and food / For future years'.[23]

The 'dim abode' also finds a notable echo in 'Tintern Abbey', where the speaker claims that Dorothy's present experiences

> shall be matured
> Into a sober pleasure, when thy mind
> Shall be a mansion for all lovely forms,
> Thy memory be as a dwelling-place
> For all sweet sounds and harmonies.[24]

Although the conception of memory as a space or room of storage is a recurring trope within the tradition of Western thought, Wordsworth's own version of this is both singular and significant. The tropology of Wordsworthian memory differs from significant precursors – such as Locke's storehouse image and Hume's mental theatre – by how it insists we inhabit our memories. Memories are not just an inner resource that can be drawn upon for diversion or comfort; rather, they ground our existence by constituting our identity. Furthermore, a poem such as 'Home at Grasmere' shows that for Wordsworth this involves a complex dialectic between memory and specific places. This entire dimension of Wordsworthian memory – too rich to be explored at sufficient length here – is short-changed if one too hastily reduces the spaces of memory to the pure mechanics of rhetoric. For Wordsworth's conception of memory both takes place in a diversified medium (linguistic and phenomenal, spatial and temporal) and encompasses a variety of forms of experience (natural and supernatural, personal and social). One of Wordsworth's most insightful readers, David Bromwich, has pointed towards this complexity, noting the 'arbitrariness' of this poet's recollections. Wordsworth, Bromwich has argued, 'cannot say what drives the compulsion [of a particular memory], or what it was that made him seize a particular moment'.[25] Yet the methodology of Bromwich's own reading of Wordsworth is itself oddly out of tune with such open-endedness. For, despite distancing himself from the finger-pointing moralism of many of Wordsworth's New Historicist critics, Bromwich follows them in his tending to identify particular events of the French Revolution as a single, traumatizing referent for this poet.[26]

Wordsworth's understanding of memory, as it has been presented so far, should itself be a sufficient deterrent towards such monological reductions of the poems in question. Yet there is still one more fundamental problem that we have not confronted, which indeed renders an informed, critical recollection of Wordsworth's accomplishment even more difficult. It concerns not an internal difference in the make-up and form of memory, but an *external* difference in its very own identity. For Wordsworthian memory transcends itself: in its most radical conception, it engages with something inscrutable – with what will not, indeed cannot, be remembered. This intractable dimension crops up when his writings deal with the failings and obscurities that resist being fully recovered by the powers of memory. A general scepticism towards any genealogical activity comes across in the lines immediately preceding the 'Blessed Babe' passage:

> Not only general habits and desires,
> But each most obvious and particular thought–
> Not in a mystical and idle sense
> But in the words of reason deeply weighed–
> Hath no beginning.
>
> (II, 233–237)

Here Wordsworth almost retracts his own archaeology of identity prior to presenting it. The blessings of the babe are, perhaps, not the first blessings after all. There is always some prior event, some earlier instance or *milieu*, which supplements the beginnings we fasten on to as significant or decisive.

In the above quote, one can glimpse Wordsworth's characteristic defence of the quotidian. Poetry has to romanticize our lives by showing the ordinary in an extraordinary way, yet this does not involve a mystification of existence. Even the 'most obvious and particular' things have an infinite richness in them. Hence even the slightest, seemingly most insignificant details of a life are memorable, if one only gives them their due attention – an attention which itself is identical to the meditation inherent in 'recollection in tranquillity'. One can sense a certain defensiveness when Wordsworth insists in the first book of *The Prelude* that in his childhood the 'common face of Nature spake to me / Remembrable things' (I, 615–616). A similar anticipation of criticism would seem to be present in a passage which comes soon after:

> I began
> My story early, feeling, as I fear,
> The weakness of a human love for days

> Disowned by memory – ere the birth of spring
> Planting my snowdrops among winter snows.
>
> (I, 640–644)

Wordsworth seems to be indicting himself here, for indulging in a form of sentimental nostalgia. Yet more than this is at stake. Something radically foreign to memory is being evoked: not the value of these memories, but their accessibility as such seems to be the issue. In the final, 1850 version of *The Prelude*, Wordsworth rewrites the passage and effectively denies what he suggests in the earlier version: in the later version, he is 'not misled, I trust / By an infirmity of love for days / Disowned by memory'.[27] This emendation occludes the connection between the resistance of memory and the evocative image of the poet 'Planting my snowdrops'. For the latter metaphor would seem to indicate some kind of radical unity without distinctions (indistinct as 'snowdrops among winter snows') which exists prior to any form of conscious life ('ere the birth of spring'). It suggests a heightened state of diffuse unity – an oceanic form of presence prior to any murderous dissection – that is foreign to the divisions and conceptualizations inherent in any use of the faculty of understanding. Some experiences are so unified, Wordsworth (in the earlier version of the poem) seems to be saying, one cannot hope to recall them: one might as well try to locate one particular snowdrop in a field of snow. By 1850, he seems to either have forgotten this insight, or arrived at the view that the power of forgetting is best left alone.

In the early writings, however, memory remains drawn towards an experience of immediacy, which it can only disclose through a form of dissimulation. In a crucial passage in Book II of *The Prelude* the potential futility of this obscure experience is both raised and dismissed:

> I deem not profitless those fleeting moods
> Of shadowy exultation; not for this,
> That they are kindred to our purer mind
> And intellectual life, but that the soul –
> Remembering how she felt, but what she felt
> Remembering not – retains an obscure sense
> Of possible sublimity, to which
> With growing faculties she doth aspire,
> With faculties still growing, feelings still
> That whatsoever point they gain they still
> Have something to pursue.
>
> (II, 331–341)

The intensities of the past are irredeemably lost, yet they are nevertheless spurs for action directed towards the future. Hope takes its bearings from the obscurities of oblivion, the ineluctable pastness of the past. Wordsworth confronts, in his own way, that which Nietzsche would later indicate to be the major repressed of Western civilization – the ephemerality of the 'it was [Es war]' of the past[28] – yet does not give in to nostalgia.

Although this strand of Wordsworth's thought presents reminiscence as ultimately an impossible undertaking, one should be wary of presenting him as a radical and unerring sceptic. Even while he attests to some of the crises and aporias of memory that will persist long after romanticism, he also seeks to give affirmative accounts of both the content and the formal workings of memory. Wordsworth cannot be used as a representative for any single and unambiguous theory of how we bring back (or fail to bring back) the ghosts of our past. As a precursor, he does not exclusively endorse a personal or individualist account of memory, but also taps into its more inclusive, social forms. Furthermore, the sheer multiplicity of his example will align some very differing deployments of memory, among the later poets discussed in subsequent chapters of this study, with his crucial precedent: while the influence on figures such as Hardy and Heaney might seem straightforward, even a declared opponent such as T. S. Eliot will have trouble leaving Wordsworthian memory behind. At the same time, the slipperiness of Wordsworth's poetic practice of memory is such that it constantly tempts both critics and poets to simplify and abridge its rich treasures.

All in all, Wordsworth's poetry can be said to evince an open-minded multiplicity that goes contrary both to what is the received opinion, and to the critical, recollective practice of many of his modern-day readers. Certainly, it will not do to enlist Wordsworth as a spokesman for a canonical version of literary history, where a form of personal voluntarism constitutes an unquestioned foundation. Contrary to what Harold Bloom has recently claimed, Wordsworth's memory is not a canonical memory that tells us 'what and how to remember'.[29] Rather, it is a scrupulous memory that is so radically uncertain about what and how one should remember that the notion of a canon – and that includes a canon in which Wordsworth is designated as the inaugurator of modernity – is challenged by it. Wordsworthian recollection is never a process that returns us straightforwardly to the given facts of history: one has to remember, and yet one will never really remember. For the blessing, as well as the bane, of finitude, as experienced by this poet, involves inhabiting a mysterious unknown, a dim abode in distant winds.

Christina Rossetti's renunciations

Memory is of the past. Yet, as indeed Wordsworth demonstrates so viv-
idly, the ways in which poetry responds to the past can vary widely.
Some foothold for reflection can be gained from the fact that the past
is always filtered or mediated: we remember on the basis of where and
who we are *now*, our current horizons framing any recourse to the riches
of recollection. Yet even such formulations need to be modulated and
expanded. For the present and the past do not encounter each other in
isolation, like two lovers isolated in a cocoon of intimacy. This duo is
always shadowed by a third: like a voyeur or hidden backdrop to their
assignations, the future is a dimension that inexorably impinges upon
how past and present interact with each other. If we remember, we do
so in order to act upon the future in some way. This lesson is perhaps
most tellingly developed by Martin Heidegger in *Being and Time*, where
he not only clarifies the imbrication of the three ecstasies of time, but
also insists upon the future's decisive role in all temporal unfolding.[30]
   It is particularly worthwhile reminding oneself of the future-
directedness of memory when reading authors active during the reign of
Queen Victoria. Victorian literature has almost invariably attracted the
stigma of being overly nostalgic, its heavy investments in tradition and
history being particularly stringently dismissed by modernist authors
eager to free themselves of the yoke of the past. Such a view would
invite us to see Victorianism as a fundamental betrayal of the multiplicity characteristic of Wordsworth's dealings with memory. But beyond
generalizing too vaguely about the complex phenomenon of Victorian
nostalgia, which I will return to in the next chapter,[31] this view also
entails ignoring or rationalizing away much of what was going on in
the nineteenth century. Not only was this a century that included a
proto-modernist like Baudelaire, but also the supposedly staid Victorian
verse of Elizabeth Barrett Browning – here in book V of *Aurora Leigh* –
embraces the passing moment:

> if there's room for poets in the world
> A little overgrown (I think there is),
> Their sole work is to represent the age,
> Their age, not Charlemagne's – this live, throbbing age,
> That brawls, cheats, maddens, calculates, aspires,
> And spends more passion, more heroic heat,
> Betwixt the mirrors of its drawing rooms,
> Than Roland with his knights at Roncesvalles.[32]

Given that received opinion tends to identify the temporality of Victorianism with a misty-eyed yearning for the past, Christina Rossetti's poem 'Song ("When I Am Dead, My Dearest")' comes across as something of an odd specimen. Written when Rossetti was only eighteen, on 12 December 1848, the text was later included in her volume *Goblin Market and Other Poems* (1862). The opening lines spell out the apparent disdain with which the speaker confronts prevalent rites of mourning:

> When I am dead, my dearest,
>   Sing no sad songs for me;
> Plant thou no roses at my head,
>   Nor shady cypress tree.
>
>   (1–4)[33]

No tokens of love or grief, nor any vocal expression of loss, are required or even allowed to be apposite. One might expect the speaker to contrast inner safekeeping of memories to the ephemerality of passing shows, but instead she goes on to express equanimity concerning the mental act of memory, too: 'And if thou wilt, remember, / And if thou wilt, forget' (7–8). There is no contrast between the ritual deeds and inner faithfulness of recollection here; all is swept away, it seems, by the absolute and puzzling indifference of the speaker's peculiar voice.

The conviction and eerie lucidity of this voice is such that one might forget that Rossetti is a Victorian, forget that even her late, devotional *Verses* owned up to a 'Scarce tolerable life, which all life long / Is dominated by one dread of death' ('Scarce tolerable life, which all life long', 1–2). Should one hastily contextualize and explain away the puzzle? Forbidding mourning, 'Song' seems to call for a complete severance with all that is known of life, never mind the particulars of a specific historical era. This desire for a new beginning is accompanied by a mellifluousness that seems as old as the hills, and has as its premise the use, on a multitude of levels, of repetition. Some of these forms of repetition can be quickly evoked: the opening lines are rich with the aural recurrences of alliteration and assonance that help underpin the poem's deliberate evocation of song: 'When I am dead, my dearest / Sing no sad songs for me.' Later, there is a repeated use of anaphora, most insistently perhaps in the repetition of 'I shall not' in lines nine to eleven. In addition, the sixteen lines of the text can be broken into four quatrains utilizing the ballad rhyme of xaxa. The ballad form's alternation of eight and six-syllable lines is also lurking behind the skeleton of

Rossetti's lines, albeit set aside for two successive lines of six syllables at the end of both stanzas. The endings of the stanzas are also, fittingly, the place where the rhythmic repetition of the iambic metre attains its most insistent regularity, as the speaker hammers home her lesson in temporality.

Perhaps the most important form of repetition in this poem, however, is located in the symmetrical disposition of its argument. Where the first stanza directs itself to 'my dearest' (1) – an interlocutor who may be, at first sight, either a lover, a friend, or a family member – the second one is exclusively devoted to the speaker's own future. Reading the second stanza, the reader is reminded of the first, creating a verbal palimpsest of sorts. This repetition is far from a simple restatement or doubling: if one were forced to choose between Gilles Deleuze's opposition between Platonic repetition (which effects semblance and strives towards unity) and Nietzschean repetition (said to primarily set to work divergence and difference),[34] then the latter would probably provide the most fitting template. But any simple opposition between identity and difference fails to fully account for the effect here. On the one hand, 'Song' seems like an oddly static poem, judging by the obduracy with which the speaker insists upon her unorthodox views on mourning. On the other hand, the distinction between her and her interlocutor is a fundamental one, contributing to a skewed relation between the poem's two parts. This is perhaps most clearly seen in the endings of the two stanzas: although we are presented with something that comes across as a slightly varying refrain, the temporality of the two endings is crucially different. In the first stanza, the commas after 'if thou wilt' in lines seven and eight create important breaks, replete with hesitation. The speaker cannot know what her interlocutor will do; hence these caesurae indicate that – even if she is trying to fully anticipate any possible stance he might take – there is something unknown and unpredictable at hand. Further, the verb 'wilt' gains weight and pregnancy from these pauses, alerting the reader not only to the attempt to sidestep the powers of the will, but also to a metonymic nod in the direction of the same word's sense of becoming limp or losing energy. Given that the speaker has just made reference to roses, trees, and green grass, the reader is tacitly encouraged to see her addressee as a potentially wilting flower.

Despite the risk of anachronism inherent in projecting contemporary social configurations onto Victorian texts, a certain – if muted – feminism may be at work. Rossetti's later preface to the 'Monna Innominata' sonnet sequence toyed with the idea of what might have happened had Dante and Petrarch's female muses been given a voice: 'Had such a lady spoken for herself, the portrait left us might have appeared more tender, if less dignified, than any drawn even by a devoted friend.'[35] Even if she seems to be at death's door, the speaker of 'Song' is quietly empowered vis-à-vis her addressee through being the only speaker. If the interlocutor is in a passive position, lacking not only a voice but also any power to direct proceedings, the speaker has much more room in which to manoeuvre. No caesura is present in the final two lines, as her future state – although unsure – can be approached with equanimity: 'Haply I may remember / And haply may forget' (15–16). There is no insistence upon the gap between present thoughts and future actions here, as she instead envisages her own unfolding temporality as a seamless continuum. Eric Griffiths has claimed that the 'rhythmic catch' in Rossetti's voice 'is instinct with the experience of time, particularly with the experience of waiting, during which time most makes itself felt'.[36] The entirety of 'Song' unfolds in the space between present and future, waiting for the end, but through its rhythm it nevertheless distinguishes between different experiences of that waiting, contrasting the unpredictability of the other (i.e. the unheard interlocutor) with the conviction of the self (the speaking, lyrical 'I').

The adverb 'if' is significantly missing at the end of the poem, replaced by the more temperate 'may'. In a different poem, 'Another Spring', Rossetti allows her speaker to unpack the temporal heart of this word: 'If I might see another Spring– / Oh stinging comment on my past / That all my past results in "if"' (17–19). No such 'stinging comment' affects the speaker of 'When I am dead, my dearest': the entire poem is framed by the near-inevitability of its opening 'When', rather than by the uncertainty of an open future. This does not mean that the future is fully foreclosed or decided, since, after all, this is a poem that concludes with an alternative between forgetting and remembering. Still, the speaker can approach the issue of her own death with resolute steadfastness, something which is perhaps hinted at in the way 'haply', at the end of the second stanza, provides a surprising counterpoint for the first stanza's 'wilt'. As commentators have pointed out, while the immediate meaning of 'haply' refers to that which may occur by chance or accident (as in line ninety-seven of Gray's churchyard elegy: 'Haply some hoary-haired swain may say'), it is hard to avoid the association of 'happily' at this juncture. Even if Angela Leighton uses this poem to argue that Rossetti was, 'at some level of consciousness, profoundly indifferent to both love and faith, past and future',[37] indifference is not the sole emotion on display here. The very wavering between happenstance and happiness indicates that the speaker is balancing between something akin to the sepulchral neutrality entertained in Wordsworth's Lucy Gray poems, on the one hand, and a more jubilant affirmation of the afterlife on the other.

If the speaker of 'Song' is jubilant, it may be because the past and present are dwarfed by the future prospect of a Christian heaven. Memory fades to insignificance when compared with the last things. Certainly, the afterlife envisaged by the poem may seem a peculiar or even mysterious one. We are told that the speaker will be 'dreaming through the twilight / That doth not rise nor set' (13–14). No further specification of her afterlife is given, though, as the poem mainly dwells on her renunciation of the life and existence she is about to leave behind. Some commentators have been keen to dispel the oddity of the vision of a twilit afterlife through contextualization, arguing that the message of the poem is more orthodox than it appears. The twilight of the poem is, they argue, that of 'Soul Sleep', a state explained by Betty S. Flowers as follows:

> the theological doctrine of 'soul sleep' [denotes] the state of the soul between death and Judgement Day in which the soul 'sleeps' and dreams of Paradise. The Order for the Burial of the Dead in the *Book of Common Prayer* characterizes Christ as the 'First-fruits of them that slept' (1 Cor. 15:20). CR [i.e. Christina Rossetti] refers to 'them which sleep in Jesus' (I Thes. iv:14) [in *Seek and Find*].[38]

Such a reading is justified, if one grants that, in critical retrospect, all the various parts of Rossetti's *oeuvre* must conform to a unified world view. The speaker of a later poem by Rossetti, 'The Poor Ghost', begs, for instance, to be allowed to 'sleep now till the Judgment Day' (36). There is no doubt that the later stages of Rossetti's career present only a Christian alternative to a meaningless or materialist explanation of death, and finds the former a source of solace: 'Death is not death, and therefore do I hope' ('It is not Death, O Christ, to die for Thee', 9–10). The individual and time-bound nature of human memory is also far less compelling a topic, in her final lyrics, than the reciprocal relations of recollection that exist between godhead and believer. A line from 'A Martyr: The Vigil of the Feast' neatly encapsulates this two-way traffic: 'Me, Lord, remember who remember Thee' (10).

To explain the early Rossetti on the evidence of her later work is to place a premium on hindsight – to remember forwards or teleologically. It is to engage in critical recollection of a particularly unifying and goal-oriented kind, which Rossetti herself crucially adumbrated in the poem published at the end of her very last volume, *Verses* (1893):

> Looking back along life's trodden way
>   Gleams and greenness linger on the track;
> Distance melts and mellows all today,
>   Looking back.
>
> Rose and purple and a silvery grey,
>   Is that cloud the cloud we called so black?
> Evening harmonizes all today.
>   Looking back.
>
> Foolish feet so prone to halt or stray,
>   Foolish heart so restive on the rack!
> Yesterday we sighed, but not today
>   Looking back.

Not all commentators have felt bound to follow this rationale. Even if she does not stress the difference between the early and late work, Angela Leighton is effectively defending the former against being interpreted in light of *Verses* and other late works, when she, in an arresting reading, declares that 'it is not heaven, but entombment, which fascinates Rossetti; it is not "Soul Sleep" which characterizes the state of death for her, but a disturbing sleeplessness of the mind and an accompanying corruption of the body.'[39] To support this claim, Leighton refers to what she characterizes as 'facts which strike any reader of the poet's work',[40] arguably ignoring the religious 'facts' that are just as prevalent in the same *oeuvre*.

It should however be hard to ignore that 'Song' dwells more upon the negativity of death, through the motif of a deathbed renunciation, than upon any immediately recognizable conception of a Christian afterlife. At the very beginning of the poem, the proximity of 'dead' to 'dearest' in the first line might be seen as giving some support to Leighton's reading: it is as if intimacy and death are linked by the strongest of associative links, a link supported by many centuries of poetic thought upon the self-obliteration risked in sexual ecstasy or identification. We are not far from pre-Raphaelitism here, although an even more immediate context than that provided by Rossetti's contemporaries nudges us in a similar direction. For, if it is tempting to interpret 'Song' on the basis of later work by its author, this temptation can be balanced by having recourse to her *earlier* work – we can just as justifiably choose to remember backwards as forwards, utilizing what one might call an archaeological rather than teleological memory. What appears to be a genetic source of the kind typically privileged by biographical and historical approaches is readily available to assist us. Composed on 7 December 1848 – only five days before 'Song' – the unpublished poem 'What Sappho Would Have Said Had Her Leap Cured Instead of Killing Her' anticipates 'Song' in a number of ways. Based on the legend that the Greek poet Sappho – believed, at this point in history, to be heterosexual – committed suicide due to a broken heart, this text envisages a less tragic outcome. At the end of the poem, the speaker admits that 'His footsteps left a smouldering track / When he went forth, that still doth burn' (63–64), yet nevertheless resists utter despondency: 'I must go forth and bear my pain' (60).

'What Sappho Would Have Said' differs fundamentally from 'Song' by presenting death as a possibility that can be set aside, rather than as inevitable. It also differs in how it frames its love story, opting for a third person reference to a lost lover rather than addressing an unspecified interlocutor in the second person. Yet the middle section, where Sappho envisages her own death by a 'river side / Where the low willows touch the stream' (19–20), has several formulations which strikingly anticipate 'Song'. In the sixth stanza, the 'holy hushedness' of Sappho's surroundings are compared to a dove that 'would fain / not wake, but drowse on without pain' (35–36), foreshadowing the nightingale in 'Song' that will 'Sing on, as if in pain' (12). Not only the latter poem's descriptive enumeration of the 'green grass above me / With showers and dewdrops wet' (5–6) but also other particulars of death's sylvan setting are paralleled by Sappho's imagining that

> My pillow underneath my head
>   Shall be green grass; thick fragrant leaves
>   My canopy; the spider weaves
> Meet curtains for my narrow bed;
> And the dew can but cool my brow
> That is so dry and burning now.
>
> (49–54)

Perhaps most importantly, in this context, 'Song''s enigmatic reference to 'the twilight / That does not rise nor set' (15–16) has a counterpart in Sappho's sense that 'the race / Of time seems to stand still, for here / Is night or twilight all the year' (28–30).

'What Sappho Would Have Said' is in fact Rossetti's second poem on the death of the Greek poet. Two years earlier, in September 1846, she wrote a sonnet simply entitled 'Sappho'. There, a speaker's death wish once more fastens on a vision of the afterlife:

> Oh! it were better far to die
> Than thus for ever mourn and sigh,
> And in death's dreamless sleep to be
> Unconscious that none weep for me;
> Eased from my weight of heaviness,
> Forgetful of forgetfulness,
> Resting from pain and care and sorrow
> Thro' the long night that knows no morrow.
>
> (5–12)

Even more explicitly than in the later poem on Sappho, the speaker here develops a decidedly non-Christian account of death's aftermath as a dream without end. Unlike what is the case in her later religious work, this night 'knows no morrow'.

On the basis of all these verbal echoes, it is hard to avoid seeing 'What Sappho Would Have Said' and 'Sappho' as compositional germs from which Rossetti developed 'Song'. They cast interesting light on the rather open-ended relationship between the speaker and her interlocutor in the latter poem, suggesting that the speaker's surprising equanimity can be interpreted as a stoic reaction to lost love as well as impending death. To borrow the words of the poem 'Sappho', she is 'Forgetful of forgetfulness', rather than blithely indifferent towards the whole issue of memory *per se*. In this context, her denial of mourning comes across as a staunchly reactive gesture, and the mask of equanimity appears to be more of a heroic or tragic choice than a simple denial of temporality.[41] She is anti-Victorian in the way so many Victorians were: combating the backward glance prevalent during her age, she is nevertheless, willy-nilly, subject to it. The truth of 'Song' is, according to such a reading, not to be found on the surface of the poem's content, but below it, or in a contiguous work of Rossetti's such as 'At Home', also included *Goblin Market and Other Poems*. In the latter poem, the speaker visits her friends after her death, as a ghost, and is distraught at how easily they have recovered from their grief:

> I all-forgotten shivered, sad
> To stay and yet to part how loth:
> I passed from the familiar room,

> I who from love had passed away,
> Like the remembrance of a guest
> That tarrieth but a day.
>
> (27–32)

If 'Song' protests too much, that act of protest may of course have something to do with underlying matters of gender. Gilbert and Gubar have described Rossetti and Elizabeth Barrett Browning as 'the great nineteenth-century women singers of renunciation as necessity's highest and noblest virtue'. This renunciation has, these critics claim, an obvious cause in 'the maze of societal constraints by which women poets have been surrounded since Anne Finch's day'.[42] And it certainly does seem perverse to ignore the compatibility of Rossetti's characteristic stance of recalcitrance, dubbed a 'decorum of omission' by Constance W. Hassett,[43] with the societal norms that constrained female poets in the nineteenth century. This is a context larger than that of individual biography, transcending the possible link between what Jan Marsh has called the 'peculiarly serene pathos' of 'Song', on the one hand, and Rossetti's ultimately terminated engagement with James Collinson on the other.[44]

As Lawrence Lipking has shown, there is a long tradition – originating in the eighteenth century – of British female poets writing about Sappho's desertion in a way that reflects back upon their society's gender politics.[45] Written on the margins of this tradition, 'Song' is bolstered by something of its impetus. It certainly is possible to interpret the poem as providing one of many instances of what Jerome McGann understands as the dominant tenor of Rossetti's poetry:

> The great value of Christina Rossetti's work – and in this she is like no other woman writer of the period – lies in its pitiless sense that the world is a scene of betrayal and that the betrayal appears most clearly, and most terribly, in the relations between men and women.[46]

Despite the danger of reductionism in such a statement, though, McGann also allows that Rossetti's poems present obstacles to simplification: 'they test and trouble the reader by manipulating sets of ambiguous symbols and linguistic structures.'[47] Another poem from the *Goblin Market* volume, 'Winter: My Secret', is, quite literally, the *piece de resistance* of this tendency. The speaker of that text insists upon having a secret, but will not divulge its contents. She rings the changes on the four seasons, but only slightly modulates her intransigence: from 'my secret's mine, and I won't tell' (6), she drifts to the only marginally forthcoming finale of 'Perhaps my secret I may say, / Or you may guess' (33–34). As in many of Rossetti's poems, another of the author's texts lurks in the vicinity of these words: in this case, 'Song''s ending of 'Haply I may remember / And haply I may forget' provides an interesting echo.

Both 'Winter: My Secret' and 'Song' belong to a larger group of Rossetti's poems, in which the speaker inhabits a position of solitude that makes her seemingly unassailable to the world. Another example is found in the second section of 'Memory', included in the 1866 volume *The Prince's Progress and Other Poems*, where the speaker declares that 'I have a room whereinto not one enters / Save I myself alone' (1–2). We are going to encounter related instances of the spatialization of memory's innerness in Tennyson's *In Memoriam* and other poems discussed later on in this study. In the case of 'Memory', the inner space is one in which the speaker has interred the memory of a lost love: 'If any should force entrance he might see there / One buried yet not dead' (29–30). Here there is a close thematic connection to 'Song': for the latter, too, can be read as an attempt to transcend what might be a tale of lost love, and a sceptical reading of the poem might insist upon unearthing the speaker's elusive memories rather than endorsing her self-willed amnesia. Yet the movement towards self-transcendence is more forceful in 'Song' than in most comparable poems in Rossetti's *oeuvre*.

If this movement is unconvincing read in the context of biography or the tradition of the abandoned woman, more compelling force in the same direction is gained by the poem's grafting of itself upon the ballad genre. As was later demonstrated by the German modernist Stefan George, folk poetry need not function as an expression of the demotic, but can also etherealize its material. In Rossetti's poem, the utilization of the traditions of song and ballad further the speaker's desired severance from the given particulars of lived human existence. Paradoxically, Rossetti's reiteration of past forms allows for some assurance in the dismissal of the past: the speaker haply forgets, precisely because she haply remembers. Related to the 'structural dependence of expression and repression upon one another' that Isobel Armstrong has identified both in 'Goblin Market' specifically and in Rossetti's work more generally,[48] remembrance and oblivion both rely upon one another and cancel each other out.

Similarly, the poem's ability to soar as a lyric utterance gains impetus from how it both refers to and denies other instances of song. If the speaker wants no 'sad songs for me' (2) and insists that she will 'not hear the nightingale / Sing on, as if in pain' (11–12) – circumspectly echoing Coleridge's scepticism about the nightingale's alleged melancholia in 'The Nightingale' – her own song nevertheless gains a transcending timbre from its contiguity to these instances of song. The reference to the nightingale interestingly hedges its bets on the issue of the possible melancholia of this bird. Whereas Milton's 'Il Pensoroso' insisted upon the mournfulness of the nightingale, Coleridge's 'The Nightingale' started a new tradition (that includes Keats's 'Ode on a Nightingale') by affirming its joyfulness. Rossetti's references to nightingales inherit this question, and often seem to dither and contradict one another, but in 'Song' her open-ended formulation, whereby the 'pain' is qualified as metaphorical, can be read as impartially appropriating the entirety of the tradition, carefully avoiding any partisan position.

Song is, however, not only a motif, but also a matter of genre. The success of Rossetti's use of the song format can be measured by the plethora of musical versions of her poems. Hers is a voice that is eminently singable, and therefore also singularly amenable to the oddly intertextual drift towards autonomy that comes with lyric and song-like structures. As Hassett observes:

> lyric says what it already hears, and poems listen for and return 'musical echoes' of other poems. Thus it happens that when first imagining a speaker completely lost in love and relieved by death of an individual identity, Rossetti abandons particularizing language and succumbs to the general music of featureless soulfulness, i. e., general among lyric writers.[49]

Thus one can easily read 'Song' as a meta-poem, celebrating how the transcendental ego of the poet's speaker will survive the empirical self of Rossetti. As many poets have remarked, the aesthetic memory or afterlife of a poem is not a rebirth – for no reading of a poem will bring its author literally back to life – but rather a more puzzling and paradoxical combination of presence and absence. If the author is not completely dead, then she is at least transformed into something or someone more ethereal or virtual. In Rossetti's text, a form of selective amnesia facilitates aesthetic autonomy: through forgetting the particulars of context – but not disallowing memories of a textual nature – the text aspires to the status of a freestanding entity.

'Song' might remind one of 'Goblin Market' by the way in which it engages in a rich sensuousness, only to seemingly refuse the pleasures of the senses. The series of 'I shall not see … / I shall not feel … / I shall not hear' (9–11) draws attention to the ordered, almost systematic, nature of its act of renunciation. Yet the senses are deployed in a manner that orchestrates a very particular kind of setting: Rossetti's poem carefully negotiates mourning's investment in place. The details of the graveyard and its environs – the roses, the cypress tree, the 'green grass above me' (5) – are evoked, only to be resolutely dismissed. Death is unmoored from the physical anchor of the mementoes and rites of the graveyard, powered by a desire which only will stop – with the enigmatic reference to 'the twilight / That doth not rise nor set' (13–14) – at the most sketchy, unearthly and allegorical of admissions to the claims of place. Freed from memory, the poem stages an autonomy that also wishes to be liberated from the weight of place.

Still, as this reading of Rossetti's poem has shown, the road to autonomy is one fraught with uncertainties and alternatives. Looking back, one might follow the example of the speaker of 'Looking back along life's trodden way', and attempt to submit all to the mellowing, harmonious hindsight of aesthetic transcendence. Yet there is no reason to sing a sad song – or happy song, for that matter – concerning the necessary eclipse of the given in light of the text's internal, formal configuration. For the memories of other paths remain: what Hillis Miller has called 'the linguistic moment' of a text cannot banish all the other moments.[50] The remembering reader cannot forget all in an oblivious act of interpretation. As a result, 'Song' remains ambivalently poised between warring memories – some going archaeologically backwards to presumed origins, others moving forwards to constructed teleological goals – as well as between memory and forgetfulness. In a somewhat different form, Rossetti confirms the multiplicity of memory established by Wordsworth. Haply, the reader may choose, or be forced to, remember or forget – yet her song includes latent potentialities that are ready to be unearthed, anew, with every rereading.

Tennyson's *In Memoriam* and 'This Wide Whisper'

With Lord Alfred Tennyson's *In Memoriam* (1850), we encounter a much more extensive confrontation with memory and its role in the workings of mourning. Tennyson's poem also deals quite differently with the multiplicity of memory. Where Wordsworth's precedent demonstrates the multiplicity of memory's foundations through a rich deployment of metaphor, and the interpretation of Rossetti's poem is forced to hold various stances to memory in an uneasy balance, the author of

In Memoriam tries to more forcefully appropriate the power of memory in a univocal way. Unlike Rossetti's 'Song', Tennyson's elegy will make extensive use of space. Yet the complexity of spatial relations in *In Memoriam* will arguably return the poem to the very multiplicity and dismemberment it is trying to banish. As such, its inner spaces will be shown to be an insufficient basis for memorial architectonics, calling for the supplement of the exterior spaces of *Idylls of the King*, which we will address in Chapter 3.

Although Tennyson is a poet prodigiously interested in memory, he seems resistant to pursue its ravel beyond a certain point. A melancholia of memory holds his speakers in a spell, which many of the poems neither contextualize nor explain. Although overly irreverent, perhaps Auden's mocking evaluation of his Victorian predecessor can be of help here. Tennyson, he famously wrote, 'had the finest ear, perhaps, of any English poet; he was also undoubtedly the stupidest; there was little about melancholia that he didn't know; there was little else that he did'.[51] Flippancy aside, there is some point to this estimate. For there is a resistance to thought, of sorts, in Tennyson's obsession with all things gone by, which one might be tempted to link to the more general phenomenon of Victorian nostalgia, insofar as it involves seeking a closed refuge from the more fragmenting dimensions of time and identity.[52] But it is not certain that Tennyson's exposure to the past can be straightforwardly and exhaustively described as a defensive or limiting gesture, even if involves a blockage of thought. This is hinted at in 1831 when Arthur Hallam, writing to Tennyson, says he is 'not without knowledge and experience of your *passion for the past'*.[53] Tennyson was himself to use a similar formulation at a later date, appropriating his late friend's choice of words.[54] Now a passion is something more than a mere interest, but also something rather different from reflection. Tennyson's poetry seems to frequently be beset by memories, implicitly recalling the Latin root of the word passion: *pati*, meaning 'to suffer'. The protagonists of the poems suffer their memories, having no other choice than to be inundated by the compelling evidence of the past.

Part of the reason for this passivity resides in the fact that memory is here understood to be the very element of thought and action, rather than a limited faculty one can make use of at will. Tennyson at one point writes of how the dead will have access to the 'eternal landscape of the past' (xlvi, 8): all their past experiences will be laid out before them, presumably as well-organized and accessible as all the varied features of nature's scenery in a painting by Claude or Poussin. Such are the dealings of the dead. Even if the temporal experience of the living is different, for them too the past doesn't simply pass away. Tennyson is here close to Antonio Negri's claim that the past is 'eternal', since it is 'indeed the power of accumulated life, of an irreversible and indestructible temporality'.[55]

Whereas Proust would later present his conception of involuntary memory as the result of a revelatory discovery, Tennyson in many ways presents the passion of memory as a starting point and problem rather than a solution. The poet's challenge is to transform passive suffering into active mastery. *In Memoriam* is a poem that gradually affirms the value of large-scale structures ordering the passing behaviour of individuals. More specifically, it affirms the order of ritual. Insofar as mourning Hallam is Tennyson's own poetical 'ritual of the dead' (xviii, 12), it is a process that follows its own linear logic, like a funeral procession. The cathartic passage from wild despair to a calmer form of sorrow, and then on to the relative contentment of the close of the poem, creates an orderly, even schematic, backdrop – amenable to the psychological and generic explanations later favoured by Freud and Sacks – for the interspersed eccentricities of its depictions of Victorian domesticity.[56] In 'To J. S.', the poem commiserating with James Spedding's loss of his brother, there is a hint towards the inevitability of such a development: it is asserted that outsiders should not meddle too much with the process of mourning, since 'Great Nature' (line 35) governs its necessary, teleological course.[57] The natural imagery of *In Memoriam*, spread throughout the poem, embodies the workings of this great nature. Nature's organic growth from seed to flower, onward to death and then to another rebirth, is the guarantee, as it were, not only for the inevitable rewards of mourning ('sorrow makes us wise'; cxiii, 1), but also for the larger concern of the gradual perfectibility of man, and the transition from earthly life to paradisiacal afterlife. In all of these there is a process of purification, which makes it possible that 'men may rise on stepping stones / Of their dead selves to higher things' (I, 3–4). Such purification is also the underlying premise for the speaker's attempt to free himself from an overly obsessive dwelling upon the past: organic structure is a means by which Tennyson attempts to control the force of memory.

At first sight, the spiritual and religious leanings of Tennyson's poem might seem to entail a denial of all organic teleology, akin to the renunciation of the graveyard landscape in Rossetti's 'Song'. The well-documented struggle between religious faith and nineteenth century science (particularly the geology of Chambers and Lyell) would seem to imply that the mourning speaker's ways in *In Memoriam* cannot be those of ruthless nature, 'red in tooth and claw' (lvii, 15).

This is evident early on in the poem (even before the explicit discussion of the new scientific discoveries), where nature's quiescence is taken as a false exemplar for the speaker, providing a source of identification which comforts him but ultimately doesn't do him any good. The yew tree of section ii, 'Who changest not in any gale' (ii, 10), thus embodies an unchangeable fixity which can only lead the speaker to self-indulgent apathy. Similarly, the cold fatality of nature in section xi provides a recipe for impassive quiescence rather than self-improvement:

> Calm and deep peace in this wide air,
>   These leaves that redden to the fall;
>   And in my heart, if calm at all,
> If any calm, a calm despair.
>
>   (xi, 13–16)

This is only a passing stage, more indicative of the speaker's subjective state of crushing sorrow than any deep-seated scheme of things. More fundamental problems with natural development come to the surface later on in the poem. This is particularly true of section lv, where nature's own goal-bound activity reveals itself to be far less systematic than the romantics believed it to be:

> The wish, that of the living whole
>   No life may fail beyond the grave,
>   Derives it not from what we have
> The likest God within the soul?
>
> Are God and Nature then at strife,
>   That Nature lends such evil dreams?
>   So careful of the type she seems,
> So careless of the single life;
>
> That I, considering everywhere
>   Her secret meaning in her deeds,
>   And finding that of fifty seeds
> She often brings but one to bear,
>
> I falter where I firmly trod.
>
>   (lv, 1–13)

The Manichaeism of this vision of God and nature being 'at strife' does not, though, preclude the endorsement of organicism at an abstract, generalized level, which will order the inner spatiality of the poem's developmental scheme. The problem with nature is not that it is organic, but rather that it is not nearly organic enough: bringing only one out of fifty seeds to fruition, it does not fulfil its teleological task. This is the reason why the speaker soon after insists that 'I curse not nature, no, nor death; / For nothing is that errs from law' (lxxiii, 7–8). Nature's deficits are covered in a more general economical scheme, and, if the rational goal of current events may be hard to glimpse, it must nevertheless be out there somewhere:

> We pass; the path that each man trod
> Is dim, or will be dim, with weeds:
> What fame is left for human deeds
> In endless age? It rests with God.
>
> (lxxiii, 9–12)

The result is a *deferred* teleology, where the final aim is left in obscurity but retained as a matter of faith. According to section lxxvii, this deferring of ends also affects the very being of the poem: as life's final goal is obscure, so is the fate of every instance of 'modern rhyme' (lxxvii, 1).

Organicism is retained on several fronts. Hallam's progress is described as a process of growth (in section cxiv), and the speaker's mourning is figured as attuned to nature's ideally organic processes in how it 'Becomes an April violet, / And buds and blossoms like the rest' (cxv, 19–20). Even more forcefully, the closing of the poem not only combines an organic stress on ordered development, but also hypostasizes the goal of that movement:

> No longer half-akin to brute,
>   For all we thought and loved and did,
>   And hoped, and suffer'd, is but seed
> Of what in them is flower and fruit;
>
> Whereof the man, that with me trod
>   This planet, was a noble type
>   Appearing ere the times were ripe,
> That friend of mine who lives in God,

> That God, which ever lives and loves,
> One God, one law, one element,
> And one far-off divine event,
> To which the whole creation moves.
>   (Epilogue, 133–144)

When Tennyson writes of 'That God' in the final stanza, we are tempted – keeping in mind his characteristic tendency to err from the well-travelled highways of traditional Christian dogma – to ask: 'which one?' The answer propounded here seems to be close to that most organic of philosophers, Aristotle, who demanded of divinity nothing else than that it needs must be – as an unmoved mover – the aim of the inherent development of all finite entities.

The most obviously organic device utilized by the poem is the recurring emphasis on annual seasons. While Hallam's experience of paradise is presumed to be of a place where 'All knowledge that the sons of flesh / Shall gather in the cycled times' (lxxxv, 27–28), it is also true that all life before that, too, is of a circular nature. The friendship of Hallam and Tennyson is linked to this circle, since they were 'crown'd with all the season lent, / From April on to April went, / And glad at heart from May to May' (xxii, 6–8). More fundamentally, the poem's underlying scheme of rebirth out of destitution is figured on the basis of seasonal change. The maturation of Tennyson's voice is ineluctably linked with budding nature:

> O thou, new-year, delaying long,
> Delayest the sorrow in my blood,
> That longs to burst a frozen bud
> And flood a fresher throat with song.
>   (lxxxiii, 13–16)

Section lxxxv makes the link between the seasons and the triggering of memories: 'change of light or gloom' causes a reawakening of 'My old affection of the tomb, / And my prime passion in the grave' (lxxxv, 74–76). In establishing this bond between the fraught development of its speaker and the rhythms of nature, *In Memoriam* is similar to 'Mariana'. Whereas the latter, shorter poem uses the different phases of the day (morning, noon, evening, dusk) to vary its desolate stillness, the longer poem employs the seasons of the year to mark the passing of time. Although one can find ample evidence of hesitation and lack of direction in both 'Mariana' and *In Memoriam*,[58] the latter is of course by far the more hopeful text: the mourning speaker gradually distances himself from his loss, and gains a sense of consolation, while Mariana ends up returning to her refrain (if with minor variations): 'She wept, "I am aweary, aweary, / O God, that I were dead!" ' (lines 83–84). While she is 'without hope of change' (line 29), *In Memoriam* uses the word 'change' as one of its key, recurring rhyme-words, ceaselessly toiling on with the sublimation of grief and the freeing of the mind from the fixations of memory.

In some respects, *In Memoriam* enacts a rectifying of the skewed natural rhythm inherent in 'Mariana'. Yet, as has frequently been the case with Wordsworth, there is always the risk of making the works of the mature Tennyson a too stolid counterpart to those of his own younger poetical self. Angela Leighton has commented that the

> strain of 'pure aestheticism' in Tennyson does not stop with the earthly paradises of 'The Lotos-Eaters' and 'The Palace of Art'. It runs all through his work, turning up in those islanded moments, when beauty for its own sake becomes separated from the moral and narrative action of the poem.[59]

Related to that aestheticism, there is not only a formal arrest in the progress of the poems, but also various forms of thematic suspension of organic schemas. Particularly clear in Walter Pater's celebrations of decadence, this is likewise evident in section lxxii of *In Memoriam*, where the 'dim dawn' (lxxii, 1) brings with it echoes of 'that reverse of doom, / Which sicken'd every living bloom, / And blurr'd the splendour of the sun' (lxxii, 6–8). In this skewed and perverted state, nature is twisted out of its lawful shape. The 'tears' of rain 'make the rose / Pull sideways, and the daisy close / Her crimson fringes to the shower' (lxxii, 10–12).

This form of natural perversion poses a serious threat to the ordered progression of organic nature otherwise so prevalent in the poem. It also opens up for an economy of waste and depletion that is in contrast to organism's economy of growth. Certainly, the speaker of the poem desires some kind of reward for his toils. When he asks 'What profit lies in barren faith, / And vacant learning' (cviii, 5–6), he is not only reiterating a Faustian disillusionment with the ways of the world, but also revealing the text's deep structure of investment and reward. If a profound immersion into his memories of Hallam seems the best course of action for a while, it is because he will 'rather take what fruit may be / Of sorrow under human skies' (cviii, 13–14). While the poem does not quite follow the eighteenth century's faith in a rather straightforward process of human perfectibility, it nonetheless does adhere to a Victorian faith in human improvement that obeys the gradual (and varying) progress of natural fruition. In the following century, another major religious poem – Eliot's *Four Quartets*, which will be addressed in Chapter 4 – will feel itself forced to dismiss both of these schemas.

In Memoriam's scheme of maturation has a crucial impact on how the poem frames its understanding and use of memory. If one believes in the necessity of a narrative of development through retrospection, then it will indeed be 'natural' to interpret the poem's self-remembering benignly – as Robert Douglas-Fairhurst does – as a process of maturation 'creating the sound of a mind raising its past, and itself on that past'.[60] We have a teleological memory of the kind deployed by critics who attempt to solve the interpretive cruxes of the early work of Christina Rossetti in light of her later, more consistently orthodox poetry. Yet a somewhat different, perhaps less credulous, approach to *In Memoriam* is also available, which would draw attention to the sacrifices and deprivations inherent in all progression – effectively highlighting the multiple resistances to unifying accounts of the poem's movement.

In the nine extant fragments excluded from the poem, all written in the same verse form as the rest of *In Memoriam*, one can trace something of this resistance. These fragments are the dross of Tennyson's work of mourning, expressions of an abstract negativity that could not be completely assimilated to the published version. In them, the body of *In Memoriam* is stretched to a breaking point, to a prosthetic site where it is hard to separate an *oeuvre*'s amputations and abortions – the 'indigestions of the brain'[61] – from its vital, living limbs. They might even be said to represent the corpse of the poem: for a poem about death and mourning, *In Memoriam* is strikingly silent about the materiality of the corpse. It is as if the traditional taboo against touching the corpse is here transformed into a verbal interdiction: the poet shall not dwell upon the singular impersonality and haunting liminality of the corpse; he shall not even deign to mention it. However ambiguous and virtual the poem's repeated references to the hand of Hallam may be,[62] those references still are obfuscations of a sort. As Maurice Blanchot has written of Rilke, this is a poet who is 'unwilling to restore to death the lowly impersonality which would make of it something less than personal, something always improper'.[63]

The following discarded fragment can bring this process of denial into clearer focus:

> Let Death and Memory keep the face
>   Of three and twenty summers, fair.
>   I see it and no grief is there,
> Nor time can wrong the youthful grace.
>
> I see it and I scarce repine.
>   I hear the voice that held me fast.
>   The voice is pleasant in the past,
> It speaks to me of me and mine.
>
> The face is bright, the lips are bland,
>   He smiles upon me eye to eye,
>   And in my thoughts with scarce a sigh
> I take the pressure of his hand.

Here the look 'eye to eye' in the final stanza may lead one to think of Walter Benjamin's concept of the aura, which strongly privileges a community of glances, a form of ocular sociality.[64] But for Tennyson it is the following reference to 'the pressure of his hand' that bears the brunt of the verse's emotional investment, giving tactility a characteristic pride of place.

As Christopher Ricks's notes point out,[65] this fragment was plundered for two different sections of the final version of *In Memoriam*. Lines 7–8 were transformed into the following: 'And that dear voice, I once have known, / Still speak to me of me and mine' (cxvi, 11–12). The final four lines crop up elsewhere, as

> And bless thee, for thy lips are bland,
> And bright the friendship of thine eye;
> And in my thoughts with scarce a sigh
> I take the pressure of thine hand.
>   (cxix, 9–12)

The references to the bright face, the smile, as well as the intensity of the mirroring 'eye to eye' are removed. More generally, the published fragments fail to recover the way in which this unpublished discard travels across the length and breadth of Hallam's body, creating a veritable catalogue of sensuous immediacy. Yet it *is* a fragmentary catalogue; more a fetishistic roll call of bodily impressions than an evocation of a unified totality. Severing the links of this *ensemble*, the writing of *In Memoriam* can be said to register a recoiling from the incompleteness of the disorganized body. Arguably, it is precisely the broken nature of this fragment that causes it to splinter the organic unity of the work of art where 'all ... / Is toil cöoperant to an end' (cxxviii, 23–24). When some parts are splintered or discarded, the sense that all contributes to the whole is at best an inexplicable faith, at worst a misguided and misguiding illusion.

The question of *In Memoriam*'s structure, or the lack thereof, has been one of the major focuses of the criticism of the poem. It certainly has a far from negligible bearing on the question of memory's role in the text. For in many ways this is a poem fragmented by memory: its disjointedness stems from the very multiplicity of its embodied memories. Nicholas Dames has claimed that 'the bursting of an unassimi- lated and still-powerful past into the present' is by design 'forgotten' by the controlled nostalgia of the Victorian novel.[66] In this respect, *In Memoriam*'s struggles to frame a niggling, overwhelming past is less a period piece of Victorian nostalgia than an anticipation of the chaotic plurality of an exhaustive, everyday memory Dames sees char- acteristic of the literary modernism of Woolf and Joyce. This feature links it to Tennyson's preceding long poem, *The Princess*, published in 1847. *The Princess* is notoriously diverse, spanning many different moods and registers. Not only does it consist of different narratives, thus constituting – as its extended title also insists – a medley, but furthermore there is the heterogeneity of the framing narrative, set in the gardens of Sir Walter Vivian, and the interspersed songs. The songs were a late addition, intended to solder the poem into a more tightly knit whole. Arguably, they have had quite the opposite effect, as later anthologies have tended to feature songs such as 'Tears, Idle Tears' and 'Come down, O maid, from yonder mountain height' completely sev- ered from the surrounding poem: these texts function as detachable units, originally welded to a larger whole but now to a large degree remembered as independent lyrical utterances.

Their status is additionally complicated by the fact that they are themselves carriers of memories. 'The splendour falls on castle walls', also known as the bugle song, is famously linked with Tennyson's sightseeing experience of Killarney, an association that considerably boosted the Irish tourist industry. The landscape verbally painted in 'Come down, O maid' was said by Hallam Tennyson to be 'written in

Switzerland – chiefly at Lauterbrunnen and Grindelwald – and descriptive of the waste Alpine heights and gorges and of the sweet valleys below'.[67] A more complex process of remembering is linked with 'Tears, Idle Tears', which Tennyson admitted writing close to Tintern Abbey – a place which resonates not only of Wordsworth's own act of poetical remembering, but also of Hallam, who was buried in nearby Clevedon.

In all such cases, the songs function not only as elements of a larger whole, but also as both memorable in their own right *and* significantly linked to one or more personal memories heterogeneous to the plot of *The Princess*. Not only is 'Tears, Idle Tears' a poem not devoid of its own integrity, but it also constitutes (through the association with Hallam) a subterranean mnemonic link between the larger bodies of *The Princess* and *In Memoriam*. In the former poem, Tennyson elegantly compares living poetry, the kind of verse which survives in the memory of its audience, with 'jewels five-words-long / That on the stretch'd forefinger of all Time / Sparkle forever' (*The Princess*, ii, 355–357). Exemplifying what it pronounces, this fragment implicitly figures memory as a something of a dissevering force, or even as something of an elusive jewellery thief: memory does not reconfigure a whole – it does not construct a palace – but rather unearths small, isolated gems.[68] It wheels and deals with the surface ornaments of the edifice, neglecting both the heart and the deep-seated skeleton of the matter however it sees fit.

In the age of the Arnoldian touchstone, Tennyson's poetic stepping-stones have a slippery, punctual power that can stop one in one's tracks, as well as provide poetical transport. As such, their logic is related to how the poem remembers Hallam himself. When the poem hardly mentions Hallam's name, and in the end subsumes him as both part of a spiritual universe and as a quasi-Christ figure, these are gestures which indicate that the poem risks being more interested in 'The Way of the Soul' (a discarded title of the poem) than its purported subject. This particular forgetting of Hallam is thematized, and thus remembered, within the text itself. It is as if the speaker remembers that he is forgetting his friend, which is something quite other than letting him slip his mind completely.

This paradox of a kind of forgetful memory, reminiscent of what we saw occurring in Rossetti's 'Song', relates to the entirety of *In Memoriam*. This is not to say that the poem involves a light-hearted dealing with its weighty subject. Quite to the contrary, it does not neglect the 'sense of duty' Tennyson believed to be inherent in literature, a duty 'not only to the living and the unborn, but also, in a very marked degree, to the dead'.[69] Yet this duty involves one in a complex double bind: the best way to remember Hallam, one might say, is to forget him. Hence when the speaker tries to imagine how Hallam would react to grief, he finds a precedent for his own act of mourning – as well as some solace – in his belief that Hallam would not overdo it.

This is an act of imitation more encompassing than the verbal echoes of passages from Hallam's writings, which have recently been identified by commentators on *In Memoriam*. From his friend, Tennyson wishes to inherit a temperate form of forgetting that ensures that his mourning is not self-indulgent, that he is getting solidly to grips with the matters at hand. This is the most important way in which Tennyson's use of memory is consciously critical. A parallel can be once more drawn to *The Princess*: after having 'Tears, Idle Tears' sung to her, Princess Ida declares that there are times one must let 'the past be the past' and 'let old bygones be', since all hinges on the fulfilment of Millennial harmony: 'all things serve their time / Toward that great year of equal mights and rights.'[70] Seizing not only the moment of the present, but also the past, entails an act of organization, of structuring experience, and also here Tennyson has Hallam as his own exemplar: he admires his old friend for how he 'large elements in order brought' (cxii, 13). This is the kind of control that Tennyson must find within himself in the writing of *In Memoriam*, for how else can he avoid becoming

> that delirious man
> Whose fancy fuses old and new,
> And flashes into false and true,
> And mingles all without a plan?
> (xvi, 17–20)

When Tennyson tries to organize his long, elegiac poem into more than stray fragments, he is allowing his own 'imitative will' (cx, 20) to be spurred by his old friend. There is, however, the danger the resulting edifice will hardly bear any legible inscription in memory of Hallam.

As is well known, Tennyson neither attended his friend's funeral nor managed to respond to Hallam's father's request for a biographical contribution to the publishing of his son's literary remains. The fact that eighteen years passed in between Hallam's death and the publishing of *In Memoriam* makes the poem twice as belated as Spenser's mourning of Sidney in 'Astrophel', another famously deferred act of poetical mourning. In light of Tennyson's extreme hesitation over publishing it, one might see the text as constituting a kind of substitute object, a fetish or a relic, feigning a sense of the enduring presence of one particular past person. As Edward S. Casey has pointed out, it is a common activity to 'commemorate ... by *remembering through* specific commemorative vehicles such as rituals or texts – or any other available *commemorabilia*'.[71] Certainly *In Memoriam* contains within itself several references to various objects functioning as such vehicles. Timothy Peltason has justly remarked upon how the memory of Hallam does not 'do its work unaided in the poem', but is triggered by significant objects such as 'landscapes, houses, and significant places, [as well as] in his letters'.[72] Yet one should not forget the poem itself: Tennyson's manuscripts are, among other things, material objects. As such, they are comparable, say, to the drawing of Hallam by one of the Sellwood sisters that the author of *In Memoriam* always kept in view. By hanging on to these manuscripts for so long, rather than sharing them with a larger public, Tennyson was neither simply evincing shyness nor just demonstrating how a combination of critical denigration and oversensitivity contributed to his long-term withdrawal from the literary scene: he was also holding on to and prolonging the ritualized presence of Hallam.

There is a parallel to Mallarmé's unfinished elegy for his son, Anatole, who died at the age of eight. Mallarmé's fragments suggest that the graveyard is not the exclusive, or perhaps even primary, site of mourning: 'true mourning in / the apartment / – not cemetery – // furniture'.[73] Tennyson's poem does not significantly reflect upon on the bourgeois fixation on furniture so evident in the nineteenth century novel, but he does anticipate Mallarmé's very conscious investment of his memories of loss in the paraphernalia of the everyday. Tennyson's poetic act of remembrance is also like the French symbolist's internalizing act of grief, in that it too can be read as functioning as a personal gravestone, of sorts, made by a poet in remembrance of a lost one. For not only is *In Memoriam* intricately bound with the process of mourning, but it is also – at least in part – a material object, and one which Tennyson kept returning to in an extended process of working through his grief.

Perhaps, though, a gravestone is too modest a figure to capture the obsessive power of the text's amassing of affect. For the regimentation of space in Tennyson's sprawling poem makes its phenomenology of mourning more similar, in some ways, to that of an entire graveyard than just one gravestone. The way in which the Victorians tried to give grief its pride of place in their elaborate graveyards (of which Highgate and Kensal Green are perhaps two of the most illustrious examples), yet still displace death's more unhealthy side-effects from the centres of their cities (by opting for more marginal and rural sites), parallels the way in which Tennyson's poem both confronts and sublimates the speaker's sorrow. This parallel can be given more specificity: the initial drafts of *In Memoriam* reveal that the text was initially meant to contain sections of a regular length, indicating that the poet was planning to map his grief onto something akin to tidy, symmetrical plots of ground. Thus the Trinity Notebook, containing some of the earliest drafts of the poem, starts off with what would become section xxx in the published version. This section is subsequently followed by numbers ix, xvii, xviii, and xxxi. All of the latter consist of precisely five stanzas of the poem's characteristic quatrains, and numbers xvii and xviii are headed 'II' and 'III' respectively.

There is some evidence, then, that the earliest formal conception of the poem involves a series of short poems of the same length. This conception is quickly shattered by the next poem in the Trinity Notebook, a version of section lxxxv, which, despite seeming to build on the same scheme, soon grows to become far longer than the preceding units. Yet even this section may have been of five stanzas originally, with the remainder added on later; a thesis which is supported by the fact that the subsequent section (number xxviii) is again five stanzas long. In any case, evidence suggests that *In Memoriam* as a whole was originally conceived of as a stanzaically regular poem. The geometry of this literary burying of the poet's friend soon lost its tidiness, however, and became more similar to that of an old, time-worn cemetery – the kind which the more rationally structured Victorian graveyards were meant to leave behind – overflowing with keepsakes of the dead and with the odd administrative building dotted around its landscape. Thus Mallarmé's comment that '*In Memoriam* is a cemetery for one single dead man' is valid beyond its immediate, rather ironic, level.[74] In concordance with this parallel, the growth of *In Memoriam* is a mirror image of the kind of congestion that overtook the cemeteries of the day, as even the new and spacious cemeteries run by private enterprises began to fill up. James Stevens Curl claims that, by the 1870s,

> it had become apparent to many observers that the new hygienic cemeteries were bound to create difficulties as they, too, filled with bodies. There were growing murmurs about pollution of rivers, and the masses of human remains packed into London clay caused great concern. ... Furthermore, the early idea of cemeteries as landscaped parks with mausolea and monuments tastefully placed within them had failed as they had more and more memorials crammed into a limited space.[75]

Similarly, Tennyson may have started out wanting to swiftly order his experience of death in an orderly, spatial schematic, but he soon found himself obeying death's own drawn-out and labyrinthine logic. While he once was Hallam's 'partner in the flowery walk / Of letters' (lxxxiv, 22–23), the process of writing *In Memoriam* involved him in meandering peregrinations on obscure paths, amid tangled growths, outlined by the virtual body of his deceased friend.

Tennyson's poem can be read as an act of compensation, the formation of a sprawling graveyard-like space of language where the poet could confront and explicate his own grief without letting go of the past. Yet it also tends towards being an act of substitution, replacing Hallam with alternative entities and spaces. The process of mourning is in some respects exemplary for memory in general: arguably, no other human act (or passion) is equally fitted to bring out the dimension of loss inherent in all memory. You can't go home again: to remember is to engage with past presents that will never return with anything of the immediacy they once had. Rather than constituting a transparent reproduction of perception, memory relates to an underlying sense of loss, which becomes especially acute and final when the memories involved relate to someone who has passed away.

This last reading has shown how Tennyson, in *In Memoriam*, attempts to combat the passing away of Arthur Hallam with substitution formations. Time's flux is given shape and structure by spatial structures of varying innerness. When the poem itself functions as a fetish object, it aspires to a kind of literary autonomy that we saw Christina Rossetti approximate in her 'Song'. Yet neither the materiality of the fetish object, the structure of organic maturation, nor the symmetrical plots of the graveyard are fully commensurate to the task with which Tennyson grappled. None of these is immune to the kinds of multiplicity that Wordsworth embraced as central to the workings of poetic memory. In the next chapter, I will show how, by wedding internal space more emphatically to outer places in *Idylls of the King*, Tennyson later attempted to give both more solidity and permanence to poetic memory. The latter text will be addressed together with other poems that look at mythical or legendary memories: together with Hardy's 'Poems of 1912–13' and Yeats's 'Under Ben Bulben', the *Idylls* will also be shown to approach the issue of collective, rather than primarily individual, memory.

3
Weird Wests: Victorian and Post-Victorian Displacements of Nostalgia

Must memory be shared and externalized in order for it to survive, or be handled, with any force? And once recollection is exposed to external sites and vessels, can it be adequately controlled? These are questions encountered by poets who either are suspicious of, or suffer the detrimental effects of, the extremes of romantic innerness. Memory may seem more unassailable and untainted when safely lodged in the interior recesses of the sole psyche, and yet so much recollective verse reveals, of course, that the individual is transitory, too. Although elegy may provoke the poet to batten down the hatches of interior fastnesses, elegy also reminds us that such storing places may, sooner rather than later, be ruined by the unimaginable touch of time. In this chapter, attempts to link memory with more concrete and collective forms of spatial extension will be addressed. First, Tennyson's *Idylls of the King* will be seen to balance an embrace of collective, localized memory with a distrust of how such memory involves one in a logic of images. As such, the Victorian Poet Laureate's fragmented epic does not fully complete the movement towards exteriority already glimpsed in *In Memoriam*. In the second reading of this chapter, Thomas Hardy's 'Poems of 1912–13' will be seen to build on the precedent of the *Idylls*, using Arthurian legend as a template for the forging of a mystical connection between the memory and the west of England. Hardy's sequence will prove to be more individualistic than Tennyson's poem, though, and its affirmations of romance in a Cornish setting will be accompanied by an anguished scepticism with regard to memory's ability to make the past fully present once again. In the third and final reading, William Butler Yeats's 'Under Ben Bulben' will be presented as transcending his predecessors in scope and idealist ambition, yet doing so at a price. Our reading of 'Under Ben Bulben' will tease out what is left by the wayside of Yeats's grand testamentary performance, focussing particularly on the relationship between the poem and the poet's epitaph, as well as the latter's address to an unidentified horseman.

When poetry turns to memories linked with fateful places of long tradition, is the upshot necessarily an unequivocal bolstering or protecting of the self? By linking memory to returns to western places imbued with the aural trappings of origin, all three of the Victorian and post-Victorian works that will be addressed here come close to the ambit of nostalgia (from the Greek, *nostos* meaning 'return home' and *algos* meaning 'pain'). The west is approached as something akin to a long-lost home, tantalizing each of these poets in turn. In a recent study, Linda M. Austin has detailed nostalgia's transformation, during the period from 1780 to 1917, from being a pathological state of homesickness to a more generally accepted aesthetic phenomenon involving a pleasurable recollection of the past. Interpreting literary and cultural texts as reflections of psychophysiological thought of the period, she traces a general shift from understanding memory as a mental activity to a phenomenon rooted in a particular conception of the body: 'taking up long suppressed materialist ideas to locate a memory beyond consciousness in the body's motor-sensory mechanisms, psychophysiology reconfigured the traditional dualism between mind (or soul) and body'.[1] Austin's readings of Victorian poetry trace an itinerary whereby 'a focus on verifying the identity of objects from the past' yields to 'an exercise in spatial, egocentric, and instantly verifying repetition'.[2] In her account, nostalgia gradually loosens 'its overt ties to the content or truth-value of the past,' instead relying on therapeutic use of 'sensation and bodily practices'.[3] Nostalgic rememberings are, she claims, generally 'autoreferential', and 'often reflect, as content, their own production'.[4] My own readings of Tennyson, Hardy, and Yeats in this chapter will parallel Austin, insofar as memory is seen as being increasingly linked to extramental sites. All three poets can be read as negotiating with nostalgia's desiring look backwards, but what Austin terms nostalgia's 'idyllic hyperbole' will in each case, here, be undermined by a troubling weirdness that challenges the ego.[5] Crucially, it will be shown how these poets' investing of memory in external places and objects exposes it to processes of displacement – i.e., expansions and slippages of meaning ultimately beyond the ken of nostalgia.[6] While disturbance comes from without for Yeats, in both Tennyson and Hardy displacement surfaces in the texts themselves, as these readings go beyond autoreferential nostalgia to critical uses of memory.

The contentious image in *Idylls of the King*

Alfred, Lord Tennyson's *Idylls of the King* insists upon understanding memory as consisting of memory-images, yet it also raises questions about the very process of image-making. The title of this work signifies not only diminutive size (compared with a fuller epic treatment), but also that it is a collection of images: the *eidyllion* are innately linked to the Greek *eidos*, and thus also to the venerable tradition that sees literature as a form of mimetic picturing. Even at their most linguistically challenging level, the *Idylls* adhere to the logic of the image. In this Tennyson's respect, epic may be considered as providing a more conservative, or more limited, account of memory than that found in *In Memoriam*, as the latter did not place such a strong emphasis on imagistic copying.

The understanding of recollection as a mental copy of an original impression has arguably been sidelined, or superseded, in recent years by a more contextual emphasis on the place and performative efficacy of memory. Thus Norman Malcolm could, in 1970, utilize Wittgenstein's critique of representative conceptions of thought to question the understanding of memory as image. Malcolm showed that nineteenth and twentieth century thinkers in Britain and America had seemingly been obsessed by this model: 'It is as if Russell, Price, James, Hume and the rest thought like this: There certainly has to be in our remembering a copy of the past event we remember, and what could this copy be if not an image?'[7] Yet neither the image, the structural copy of an original impression, nor the idea of a memory trace satisfied Malcolm: all of these conceptions insisted upon the universal presence of memory images in recollection, even if only a limited number of acts of memory actually involve anything of the sort.

Still, even if it has its shortcomings, the image theory has the advantage of providing grounds for a comparison between the memory and the object or state of affairs upon which it is based. Hence the pervasiveness of the idea, which received venerable ancient formulations in Plato's *Theaetetus* and Aristotle's *On Memory and Reminiscence* (*Peri mnemes kai anamnesis*). What Tennyson's idylls share with the tradition of writings on the memory-image is an intense interest in the misfirings of memory. One could say that a distrust of memory, as well as of language, pushes him towards a wholehearted embrace of the image. Yet Tennyson is also attuned to the image's poetical riches. His defence of *Idylls of the King* against some readers' overzealous application of allegory is also a defence of the image: 'the thought within the image is much more than any one interpretation.'[8] Though bound to the image, it must be emphasized that this poem is not an exponent of a simpleminded mimeticism – Tennyson's own distaste for contemporary realism indicates as much – but rather explores the problems and possibilities of *mimesis*, an exploration that gains amplitude through its own complex imitating of mediaeval manners and legends through a modern prism.

In focusing upon the memory image, this reading will mainly concentrate on two of the twelve idylls that together make up Tennyson's *Idylls of the King*: 'Balin and Balan' and 'The Passing of Arthur' have been chosen because they arguably contain the most sustained meditations on memory present in the poem. Apart from including what is perhaps the most subtle meditation on the status of the image in the entirety of the *Idylls*, 'Balin and Balan' also presents the most incisive deliberation over the stakes involved in connecting interior memories to outer spaces. In this, the fifth of the idylls, Tennyson presents us with not only the advantages but also the risks of externalizing memory. As such, it constitutes a transition between recollection as individual innerness, which we confronted in the previous chapter, and the attempts at embodying memory in collective localities that will loom large in this one.

When we first meet the knight Balin in Tennyson's text, he is a man with a past. Three years previous to the commencement of the narrative, he and his brother, Balan, were exiled from Arthur's court as a result of his hot temper. When Arthur wins him back to the court at the beginning of the idyll, this is done in order to deliver him from a tainted life. As Balin declares to Arthur,

> I smote upon the naked skull
> A thrall of thine in open hall, my hand
> Was gauntleted, half slew him; for I heard
> He had spoken evil of me; thy just wrath
> Sent me a three-years' exile from thine eyes.
> (53–57)[9]

Although the idyll repeatedly returns to the problem of Balin's violent temper as his major failing, it should be noted that the cause for his original exile is, in a fashion, only a heightened adherence to Arthur's precepts. For both Arthur and Balin will not countenance slander. Yet Balin will meet misfortune precisely because of the disfiguring effects of slander, and his inability to construct a beneficent memory-image that will help him leave his past behind.

Arthur's attempted redemption of this erring knight is emblematic of a larger project. Balin is a particularly arresting other of Arthur's community. By bringing him to Camelot and the Round Table from the outskirts, where he long has wreaked havoc with his brother Balan, Arthur is attempting to enforce a sublimating measure. The instinctual violence of the community will not be permitted to harass it from the outside, but must be transformed into a potent – if markedly gentler – force for the good. At the heart of this transformation lie both an act of forgetting and the construction of a new memory-image: the radicalness of the change envisaged links Balin's case both backwards to the Christian idea of rebirth and forwards to modernist' attempts to break free of the past. Within the *Idylls of the King*, his problems are paralleled by the moral struggles of King Arthur's adulterous wife. Wrestling with her conscience, the troubled Guinevere will describe 'true repentance' as a state in which one cannot even allow oneself to 'Think again [of] / The sins that made the past so pleasant to us' ('Guinevere', 371–373). Yet such an attempted self-censorship is doomed to fail, since memory is not completely under the dominion of the will. Soon after this claim, she is described as 'moving thro' the past unconsciously' ('Guinevere', 398–399), dwelling with relish upon her first encounter with Lancelot. Balin's attempt to atone for his past is both more desperate and more radical: he will not merely try to hold the past at bay, but will seek to eradicate it completely.

In order to leave behind the 'too fierce manhood' (71) of his past, Balin strives to imitate Lancelot's gentleness. Linked to this use of his fellow knight as an ideal precedent, he also exchanges the insignia of his old shield for a new one. In place of the 'rough beast' that previously graced his shield (192), he opts for an image of the unattainable object of his love: 'Some goodly cognizance of Guinevere' (191). The term 'cognizance' – referring to an identifying, heraldic emblem – recurs in the poem. Stemming from the Latin *cognoscere*, roughly meaning 'to get to know', the word obviously refers to a particularly iconic instance of perception. But it is a perception which is meant to be lodged deep into the inner recesses of Balin's being, thus becoming a firmly recoverable memory-image. It is, however, also a constructed and external object; existing on Balin's shield, it attempts to solidify and purify inner memory through recourse to an external substitute.

As a memory image, the 'cognizance' is meant to *both* replace Balin's old image of himself *and* assuage his own frustrated desire for the queen:

> I never can be close with her, as he
> That brought her hither. Shall I pray the King
> To let me bear some token of his Queen
> Whereon to gaze, remembering her – forget
> My heats and violences? live afresh?
>
> (181–186)

Expressive of sublimated desire, this is a love token to the queen that cannot be handed over to her – only worn as a sign of distanced devotion. The emblem of self-transformation is used in an attempt to 'live afresh' by burying old self-images. By choosing to bear Guinevere's 'own crown-royal upon shield' (196), Balin hopes to attain a new form of re-cognition of his own being, the shield functioning as a reminder of his ideal self. Thus it will function roughly like a pictorial portrait, as described in 'Lancelot and Elaine':

> As when a painter, poring on a face
> Divinely thro' all hindrance finds the man
> Behind it, and so paints him that his face,
> The shape and colour of a mind and life,
> Lives for his children, ever at its best
> And fullest.
>
> ('Lancelot and Elaine', 330–335)

Balin would like to be 'the man / Behind' himself – the 'best / And fullest' to which he can aspire. Yet, at the same time, the image is not solely related to his own person. In psychoanalytical parlance, the shield may be said to instantiate relations not only with Balin's ideal ego (a narcissistic projection of an ultimate, but unattainable self) but also with his ego ideal (an other who supplies a normative role model for the self's integration into the symbolic sphere). If Balin wishes to attain a better self, it is a quest that can only be attained via an instance of mimetic desire: on the surface, his ideal self bears all the traits of Lancelot.[10] For although Balin's love for Guinevere is remembered by this sign, it also implicitly functions as an impetus to repeatedly interiorize Lancelot's desire (a presumed lofty desire, characterized by a form of disinterested gentleness) for Guinevere.

The cognizance is a reminder, but on a far more radical plane than, say, tying a knot around one's finger. By changing his shield, Balin is engaged in a profound transformation of identity through memory – it is like the forging of a new signature, or even the attempt to change one's fingerprint. But unlike the latter acts, this reinvention of the self is not a one-off. Rather than providing an instantaneous conversion, Balin's shield is involved in a longer haul that involves the changing of deep-seated habits foundational of his identity. It is an enduring and excessive exigency, demanding all the resources of even the very single-minded Balin.

It should be no surprise, then, that it fails. But why does it do so? In part, Balin's project founders because of circumstances beyond his control: he cannot know that the choice of Guinevere and Lancelot as exemplars for his own disinterested desire is misguided. The external originals for his memory-image are tainted, and therefore undermine the very inner pureness that they were meant to help safeguard. Both the lover and the beloved invested in by Balin's shield have been unable to conjure up the temperance that the knight so desperately seeks, and the manner in which their transgressive intimacy causes Balin's downfall is a forerunner for the more large-scale cataclysms of the later stages of the poem. As Lancelot cannot sustain his role of ideal other, Balin cannot manage to uphold the otherness of his brother Balan, and the latter two die, in the end, in an implosion of transgressed borders.

Matters are even more complicated than this, though. As so often in Tennyson's poem, the tidy symmetry of the plot is obscured and complicated by the way in which it mixes memory with desire, diverting its narration into a variety of contrasting channels. For Balin does not founder upon the truth about Guinevere and Lancelot's guilty love; he founders upon a lie. What finally seals his fate is not his own, rather inconclusive observations of the two lovers, but rather Vivien's fabrication of a story concerning a meeting of the two taking place in similar circumstances in Camelot: 'She lied with ease; but horror-stricken he, / Remembering that dark bower at Camelot, / Breathed in a dismal whisper "It is truth"' (517–519). He has managed to hold his own memory of their close – but not obviously carnal – relations in 'that dark bower at Camelot' at bay for a long time, and not let it overshadow the memory-image on his shield. But the testimony of Vivien's alternative memory – and its corroboration by her squire – is enough to tilt the balance.

Thus one might place the guilt squarely on Balin's own shoulders. He is precipitous in placing any credence in Vivien's mendacious version of events. He bases his ideal memory-image on the common perception of Lancelot's virtue, on the knight's fame, but lets himself be persuaded by untrustworthy testimony. Certainly, Balin blames himself at the end of the idyll. While he and Balan lie dying in one another's arms, he cries out:

> 'O Brother' answered Balin 'woe is me!
> My madness all thy life has been thy doom,
> Thy curse and darken'd all thy day; and now
> The night has come. I scarce can see thee now.
> Goodnight! for we shall never bid again
> Goodmorrow – Dark my doom was here, and dark
> It will be there. I see thee now no more.
> I would not mine again should darken thine,
> Goodnight, true brother.'
>
> (607–615)

The strong emphasis on the motif of darkness is not without precedent in 'Balin and Balan', and will reward some scrutiny. It is anticipated by a few references to the mainly malevolent workings of shadows. Shadows are particularly important in describing Sir Garlon's ghost-like attack on Balin in the woods. A 'shadow of a spear' (317) passes by, as Balin only catches a glimpse of his assailant: he sees only 'a shape / A light of armour by him flash, and pass / And vanish in the woods' (320–322). Here the 'shadow of a spear' (a phrase repeated by Balin in line 368) is not, however, so much a simple metonymical representative for utter darkness as – since it is associated with a flashing light – a more ambivalent motif. When Balin later seeks revenge on Sir Garlon, exclaiming 'So thou be a shadow, here I make thee ghost' (388), the inherent connection between shadows and liminal spaces is underlined. Like a ghost, then, we never know where we have a shadow: the only thing we can be sure of is that we cannot put our finger on it.[11]

These references to how shadows exist on the borderlines of perception and existence reflect back upon earlier uses of the motif, which more directly address the question of memory and its important role on the threshold between interiority and exteriority. To create an image or external representation of a memory, whether it be an emblem of a shield or a photograph, is here to surrender the bright light of inner evidence to the shadow play of outer spaces. One passage places the responsibility of how such shadow play undermines Balin's project squarely on his own shoulders. When he despairs of living up to the courtly codes of Camelot, we are told that Balin's discontent conjures up dastardly shadows that imaginatively disfigure the world without. The situation makes Tennyson call upon one of his characteristic deployments of Homeric simile:

> Thus, as a hearth lit in a mountain home,
> And glancing on the window, when the gloom
> Of twilight deepens round it, seems a flame
> That rages in the woodland far below,
> So when his moods were darken'd, court and King
> And all the kindly warmth of Arthur's hall
> Shadow'd an angry distance.
>
> (226–232)

In a failure of imagination, the outward shadows are mere reflections of an inner darkness, as the limitations of the subject are passed on to his world view.

Shadows are hard to escape, as a slightly earlier passage on the nature of representation makes clear. Balin asks for permission to bear the queen's cognizance on his shield:

> And Arthur, when Sir Balin sought him, said
> 'What wilt thou bear?' Balin was bold, and ask'd
> To bear her own crown-royal upon the shield,
> Whereat she smiled and turn'd her to the King,
> Who answer'd 'Thou shalt put the crown to use.
> The crown is but the shadow of the King,
> And this a shadow's shadow, let him have it,
> So this will help him of his violences!'
> 'No shadow' said Sir Balin 'O my Queen,
> But light to me! no shadow, O my King,
> But golden earnest of a gentler life!'
>
> (193–204)

The complex rhetoric of this passage leaves matters wonderfully suspended with regard to some of the most central themes of this idyll. King Arthur here displays a stance related to his disdain (not shared by his knights) for simulated battles: he is one who 'cares [not] / For triumph in our mimic wars, the jousts' ('Lancelot and Elaine', 310–311). But his lack of veneration for the shield is more than a mere individual character trait, as it echoes the traditionally Platonic denigration of representations of reality – as 'a shadow's shadow.' Yet from this premise Arthur draws a conclusion that is quite opposite to the one famously drawn by Plato in *The Republic*: the artistic representation is not harmful for being a shadow, but all the more harmless. A shadow is less effectual than a real entity, and therefore a shadow's shadow cannot possibly be the cause of much evil.

Of course the evil addressed here is primarily that of an affront to the royal personages, rather than any possible danger to Balin's own being. Ironically, the king does not discount the possibility of there being some good 'use' of the image for Balin, even if the queen's 'crown-royal' does not make any difference to the royalty itself. It is as if the image on the shield were a freely floating signifier, which could be deployed in any possible way chosen by its user. Like some mollifying, fabricated memory, invented for purely therapeutic reasons (or the nostalgic memory as described by Austin), it can function like a placebo precisely due to its lack of any deeper reality. Yet such a deeper reality is precisely that which Balin grants it: 'No shadow ... But light to me.' He will twist the sign of the crown out of its original provenance, making it signify the queen rather than the king.

Balin's later destruction of the shield provides a radical counterpoint to his early optimism. Ashamed of his own violence to Sir Garlon, he initially tries to leave it behind by hanging it 'high on a branch' (426). This is an ambivalent gesture, both an act of sacrilege and an attempted atonement. Memory is still only mixed with doubt, and not with utter despair. Yet events soon take a more drastic course. The cure for violence is itself submitted to a violent destruction, as Vivien's tale rids him of all faith in the shield's curative potential:

> his evil spirit upon him leapt,
> He ground his teeth together, sprang with a yell,
> Tore from the branch, and cast on earth, the shield,
> Drove his mail'd heel athwart the royal crown,
> Stampt all into defacement, hurl'd it from him
> Among the forest weeds, and cursed the tale,
> The told-of, and the teller.
>
> (529–535)

In an apocalyptic act of forgetting, Balin destroys the curative image – an image that itself was intended to destroy his own inborn violence. The consequences of this radically iconoclastic action are drastic, as a case of mistaken identity leads him and Balan to kill each other – indicating the radical risks run by any disavowal of representation (or what psychoanalysts call the symbolic mode) in favour of pure identity. By erasing the traces of his own past, Balin makes it impossible for Balan to accurately perceive his present identity.

At one level, Balin's disavowal of the memory-image is no more than a more pointed repetition of Arthur's previous belittling of 'a shadow's shadow'. Arthur displays some prescience with regard to what one might call the disposability of the memorial artefact, and his knight only follows suit belatedly. Thus this idyll rehearses, if in a rather more histrionic fashion, the way in which Arthur and another of his knights, Bedivere, settle their disagreement over Excalibur in 'The Passing of Arthur'. But it would be too simple to see this parallel as spelling out a straightforward message of iconoclasm at the heart of *Idylls of the King*. As we shall see, ambivalence seems to be consistently upheld in Tennyson's poem.

Where 'Balin and Balan' links memory to an instrumental object, other sections of the epic suggest that memory can be embodied in more encompassing spaces and practices. In the first idyll, 'The Coming of Arthur', the very survival of the story about Arthur is presented as building upon a combination of literary tradition and collective memory:

> so great bards of him will sing
> Hereafter; and dark sayings from of old
> Ranging and ringing thro' the minds of men,
> And echo'd by old folk beside their fires
> For comfort after their wage-work is done,
> Speak of the King.
>
> (413–418)

Read in light of this passage, which is spoken by Merlin, Tennyson's own idylls present themselves as part of a rich, widely encompassing tradition that includes, but also transcends, the merely literary sphere. Yet such an embrace of the richness of the Arthurian legacy is contradicted by the poem's concluding address 'To the Queen'. There Tennyson is at pains to differentiate his own version, presented as a gift to the queen, from all others:

> accept this old imperfect tale,
> New-old, and shadowing Sense at war with Soul,
> Ideal manhood closed in real man,
> Rather than that gray king, whose name, a ghost,

Streams like a cloud, man-shaped, from mountain peak,
And cleaves to cairn and cromlech still: or him
Of Geoffrey's book, or him of Malleor's, one
Touch'd by the adulterous finger of a time
That hover'd between war and wantonness,
And crownings and dethronements.

(36–45)

Both the ethically dubious (in Tennyson's view) account of Malory's *Le Morte D'Arthur* and that found in Geoffrey of Monmouth's writings are set aside here. More interestingly, so is the Arthur whose memory survives in the collective memory of particular localities in the British Isles. The latter's embodied presence is contrasted with the moral allegory that Tennyson's poem presents itself as 'shadowing' – confirming the centrality of that latter concept to the entire work, though not solving the vexed ontological status of shadows. Even here, though, the shadowing of the image is complicated, and takes on a life on its own: as I pointed out earlier, Tennyson was embarrassed by too straightforward allegorical readings of the poem, insisting that 'the thought within the image' transcended any given explication.[12]

Certainly Tennyson is not concerned with deracinating the legend, by ridding it of all inherited links with the English countryside. Not only does Camelot, for instance, loom large in the poem, but also Tennyson is concerned with underlining the idea that the home of the Round Table is located in a place replete with tradition and memory. As Percivale puts it in 'The Holy Grail': 'our Camelot, / Built by old kings, age after age, so old / The king himself had fears that it would fall' (339–341). Although it is a palace of art, Camelot is obviously not a figure of aesthetic self-indulgence: Arthur's abode is a building attuned to the king's spiritual and mystical aspirations. Gareth's first encounter with the gate of Camelot, in the second of the idylls, is also the reader's first experience of Camelot in the poem. Several features are stressed, including the transcendent nature of the city (which makes it disappear into the mist for its earthbound visitors) and its resplendent beauty. Both of these aspects are linked with a very particular negation of temporality. On the sides of the Lady of the Lake depicted on the keystone of the gate, the artwork attains prophetic powers:

> And in the space to the left of her, and right,
> Were Arthur's wars in weird devices done,
> New things and old co-twisted, as if Time

> Were nothing, so inveterately, that men
> Were giddy gazing there.
>   ('Gareth and Lynette', 220–224)

This transcendence of time is not a dismissal or avoidance of it, as is indicated by the subsequent description of how the gate seems to move before one's eyes. As old and new are 'co-twisted', this is an art which goes beyond time only by including it within itself: transtemporal and not atemporal, this is an overview, rather than an alternative.

The display of Arthur's wars in 'weird devices' resonates with other sections of the poem. There is an obvious link with the many heraldic devices of the poem, of which Balin's shield is one of the most prominent. Both this shield and the artwork of the gate are neither exclusively memory-images nor straightforwardly identifying markers (like names), but combine both characteristics. Furthermore, the 'weird' nature of these representations resonates with other passages in the idylls. The word itself is derived from the Old English *wyrd*, meaning fate or destiny. Yet more than mere prophecy seems to be at stake. It crops up again later in the poem: in 'Lancelot and Elaine' again with reference to the gates (the 'weirdly-sculptured gates' of line 839), and in Tristram's reference to the 'weird legend' of Arthur's birth ('The Last Tournament', 664). In neither of these does fate seem to be the main meaning, but rather the supernatural or uncanny aspects of Arthurian rule (possibly supplemented by the sense of being marvellous in an eccentric way), perhaps alluding to the traditional three 'weird sisters' appropriated by *Macbeth*. It's harder to pinpoint the exact signification of the term in 'The Passing of Arthur', when Bedivere alludes to Arthur's final battle as 'that last weird battle in the west' (29) and 'this last, dim, weird battle of the west' (95). After Arthur's departure at the end of the idyll, the word appears once more:

> The stillness of the dead world's winter dawn
> Amazed him, and he groan'd, 'The King is gone.'
> And therewithal came on him the weird rhyme,
> 'From the great deep to the great deep he goes.'
>   (442–445)

The 'rhyme' is here bound up with the fate of Arthur's reign, and his destination in 'the great deep', but its weirdness is also indicative of the gnomic abstruseness of Merlin's poem quoted in the final line. In

'The Coming of Arthur', the quoted passage completes a short riddle with which Merlin parries attempts to unravel Arthur's mysterious origins. Rumours are rife concerning the possible illegitimacy of the king, but all attempts to achieve complete clarity concerning Arthur's lineage fail. Contrasting theories about his presumed conception in 'Tintagil castle by the Cornish sea' ('The Coming of Arthur', 186) rival a more miraculous story whereby a 'naked babe' was carried onto the shore and 'rode to Merlin's feet' (ibid., 383), but no final explanation is forthcoming. The 'great deep' of Merlin's riddle may refer to the hidden reserves of Cornwall and its abutting ocean, or to a more general sense of obscurity.

If weirdness is a shared characteristic of both the grand artwork that is Camelot and the western coast that sets the scene for not only Arthur's birth but also the final battle of his reign, it is because both of these show a linking of fate and a suspension of meaning. Arthur is always a fated king, yet the significance and final issue of his fate remain suspended. Being the final idyll, 'The Passing of Arthur' is responsible for delivering this open-endedness as part of Arthur's surviving legacy, linking it closely to the west of England identified as 'Lyonnesse – / A land of old upheaven from the abyss' ('The Passing of Arthur', 82–83). Both geographically and symbolically, the abyssal deep of the west is a far cry from the kingdom's resplendent centre in Camelot, and draws sustenance from the margins of meaning and civilization.

The open-endedness of Arthur's western fate runs counter to a tendency towards teleological closure. In 'The Passing of Arthur', a desire for temporal closure is offered by the linked destinies of Bedivere and the sword Excalibur. Both are means by which Arthur's end can be linked indissolubly to his beginnings. When 'The Passing of Arthur' begins, the final showdown with Modred still has the potential of inflicting an absolute rupture with all that Arthur's life has contained until then. When Bedivere tells the troubled king to leave his worrying dreams behind and 'conquer as of old' (64), the king replies that this 'battle in the west' is 'Far other' to his previous victories (66). The ensuing challenge is to ensure that this otherness will somehow attain the character of a fruition or extension, rather than negation, of the benevolent course of Arthur's reign. The end will have to be attuned to the beginnings, and this will be taken care of by Bedivere and Excalibur in tandem.

Bedivere is the 'First made and latest left of all the knights' (2), and Arthur's leaving him grants a sense of final closure to the Round Table. He is a trustworthy assistant, the most loyal and dutiful of all

of Arthur's knights, holding up some hope for a future of knightly virtues in a changing world. By obeying Arthur's command, and throwing
Excalibur into the mere, he helps the king fulfil his mystical duty. The
duty of casting away the sword is intimated early on in the poem, in
'The Coming of Arthur':

> on one side,
> Graven in the oldest tongue of all this world,
> 'Take me,' but turn the blade and ye shall see,
> And written in the speech ye speak yourself,
> 'Cast me away!' And sad was Arthur's face
> Taking it, but old Merlin counsell'd him,
> 'Take thou and strike! the time to cast away
> Is yet far-off.'
>
> (300–307)

Later the same symmetrical pairing of the appearance and disappearance of Excalibur is linked to a work of art. In Merlin's hall in Camelot,
the eastern window depicts how 'Arthur finds the brand Excalibur'
(253), while it is intimated that the facing 'blank' (255) window of the
west awaits the corresponding image of disappearance. As with Balin's
shield, the artistic image here envelops both the coming into presence
and the fading away of reality, a wedding of processes now given an
extra twist by its link with soothsaying and teleological temporality.

Bedivere's returning the sword to the deep from which it arose is thus
in fulfilment with supernatural decree, not only remembering but also
obeying an obligation incurred at the beginning of the king's reign.
However, this gesture also represents a more ambivalent link to the past
than Bedivere's continued presence (as the first and last of knights) at
the side of his king. Later, Bedivere will become a privileged witness,
first 'Revolving many memories' (438) of Arthur's reign in solitude, and
then conveying them 'when the man was no more than a voice / In the
white winter of his age, to those / With whom he dwelt, new faces, other
minds' (3–5). One of the things that prevent Bedivere from straightaway
obliging Arthur's wish to throw Excalibur away is that he sees that the
sword could play a similar, commemorative role: if it vanishes, 'What
record, or what relic of my lord / Should be to aftertime, but empty
breath and rumours of a doubt?' (266–268). While Bedivere's narration
serves to preserve the memory of Arthur, Arthur's insistence upon the
disappearance of Excalibur threatens to condemn that same memory
to oblivion. The former seems attuned to Nietzsche's understanding of

the heroic patrimony of monumental history, while the latter (echoing Balin's destruction of his shield) is closer to the German thinker's notion of an 'active forgetting' essential to preserving the vitality and immediacy of one's existence.[13] Although Arthur surely does want to be remembered, his unbending spirituality – which combines a respect for supernatural decree with an implicit disdain for mere physical reminders of his reign – runs the risk of obliterating all memory traces associated with his rule. In short, he here encapsulates something of the entire poem's suspicion towards entrusting memory to physically given phenomena, whether those phenomena be particular places, images or (as here and in Balin's case) symbolically charged items of weaponry.

The fate of the sword is linked by metonymy to a more pressing and important issue concerning Arthur's final fate as a physical being: does he die at the conclusion of the poem, or is the 'passing' of Arthur merely his passing – on the 'dusky barge' (362), and in the company of the three queens – to the healing pastures of Avilon? Although the *Idylls of the King* leaves no doubt about the dismemberment of the Round Table, it suspends judgement on this particular question. Even Arthur himself admits to being unsure: 'I am going a long way / With these thou seëst – if indeed I go / (For all my mind is clouded with a doubt) – / To the island-valley of Avilion' (424–427).

The reason for this suspended narrative outcome is surely something more than a mere wish to remain loyal to the varying content of the many Arthurian legends: Tennyson does not hesitate, elsewhere, to make very selective use of this manifold legacy. Partly, this open-endedness creates a sense of roundedness, in that Arthur's passing is no less surrounded by the mists of myth than his coming: 'From the great deep to the great deep he goes' (445). A paradoxical result of this is that Arthur arguably becomes all the more mourned for lacking a physical grave: without any single resting place, this king can be remembered everywhere – indeed, one cannot even discount the possibility that he may not be dead at all. In addition, the fact that 'his grave should be a mystery / From all men, like his birth' ('Guinevere', 295–296) may be read as an attempt to manoeuvre around the typical problems surrounding the projection of utopias. The utopian potential of the Arthurian story was there at Tennyson's bidding from the start. As Roger Simpson has pointed out with regard to Arthur:

> his mythological aura endows him with the Messianic attribute of a promised return: he therefore remains imminent, and of perpetual modern relevance, and his second coming – itself an apt metaphor

for the Medieval Revival or Celtic Renaissance – may be constantly reinterpreted to adapt to new meliorist prescriptions.[14]

Tennyson's individual interpretation gives this utopian potential a particular inflection, and in the process attempts to circumvent a recurring Achilles heel of utopianism. For although the potential return of Arthur carries much the same inspirational value as all other utopias – readers as well as knights being expected to draw 'ensample from fair names' ('Guinevere', 487) – it also runs the same risk of seeming unrealistic. An impossible utopia or a weak messianism always risks being so distant and unthinkable that it loses all possibility of persuasion, even to the point of becoming more dispiriting than inspirational. By placing Arthur's return halfway between materiality and virtuality, Tennyson does not solve this problem, but he does allow hope and the necessities of deferral their due place, finding a not unfruitful *détente* between their respective claims.

Rather than fleeing multiplicity, the poet in this instance seeks to utilize it as a means towards an end. Without a conclusive image of the dead king, imagination is given room to play. Yet there is not free or untrammelled play. The primary limitation to Tennyson's utopianism arguably lies in how the poem tends towards a narrow form of nationalism. Particularly the concluding address 'To the Queen', with its search for the appropriate 'tone of empire' (18), tends to nudge the poem towards a form of sophisticated national epic. At least one recent critic has followed suit, claiming that Arthur 'represents the idea of the English imagination'.[15] Yet other elements of the poem point toward broader vistas: for instance, a memorandum written by Tennyson to Sir James Knowles identifies the king as being allegorical of religious faith,[16] while he also expressed approval of Knowles's own interpretation of Arthur as signifying the conscience.[17] Although Tennyson was not averse to giving the British a particularly exalted position in the universalist scheme of things, he commonly espoused the cause of a common human nature (transcending itself by aspiring towards the divine). A blend of religiosity and idealism – initiated by Kant, and subsequently passed down to the Victorians by Coleridge and Maurice – seems to have been the consistent tenor of Tennyson's later thought.[18]

Setting aside the actual content of *Idylls of the King*, though, the sophisticated way in which memory is set to work in the poem should perhaps be its most enduring legacy of all. The doubleness of the final idyll presents itself as another version of the ambivalence of the memory image, as previously encountered in 'Balin and Balan'. While the latter idyll concerned itself with its continued endurance and preservation in the present, 'The Passing of Arthur' is more directed towards understanding memory's effecting a suspended future. Paul Ricoeur has written that there 'must be an irreducible feature in the living experience of memory that explains the persistence of the confusion conveyed by the expression "memory-image" '.[19] Tennyson's version of the Arthurian legends makes a virtue of that confusion. Memory traces need not be interpreted as being 'images', but, once they are, then a powerful space of ambiguity is opened up between the projective and unpredictable play of imagination, on the one hand, and the more dutifully representative ideal of the mimetic memory-image, on the other. *Idylls of the King* links this ambivalence not only to the epistemological conundrums of art, but also to the value of instrumental objects (through the weaponry of Balin and Arthur) and the symbolism of place.

Place, romance and the past in Thomas Hardy's 'Poems of 1912–13'

No less than Tennyson, Thomas Hardy seems to have been obsessed with the presence of that which has passed by. In his poetry, both past and present risk being swallowed up by a sense of empty and meaningless succession, which also casts its ominous shadow over the future. Building on the preceding critiques from Coleridge and Carlyle on how mechanical models threaten to dominate all contemporary thought, and attacking fellow Victorians' belief in progress, Hardy laments the effects of a mechanically linear conception of time. He also explores, however, how this conception of time is countered by other factors, among which memory plays a crucial part. The third section of 'She to Him', for instance, includes a criticism of 'souls of Now, who would disjoint / The mind from memory, making Life all aim' (11–12).[20] Here it is impossible to miss what Paul Zietlow has described as 'Hardy's sense that there may be no place in the modern world, with its emphasis on production and progress, for one who remembers'.[21] In contrast to modernity, which is overwhelmed by haste and the cult of the ephemeral, Hardy casts himself in the role of a poet who takes the time to pause and meditate on that which is passing or past.

In 'Poems of 1912–13' – a sequence of poems triggered by the death of his by then estranged first wife, Emma, and published as part of *Satires of Circumstance, Lyrics and Reveries* (1914) – the battle between time's ephemerality and memory's restorative abilities comes to a particularly heightened and accomplished expression. The sequence originally consisted of eighteen poems, until Hardy added three more at its very end in 1919, subtly changing the general movement of the whole. The added poems – 'The Spell of the Rose', 'St. Launce's Revisited', and 'Where the Picnic Was' – present a more distanced view on the dead beloved. Commentators have been divided about the wisdom of this move: while Donald Davie sees it as indicative of a 'defensive small-mindedness' that leads to the depletion of the poem's original vision,[22] others have seen it as confirming important truths about mourning and textuality. M. L. Rosenthal and Sally M. Gall have, for instance, claimed that the sequence shows 'a desperate need to fix the causes, quality, and ultimate meaning of a love that promised so much yet ended in appalling distance'.[23] The addition of the three final poems, they assert, provides a satisfying end to the speaker's quest. That quest is a narrative one, and Hardy's narrative concern provides us with the motivation for the sequence's strong emphasis on geography: 'Hardy's narrative instinct helps him give his sequence a grounding in literal spaces.'[24]

Perhaps, however, the spaces involved in 'Poems of 1912–13' are neither straightforwardly literal nor simple appendages to a narrative structure? As would seem to be hinted at by the phrase 'poetry of place', used by Hardy in the poem 'After a Romantic Day' (11), narrative does not have a monopoly on space. Indeed, as we have already ascertained several times in this study, spatiality and memory tend to be consistently interwoven in poetic encounters with times past. Edward S. Casey has cogently confirmed place's importance in countering the dispersive successiveness of time in a way clearly relevant to Hardy's case:

> On a monolinear view of time, there is dispersal and disintegration as each instant arises and dies away – instantaneously. *No time is left over* in such a view: no time that might be gathered up in memory and kept therein. Thus, to say that memory is 'of the past' resolves nothing; indeed it may dissolve the effective basis for the reconnective capacity of memory itself. At the least, memory is of a non-punctiform past. But we may say more radically that memory involves something more than the purely temporal in its own makeup. ... But if memory is not simply or exclusively 'of the past,' what does it involve in addition? The very embodiment of remembering hints at an answer. To be embodied is *ipso facto* to assume a particular perspective and position; it is to have not just a point of view but a *place* in which we are situated. It is to occupy a portion of space from out of which we both undergo given experiences and remember them.[25]

Casey claims that 'memory of place, of *having been in a place*, is one of the most conspicuously neglected areas of philosophical or psychological inquiry into remembering.'[26] This may explain the reason why critics of 'Poems of 1912–13' have paid relatively scant attention to this feature, even if they have addressed – often in sophisticated and enlightening ways – other dimensions of the sequence's compelling explorations of the workings of memory.

By linking potentially revelatory acts of memory to particular, privileged places, Hardy's sequence is tacitly following in the footsteps of Wordsworth. In the latter's 'spots of time', not only the particular instances of time but also the particular places linked to those instances provide Wordsworth with the charged centres of his poetic universe – force fields from which 'our minds / Are nourished and invisibly repaired' (*The Prelude*, 1805 version, 263–264). Presumably it is no accident that the word 'spot' provides a subterranean link between Hardy's 'Poems of 1912–13' and his romantic predecessor. This *Kernwort* of sorts features no less than five times in the sequence itself, and also occurs in other related contexts. Together, these not only provide a tacit commentary on Wordsworth's poetics of place, but also can be used to outline an introductory sketch of the central features of the internal trajectory of Hardy's commemorative narrative.

In the second poem of the sequence, 'Your Last Drive', attention is drawn to the final resting place of the speaker's beloved:

> And on your left you passed the spot
> Where eight days later you were to lie,
> And be spoken of as one who was not.
>
> (7–9)

The very first 'spot' of the sequence is thus, fittingly, the place of the corpse – the burial place from which Hardy takes his bearings, and which he will have to try to leave behind for, or imaginatively transform into, more consoling and expressive locations. Where Tennyson's *In Memoriam* denied the corpse, Hardy's sequence will seek to transcend the grave. The rhyming of 'spot' with 'not' is hardly coincidental here: the woman the speaker seeks is 'not' at this spot, as presence and meaning have fled the scene. The workings of rhyme here manifest the logic of memory's returns: repetition comes as a sameness burdened with difference, the temporal doubling insisting upon a decisive swerve away from vitality, rather than a rebirth.

Yet the protagonist of 'Poems of 1912–13' is compelled to search for some kind of renaissance, however qualified or delusive. Significantly, the next occurrence of the word 'spot' takes place when another location is loaded with an emotional charge: in 'A Dream or No', memories of Cornwall press upon the speaker's consciousness, suggesting the possibility of a reinvestment of sacredness in, or at least affective recharging of, space:

> Why go to Saint-Juliot? What's Juliot to me?
>   Some strange necromancy
>   But charmed me to fancy
> That much of my life claims the spot as its key.
>   (1–4)

The allusive nod to Shakespeare ('What's Hecuba to him, or he to Hecuba'; *Hamlet*, II, ii, 532) goes via one of Hardy's own 'Poems of Pilgrimage'. Included in the latter group, and dated April 1887, 'Rome: At the Pyramid of Cestius Near the Graves of Shelley and Keats' expresses bemusement over how the commemorative obelisk for a relatively unknown Roman Tribune, Caius Cestius, looms over the grave of two of Hardy's romantic predecessors: 'Who, then, was Cestius, / And what is he to me?' (1–2) Only through an inner adjustment can the visitor make some sort of poetic justice out of the disjunctive spectacle presented by this locality. A similar movement is underway in the later poem: by claiming that 'the spot is the key', the speaker signals that the significance of place has been transformed from the forbidding indifference of 'Your Last Drive' to something more promising. The riddling or unsolved nature of the 'key' encourages imaginative recalibration (cf. 'fancy'), just as in the case of Cestius's grave: the linking of Cornwall with the memory of the dead woman can only take place on the behest of the poetic imagination.

By the third 'spot' of 'Poems of 1912–13', the protagonist has risen to the challenge, and seeks out the wellsprings of his feelings for his beloved. With 'After the Recovery', we have, in the words of Hillis Miller, moved 'from the anguished memory of the past as irremediably past to the climax of recovery'.[27] In this poem, her ghost provides momentum and direction to the protagonist's quest for a revivifying of space: 'I see what you are doing, you are leading me on / To the spots we knew when we haunted here together' (16–17). From here, it is but a short space to the attained vision celebrated at the end of

'The Phantom Horsewoman':

> A ghost-girl-rider. And though, toil-tried,
>   He withers daily,
>   Time touches her not,
>   But she still rides gaily
>   In his rapt thought
>   On that shagged and shaly
>   Atlantic spot,
>   And as when first eyed
> Draws rein and sings to the swing of the tide.
>
>   (28–36)

This consummation includes, however, the seeds of its own demise. Even if a victory seems to be won over time, closer inspection reveals that the decrepitude of 'that shagged and scaly / Atlantic spot' mirrors the bodily state of the questing lover. The latter metaphor also unflatteringly taints 'spot' with latent connotations such as fault, dirt, and littleness. Fittingly, the 'not'–'spot' rhyme also reappears, once more alerting the reader to the vulnerability and passing quality of memory's minor miracles.

It is precisely because all recollection is hampered by problems and qualifications that Hardy's sequence at times seems to be seeking to enact a transcendence of memory. As Philip Davis has observed, memory 'becomes an ironically self-isolating mode' for this poet,[28] something which is particularly painful in a series of poems that attempts to forge a connection with a lost love. Hardy's speaker therefore aspires to a kind of willing suspension of disbelief, whereby the power of memory's spaces might summon up the beloved from the beyond – and he can ignore that they are bound up with recollective acts vulnerable to forgetfulness. In short, like the speaker of Christina Rossetti's juvenile poem 'Sappho', Hardy's protagonist desires to be 'Forgetful of forgetfulness' ('Sappho', 10). In order to achieve such a state, he entertains the possibility of subtly adjusting the ontological status of the remembered individual. If he were actually being haunted by a ghost, rather than encountering a metaphorical 'phantom' from his memory, then the protagonist of 'Poems of 1912–13' could achieve a revival of the past as a new present. As it is, memory – unlike pure imagination or hallucination – can only allow the past to encroach upon the present *as past*.[29] Acknowledging this effectively entails circumscribing the desire of nostalgia. As Ann C. Colley points out, 'nostalgia is prevented from ever properly resurrecting the past because it relies on a memory that depends upon comparison and a sense of otherness.'[30]

Earlier on in 'The Phantom Horsewoman', in the second stanza, the protagonist's nostalgic attempt to sublate the present completely in the shimmering presence of the past is precisely analysed by Hardy's distanced, third person narrator:

> They say he sees as an instant thing
>   More clear than to-day,
>   A sweet soft scene
>   That was once in play
>   By that briny green;
>   Yes, notes always
>   Warm, real, and keen,
>   What his back years bring –
> A phantom of his own figuring.
>
> (10–18)

The past is here so immediate (as an 'instant thing') that it almost engulfs the present moment. By returning to the same spot where the lovers met earlier, the protagonist utilizes the power of place in order to make a phantom attain a semblance of reality. Yet even here both ecstasies of time coexist: the past is not completely immediate, since it still needs the present in order to be articulated. The term 'figuring' carries a lot of weight at the end of this stanza: most obviously, it stresses that the remembered woman is not physically present, but is as it were a figure of a memory-image traced on the mind's eye of the protagonist. In addition, though, 'figuring' alerts us to the fact that the interplay between past and present is here akin to that of rhetorical figures or tropes: the nostalgic mourner would like to elide the difference between the two, as in a daring metaphor or catachresis, but he cannot hide that the actual relation is one of similitude rather than identity. Where nostalgia, bolstered by the suggestive powers of place, would like to see the present and past simply fused, the temporal probity of Hardy's verse – critically negotiating with the very nostalgia that tempts it – insists that the present can, at best, only be like the past.

There is one final mention of a 'spot'; it occurs in the final poem of the sequence, 'Where the Picnic Was'. Revisiting the place where four friends once shared a moment of heightened togetherness, the speaker can only find the leftovers of their bonfire:

> Now a cold wind blows,
> And the grass is gray,
> But the spot still shows
> As a burnt circle – aye,
> And stick-ends, charred,
> Still strew the sward
> Whereon I stand.
>   (10–16)

No sublimity or visionary lift survives here. Wordsworth's spots of time have been rediscovered by Hardy, but now only as a passing show that is covered by a grubby palimpsest of connotations linked with dirt, moral failing, and diminution. Hardy's placing of the blessed moments subjects them to ignoble displacement. Still, despite the fact that memories are fragile and decidedly of the past, not all is lost. The ashes remain, and the 'burnt circle' is still a sign that pays tacit witness to the one-time presence of not only the speaker's friends, but also those who have been drawn into the legacy, or poetic circle, of Wordsworth.[31]

Other instances of the word in Hardy's work carry a similar ambivalence. In 'The Figure in the Scene' (published in the 1917 *Moments of Vision*), the reader may be gratified to hear that the beloved's 'form is the Genius still of the spot', only to discover the ironic counterpoint of the following rhyme: 'Though the place now knows her no more, and has known her not / Ever since that day' (16–18). Only a few lines earlier, 'blots engrained' provides a discreet hint of an internal rhyme (9). Later, 'That Moment' (in *Human Shows*) will indeed rhyme 'not' with 'blot', effectively blotting out a blessed time under these rhyming nemeses. In a much earlier volume, *Poems of the Past and the Present*, 'Tess's Lament' features a speaker longing to

> turn my memory to a blot,
> Make every relic of me rot,
> My doings be as they were not,
> And leave no trace of me!
>   (45–48)

A selective perusal of the vicissitudes of Hardy's 'spots' in 'Poems of 1912–13' can, however, only trace the outer contours of how the places of memory are treated in this sequence. For a more thorough account, attention needs to be drawn to the singularity of space at work, especially relating to how the mourning speaker of 'Poems of 1912–13' remembers via particular places. In 'The Going', the speaker's memories are triggered by a specific locality, thinking 'for a breath it is you I see / At the end of the alley of bending boughs / Where so often at dusk you used to be' (16–18). His beloved's drive home, past the spot where she after her burial 'soon would halt everlastingly' (12), is the topic of 'Your Last Drive'. A similar interplay between home and burial place is present in 'His Visitor', where the deceased leaves the graveyard to seek her husband in his nearby home: 'I come across from Mellstock while the moon wastes weaker / To behold where I lived with you for twenty years and more' (1–2). That same burial place is addressed in 'Rain on a Grave', while 'Lament' contrasts her position 'shut under grass / Where no cups flow' (19–20) with how much she would have enjoyed a party 'With table and tray / And chairs on the lawn' (4–5). In the same vein, the poem 'The Walk' focuses on how 'the hill-top tree / By the gated ways' (2–3) is irrevocably changed by her death, despite her not having visited it for a long time.

Other poems focus more on her western origins, evoking the protagonist's first meeting with her many years earlier. Where Hardy's group of 'Poems of Pilgrimage', included in *Poems of the Past and the Present* (1901), journeyed far afield in order to tap into exotic locations with a particular literary and historical charge, the speaker here makes a new pilgrimage, within the confines of England, to an area loaded with personal significance. 'I Found Her Out There' provides an important bridging function, as it creates a narrative of departure and return. The west is linked with the beloved's current place of burial: even if she left 'those haunted heights / The Atlantic smites' (18–19), to be laid 'to rest / In a noiseless rest / No sea beats near' (10–12), the speaker fancies that 'her shade, maybe, / Will creep underground' (33–34) to where her life's voyage began. Yet in terms of the sequence's narrative progress, the bridging role is filled by 'A Dream or No', where the speaker's 'dreams of that place in the West' (5), Saint-Juliot, immediately precede the following poems' description of a new visit to the area. After that, the very titles of many of the poems – 'Beeny Cliff', 'At Castle Boterel', 'Places', 'St Launce's Revisited', 'Where the Picnic Was' – indicate with what specificity topographical references are made.

In general, the spatiality of the poems is articulated by means of a dominant contrast between the speaker's present home and the west where he first met his beloved. But there is also an internal contrast within the former, between his home and the grounds where she is buried. Furthermore, there is also an opposition between the home the married couple made their own, and the 're-decked dwelling' ('His Visitor', 16) it becomes after her death. Running through all these dichotomies is an underlying conflict between home and its others. An exploration of how that which is most intimate and linked to the home becomes an instance of the uncanny (a phenomenon later scrutinized by Freud) is frequently at work, most noticeably perhaps in 'The Walk', where 'familiar ground' (12) becomes unsettlingly eerie to the speaker after his wife's death.

Even in poems where specific places are not explicitly mentioned, some spatial articulation enters nevertheless. Thus 'Without Ceremony' compares the beloved's sudden death with her tendency to 'career / Off anywhere – say to town' (6–7). In other cases, Hardy's tendency to root the process of mourning in a particular topography meets inner resistance from space itself. In 'The Voice', the speaker recalls drawing 'near to the town / Where you would wait for me' (6–7), but becomes disoriented and disheartened. What had seemed to be the sound of her voice may be reducible to a natural phenomenon:

> Or is it only the breeze, in its listlessness
> Travelling across the wet mead to me here,
> You being ever dissolved to wan wistlessness,
> Heard no more again far or near?
>
> (9–12)

Giving place its due in 'Poems of 1912–13' entails that one resists reducing the poems to purely mental, psychological, or private meanings. The speaker's mourning for his beloved is linked to the places where they met and lived their life together (and apart), as well as to the places where he now dwells upon her absence. His memories of her do not float freely, but are triggered and embodied in these sites. She cannot be easily dissociated from this material grounding. Indeed, even her current ghost-like status can be read as borrowing something of its enigma from her western origins: in 'I Found Her Out There', the speaker describes his beloved's western origins as 'By those haunted heights / The Atlantic smites' (18–19).

Further clarification of the temporal function of locality in these poems can be gleaned through Ellen Anne Lanzano's account of their setting in *Hardy: The Temporal Poetics*. Her study operates with a general contrast between the temporality of Dorset and that of Lyonnesse or

Cornwall. The former is 'under the thumb of determinist time', while the latter 'is the country of light and possibility'.[32] She is as unequivocally affirmative in her view of Hardy's Cornwall as Donald Davie was in his influential essay 'Hardy's Virgilian Purples', the latter describing the region as 'the domain of love and loyalty'.[33] Compared to 'the weary, dun terrain of Dorset', Lanzano claims, 'Cornwall has a wild, liberated energy'.[34] Within the poems addressing his wife and her death, she establishes a fundamental dichotomy:

> Hardy's Dorset perspective is materialist, based on a combination of temporal elements in a system of survival. Man on the heath is an organ of adaptation to a complex world made of parts that shift and break down.
>
> Lyonnesse, on the contrary, is an artefact of consciousness, a blend of space and time in the oneness of an idealist reverie. Poems of his relationship with Emma record impressions of a highly emotional character presented without the antinomial past-present polemic in the style of Dorset, but in the spontaneous style and full variations of a state that denies a tragic temporality.[35]

Elsewhere, Lanzano claims that Lyonnesse's blending unity comes out of an elision of divisions: it is a space where 'boundaries are not visible'.[36] as a result of how 'Hardy's dream vision smudges the boundary lines of actuality'.[37] Even when differences are noticeable, these are sublimated into a picturesque unity: 'Transitions in natural phenomena are sheltering and pleasing, and noting them is the way Hardy talks about his feelings for Emma.'[38] In short, Lyonnesse becomes a bower or haven for nostalgia, a site where the subject can have immediate access to the past, without any alienating sense of distance or regret.

If we return to Edward S. Casey's account, in *Remembering*, of how space affects memory, then he too allows for landscapes to be expressively powerful. Yet this does not necessarily have to stem from uniformity or unity. Drawing on Aristotle, Casey remarks upon how space frequently plays a delimiting role in memory. This constitutes 'place's *periechon* being, its containing/surrounding function. Place is a *mise en scene* for remembered events precisely to the extent that it guards and keeps these events within its self-delimiting perimeters.'[39] Given this function, it is striking how the Cornwall memories of 'Poems of 1912–13' are so specifically memories of a bordering place, i.e., of the site where the sea encroaches upon Beeny Cliff. It is as if Hardy has not simply chosen to highlight any place, or a singular site pertinent to a unique memory, but rather opted for a placing which acts like a meta-site of sorts – indeed, a place that actually subjects memory to an unsettling process of displacement. The meeting of cliff and sea has something emblematic about it, highlighting how memory situates itself in places where order and ground are abutted by otherness.

Is this otherness merely that of the world of romance? And if so, is romance itself a unified and entirely idealizing phenomenon that wondrously transforms everyday Cornwall to magical Lyonnesse – as it indeed appears to in Hardy's much anthologized 'When I set out for Lyonnesse'? Commentators have been quick to pick up on the intertextual links between 'Poems of 1912–13' and Hardy's early novel *A Pair of Blue Eyes* (1873) – both building on memories of the author's first encounter with his first wife. The novel may be based on happy memories, but its love triangle between Elfride Swancourt, Stephen Smith, and Henry Knight is far from uncomplicated pastoral idyll. Based on the link between the vicissitudes of Elfride's love affairs, and how 'intensity of passion attached to a particular place and time is replaced by repetition and doubt' in them,[40] Tim Armstrong has argued for a sceptical reading of Hardy's poems mourning his wife. Certainly Hardy's own characterization of the setting as a site of 'dream and mystery' must be balanced against the novel's own insistence upon 'an air of desolation' and its many terrible events, which notably include Henry Knight's visionary and humbling encounter with 'the world in its infancy' when he almost falls off the cliff.[41] Even Knight's escape from death on the cliff has unsettling consequences, as Elfride's rescuing of him causes her to jilt her former lover for his best friend, ultimately causing much unhappiness to all three parties.

Although the cliff of this momentous event is unnamed in *A Pair of Blue Eyes*, Hardy himself identified it with the Beeny Cliff mentioned in the 'Poems of 1912–13'. The cliff is used in a varied manner in the latter sequence. In the opening poem, 'The Going', the fourth stanza arguably links cliff, rider, and life in a manner not contradicting Lanzano's thesis:

> You were she who abode
> By those red-veined rocks far West,
> You were the swan-necked one who rode
> Along the beetling Beeny Crest
>   And, reining nigh me,
>   Would muse and eye me,
> While Life unrolled us its very best.
>
>   (22–28)

Where there might have been some potential for a clash between crest and sea, the final line – metaphorically comparing 'Life' to the ocean – smooths the edges in an affirmative image. Whatever the sea may roll in, the 'swan-necked' woman will surely ride it out. The verb 'reining' also has an associative link with 'reigning', suggesting royal elevation above all possible natural vicissitudes. Other poems in the sequence repeat the equestrian imagery, arguably developing an underlying contrast between the beloved's quasi-royal freedom riding horses and her celled isolation in Dorset. In the 'Phantom Horsewoman' she 'draws rein' (36), and in 'A Woman Driving', a poem from Hardy's *Late Lyrics*, the speaker admires 'How she held up the horses' heads, / Firm-lipped, with steady rein' (1–2). In 'Lament', the flipside of the muted pun is delivered: 'she would have reigned / At a dinner to-night / With ardours unfeigned' (12–14). Only a few years later, in 1923, Hardy would publish *The Famous Tragedy of the Queen of Cornwall*, set in the very same area, and the metaphors of 'Poems of 1912–13' anticipate that text's focus on female royalty.

   The Famous Tragedy of the Queen of Cornwall is not only a sad tale of a 'tragedy of dire duresse / That vexed the land of Lyonnesse' – it is more specifically the tale of an unhappy love triangle between Tristram, Iseult the Whitehanded, and the Queen of Cornwall herself – Iseult the Fair.[42] Interestingly, Hardy decided to rework some of the dialogue in *A Pair of Blue Eyes* in this later text, in the process showing some self-awareness about how he almost compulsively portrayed unhappy threesomes when writing about Cornwall. The Cornish poems of 'Poems of 1912–13' take place in the same terrain, and they too were – as Hardy's biographers have noted – written in the shadow of Hardy's divided loyalties, anguished as he was as a consequence of setting aside his affections for Emma Hardy for his new love for Florence Dugdale (whom he married in February 1914).

   Although this state of affairs does not surface explicitly in 'Poems of 1912–13', it arguably hovers unsettlingly in its margins like a tacit memory. In addition, the queenly beloved is not presented as dwelling invulnerably in the Cornish landscape of the sequence. Her later death is anticipated in 'Places', where 'free of fear, / She cantered down, as if she must fall / (Though she never did)' (18–20). 'I Found Her Out There' opens by stressing the vitalizing conflicts of the Cornish coast:

> I found her out there
> On a slope few see,

> That falls westwardly
> To the salt-edged air,
> Where the ocean breaks
> On the purple strand,
> And the hurricane shakes
> The solid land.
>
> (1–8)

Here, too, 'falls' arguably anticipates her future death, alluding subtly to Henry Knight's close shave in *A Pair of Blue Eyes*. In addition, although the threats are warded off, 'ocean' and 'strand' are no less pitted against one another than 'hurricane' and 'land'. Significantly, the sea is linked with the convulsive powers of the air, in a way that might bring to mind Shelley's 'Ode to the West Wind'. A little later on in Hardy's poem, more natural unrest is shadowed by the sorrowful stuff of legend:

> So she does not sleep
> By those haunted heights
> The Atlantic smites
> And the blind gales sweep,
> Whence she often would gaze
> At Dundagel's famed head,
> While the dipping blaze
> Dyed her face fire-red;
>
> And would sigh at the tale
> Of sunk Lyonnesse,
> As a wind-tugged tress
> Flapped her cheek like a flail.
>
> (17–28)

The speaker's memories do not reproduce a continuum or simple presence in this passage. Rather, the sorrowful break between his present and the remembered past is mirrored by how the past itself is fissured and characterized by a state of lamentation. Nature is 'blind' and 'swipes', and the wind strikes his beloved 'like a flail'. Romance itself is under erasure, as she is made melancholy by 'the tale / Of sunk Lyonnesse'. One might interpret this as a self-indulgent and even playful kind of melancholia clearly distinguishable from depression. Yet, as *The Famous Tragedy of the Queen of Cornwall* implies, there are links between the grief at the heart of 'Poems of 1912–13', on the one hand, and the legendary doom of Arthur's realm on the other.

In order to home in on how those Arthurian connotations directly involve Tennyson's precedent, let us turn to 'Beeny Cliff,' subtitled 'March 1870–March 1913'. This poem commemorates a return visit to one of the love affair's sacred sites, forty-three years later. Once more the beloved is 'riding high above', and now her hair is 'flapping free' rather than striking her in the face (2). She and the speaker can allow themselves to laugh 'light-heartedly aloft on that clear-sunned March day' (6), as poor weather quickly passes and their love seems secure. While other poems, as we have seen, use rhyme to interweave both privileged spots and their negative 'nots' with blemishing 'blots', a similar tension is seemingly resolved here, as the 'dull misfeatured stain' (8) of the Atlantic is quickly transfigured by the returning sun. If the poem's idyllic image of the West becomes doubt-ridden in the last two of the five stanzas, is that not an effect of retrospect and present grief rather than any intrinsic feature of the landscape?

IV

- Still in all its chasmal beauty bulks old Beeny to the sky,
And shall she and I not go there once again now March is nigh,
And the sweet things said in that March say anew there by and by?

V

What if still in chasmal beauty looms that wild weird western shore,
The woman now is – elsewhere – whom the ambling pony bore,
And nor knows nor cares for Beeny, and will laugh there nevermore.

(10–15)

The repeated words 'chasmal beauty' have something of the disturbing doubleness of Yeats' 'terrible beauty' (in 'Easter, 1916'). The unity of the aesthetic is enigmatically coupled with a fissure, leaving the reader uncertain whether to stress the adjective or the noun. The poem's temporal scheme suggests that original beauty has given way to the chasms of time, yet Beeny itself seems to straddle or comprehend the entire process – unless the cliff itself, and the manner in which it both joins and separates, are to be seen as a metaphor for the selfsame transformation. The phrase 'wild weird western shore' echoes the first line's 'wandering western sea': once more one might see a clear movement from innocence to more sinister overtones, as 'wild weird' arguably strikes a more discordant note than 'wandering'. Yet the movement from the first memory of 1870 to the unsettled impressions of 1913 is itself contained or anticipated in the origin: what has happened here but a process of displacement – a 'wandering'?

The evocation of a 'wild weird western shore' also undermines any recourse to an innocent or untainted sense of romance. The phrase alludes to the ending of *Idylls of the King*. Earlier in this chapter, we scrutinized Tennyson's treatment of what he called 'that last weird battle in the west' ('The Passing of Arthur', 29), and interpreted the fateful weight the word 'weird' had for that poet. The Tennysonian echoes of 'Poems 1912–13' should not be underestimated. Like *In Memoriam*, Hardy's poems constitute a sequence of poems mourning the loss of a loved one. Both sequences grapple with the idea of an afterlife in a doubt-ridden world, and both also feature speakers who admit to being overwhelmed by their grief but then achieve some measure of resolution at the end. These similarities have been noted, and commentators have identified instances of allusion – as for instance in Matthew Campbell's reading of how the 'prosodic vocabulary' in Hardy's sequence reworks that found in Tennyson's mourning for Hallam.[43] Yet the less obvious link between *Idylls of the King* and 'Poems of 1912–13' ought not to be ignored either.

Tennyson's use of the word 'weird' was intrinsically linked with the fate of King Arthur. Where *Idylls of the King* begins with the idyll 'The Coming of Arthur', and ends with 'The Passing of Arthur', Hardy's sequence opens with 'The Going' and then finishes when the speaker's process of mourning attains a semblance of equilibrium and consolation. While the latter wavers between a fully materialist account of death and more ghost-ridden visions of the deceased's return, Tennyson's text hesitates, at the end, between the king's definitive demise and hope for an enigmatic return from Avilon. There are also specific echoes in the use of locality. In *Idylls of the King*, Tintagel features implicitly in its traditional guise as the possible site of King Arthur's conception, in a story shadowed by possible adultery, but also more explicitly as a battlefield before he unified the kingdom: 'Then Uther in his wrath and heat besieged / Ygerne within Tintagil' ('The Coming of Arthur', 197–198). Hardy's sequence features nothing as dramatic and large-scale as the Arthurian battles, but the beloved's 'sigh at the tale / Of sunk Lyonnesse' takes place while she gazes 'At Dundagel's famed head' ('I Found Her Out There', 25–26 and 21–22). In addition, both 'Poems of 1912–13' and Arthur's fateful battle in 'The Passing of Arthur' are shadowed – as indeed

The Famous Tragedy of the Queen of Cornwall is to an even stronger degree – by a love triangle that unsettles a marriage. To summarize, romance is not, in Hardy's sequence, something diffuse or viewed through rose-tinted glasses: it is a domain where dreams are never fully extricable from tragedy. Set close to the putative birthplace of Arthur, and the origin of his ultimately tragic tale of death, adultery, and lost community, the 'Poems of 1912–13' are localized in a place drenched in loss and regret. The displacing force of memory checks nostalgia's desire for unity and immediacy.

The west of Cornwall is, however, much more than a simply mythical or intertextual space in Hardy's sequence. It also contributes, for instance, to a decidedly singular trait concerning the identity of the beloved. To cite Casey once more:

> Places and their memory sustain us in our everyday lives, subject as these are to fragmentation and rupture of so many sorts. Even persons (i.e., the very beings who are the sources of separation anxiety) are experienced and remembered primarily as persons-in-particular-places: 'Crawford at Asheville', 'Dan at the Handcraft Center', 'Tunie in Topeka'.[44]

There is little doubt that Emma Hardy was 'Emma of the west coast' for Hardy. In the poems set after the beloved's death, the protagonist of 'Poems of 1912–13' tries to console himself, and counter his own anxiety, precisely by stressing and exploring her link to this particular location. When she is described as living by the 'red-veined rocks far West' ('The Going', 23), the vitality of person and landscape are to be taken as identical. If, in the words of a poem written in 1913, 'She opened the door of the West to me' ('She Opened the Door', 1), it is because there is an intrinsic link between her identity and the western landscape.

Does the beloved 'embody the spirit of the landscape' to Hardy, as a recent biographer has put it,[45] or is it the other way around? Difficult as it is to answer such a question unequivocally, it is nevertheless clear that Hardy's poems present the overarching project as being one of individual memory rather than of evocation of landscape. The latter feeds, it seems, into the former. By travelling to Cornwall, the protagonist of 'Poems of 1912–13' rediscovers and safeguards the individuality of his lost love. In *Darwin's Plots*, Gillian Beer pointed out how, in general, the 'absolute gap between our finite capacities and the infinite time and space of the universe burdens Hardy's texts with a sense of malfunction and apprehension'.[46] Such an opposition between human finitude and the impersonal objectivity of the physical universe is also at work in this particular sequence. But there is also a more limited opposition at work, dealing with different temporal levels within human existence. The protagonist keeps the singular memory of his beloved secure, despite the encroaching anonymity and nothingness that threaten to consign her to oblivion. The latter oblivion is linked to the sheer mass of existing human lives, and the manner in which any individual life risks being dwarfed in comparison. A similar threat is felt by the protagonist of *Tess of the D'Urbervilles*: 'The best is not to remember that your nature and your past doings have been just like thousands' and thousands', and that your coming life and doings 'll be like thousands' and thousands'.[47] But where Tess's strategy – both in this case and in her attempts to transcend the social repercussions of Alec's rape – is to leave the past behind, the protagonist of 'Poems of 1912–13' will attempt to bolster individual memory so as to support it against its external challenges.

'At Castle Boterel' shows the speaker insisting that, despite the apparent insignificance of his and his beloved's lives in the larger frame of things, their memory nevertheless looms large:

> It filled but a minute. But was there ever
>   A time of such quality, since or before,
> In that hill's story? To one mind never,
>   Though it has been climbed, foot-swift, foot-sore
>   By thousands more.
>
>   (16–20)

Here individual memory seems to be held up as a value in itself. Unlike what will be the case with Yeats later in this chapter, Hardy is not attempting to conflate his individual memory with a larger, collective memory. Rather, as he had earlier done in the Boer war poem 'The Souls of the Slain', he brings out the conflict – later to become important in the poetry of World War I – between the two kinds of remembering, insisting upon the value of that which is only recalled by 'one mind'.[48] Still, the next two stanzas indicate that a purely subjective, internal memory may not be enough by itself. The speaker seeks verification, even if it may be of a rather fantastic kind, from outside circumstances:

> Primaeval rocks form the road's steep border,
>   And much have they faced there, first and last,

> Of the transitory in Earth's long order;
>   But what they recall in colour and cast
>   Is – that we two passed.
>
> And to me, though Time's unflinching rigour,
>   In mindless rote, has ruled from sight
> The substance now, one phantom figure
>   Remains on the slope, as when that night
>   Saw us alight.
>
>   (21–30)

Despite the rather whimsical appeal to geology, it is finally the place itself that functions as mnemonic catalyst for this revisioning of a past present.

In the subsequent poem of the sequence, 'Places', individual memory is once more contrasted to collective indifference. The speaker's private memories seem to have no public resonance whatsoever, as the three first stanzas begin 'Nobody says ...', 'Nobody thinks ...', and 'Nobody calls to mind ...'. Unlike civic, commemorative sites, the places bound up with the lovers' memories have no public significance. Nevertheless, this discrepancy does not deter the mourner:

> Nay: one there is to whom these things,
> That nobody else's mind calls back,
> Have a savour that scenes in being lack,
> And a presence more than the actual brings.
>
>   (22–26)

Mary Jacobus has identified 'the critical moment in Hardy's writing' as being 'that of imagined self-dissolution'.[49] The 'Poems of 1912–13' have a special position in his *oeuvre*, as here it is not what Jacobus calls 'the prized individual consciousness' of the poet,[50] but rather that of a seemingly unremarkable existence, which is being defended against disappearance.

The way in which Hardy safeguards individual memory against the encroaching anonymity of the crowd by linking it to a specific place might seem to have something paradoxical about it. Earlier on in this chapter, we saw how Balin risked losing his inner integrity by making it dependent upon external space, and in twentieth century philosophy (most notably in a tradition established by Heidegger and Husserl) an attempt to go beyond the individual mind has been linked precisely with attempts to explicate how being is coterminous with place. In a way, though, Hardy's 'Poems of 1912–13' reveals exactly what the later hermeneutical and phenomenological theories would express in more philosophical terms: that individual being is only fathomable in terms of its placing in a particular context and situation. As we have seen, Hardy's sequence also alerts us to the fact that an identifying place is no safe haven: by linking the beloved with the Cornwall of romance, he also identifies her with the vicissitudes and loss that are the particular freight of Arthurian legend. Even if the west is imbued with romance, it brings with it an unsettling weirdness that imbues all of its original spatiality with a sense of fateful foreboding.

Yeats and the heritages of 'Under Ben Bulben'

William Butler Yeats's poem 'Under Ben Bulben' is a grand testamentary performance. With belligerent bravado, it spells out Yeats's wish for his body to be placed in the Drumcliff churchyard near the mountain Ben Bulben. Published only five days after his death, this poem is the textual equivalent of a death mask, forged with consummate craftsmanship by a poet who is anticipating, and aiming to control, his own posthumous legacy. While the mountain of Ben Bulben 'sets the scene' (I, 11) for this drama,[51] the powerful presence of the author himself attempts to direct the attendant *dramatis personae*. There is a link back to Tennyson here: in undertaking this self-commemorative endeavour, Yeats can be said to simultaneously prolong and critically interrogate a certain Victorian fascination with the ritual trappings of the burial. The Victorian commemoration of the dead achieved, through its sumptuousness and earnestness, the condition of being an impressive and highly orchestrated spectacle. This was a widespread phenomenon, not solely linked to the upper echelons of society: 'the most elaborate ceremonials, of a kind which today would appear extravagant to the obsequies of a head of state, were matters of routine when burying a grocer or a doctor.'[52] In the reading of *Idylls of the King*, we saw that King Arthur's missing grave could be read as amplifying this phenomenon through its apparent inversion: despite seeming to contradict the pomp and circumstance of Victorian society, Tennyson's Arthur became all the more mourned, all the more remembered, for the lack of any objective tomb in his memory.

In Yeats, a figure who straddles Victorianism and high modernism, a similar tension between excess and privation makes itself felt in how he choreographs his own death through a complex act of commemoration. Although the gesture is far more self-assertive than in Christina Rossetti's 'Song', Yeats too is seeking to avoid the excess of emotion with which Victorianism invested its burials. But he does not show the equanimity of Rossetti's speaker. Even less does he aspire to disappear altogether – like the Marquis de Sade.[53] For with 'Under Ben Bulben' Yeats makes detailed preparations for the event of the poet's own death, not only dictating the exact placement of his tomb, but also supplying its epitaph. He frames an appropriate setting for the mourning of his death, attempting to circumscribe his literary heritage in the process. This he does not only by providing a form of poetical will, but also – as is indicated by the title – by attempting to delineate the correct response to, and understanding of, the surroundings of his tomb. This is a heritage that involves not only words, thoughts, and values to be handed down, but also the physical placing of the poet's memory. Linking individual memory to a particular site, Yeats follows the precedent of both how Tennyson frames Arthur's link to Cornwall and how Hardy uses the same part of England as a trigger for memories of his beloved in 'Poems of 1912–13'. In all of these three cases, elegiac memory is linked with a western site that is not only associated with the earliest memories of the deceased, but is also a place which, through its localization on the very verge where the land meets the sea, functions as a figure of liminality *per se*.

Arguably, Yeats's audacity goes beyond that of Tennyson and Hardy: not only does he deal with his own poetic memory, but he also demonstrates an ambition to conflate the recollection of an individual poet with the collective memory of the nation, rooted in its native soil, which has no parallel in their ambivalent negotiations with the legacies of the past. One should not underestimate how overdetermined, and yet elusive, an act of poetical commemoration 'Under Ben Bulben' is. Here one of the most transcendentally inclined of modern poets links his own identity with the brute mass of a concrete mountain. One might claim that all human encounters with mountains are sublimating or idealizing.[54] In the case of Yeats, though, the general self-reflectiveness of the human encounter with mountains is underlined and intensified. 'Under Ben Bulben' is a consummately idealist poem, in the sense that it posits that the materiality of the mountain and the surrounding site is only of value insofar as its significance is circumscribed by an immaterial rationale. The same goes for the poem's use of memory. Yet if 'Under Ben Bulben' presents an idealist memory, delimiting and appropriating space at the behest of the author, one need not follow its example. Yeats's appropriations of memory for poetical and autobiographical purposes are almost always forceful, but an attentive reading can point toward a tangle of memories that has been left behind by the selective process of the creative act. Despite coming across as emphatically resistant to sentimentality, Yeats will be linked – through his desire to perpetrate a self-centred act of controlled memory – to the Victorian heritage of nostalgia negotiated by Tennyson and Hardy before him. His attempt, in 'Under Ben Bulben', to use a mountain as an instrument for the commemorative creation of a harmonized and idealized self-image will be shown to be embroiled in contingencies and conflicting memories.

Evidence of Yeats's idealism can be gleaned from the material prefacing *A Vision*, where he takes time to appreciate the suggestiveness of his current physical surroundings in the small Italian town of Rapallo. The effect the mountains of Rapallo have on him is especially noted: 'these mountains under their brilliant light fill one with an emotion that is like gratitude,' Yeats writes, 'the mountain road from Rapallo to Zoagli seems like something in my own mind, something that I have discovered.'[55] Characteristically for Yeats, nature is easily elided into something transcendental and inner: it seems, as he writes, 'like something in my own mind'. Like an individualized Platonic memory, or *anamnesis*, the mountain gives back what was already the property of the mind, and is a mirroring monument of human thought's own magnificence.[56] When Yeats writes down these observations in Rapallo, in 1927, his gratitude to the mountains is no doubt due to how his recent (but still incomplete) recovery from illness has been facilitated by the protective and mild climate of this resort. He will survive the illness in question, and will later keep an association between mountains and protection against finitude.

Ben Bulben had long been associated with both protection and revelation for the local populace of the Sligo region, on the West Coast of Ireland. In an early prose text, Yeats mentions a folk rhyme celebrating the two big mountains that are on the sides of the town: 'But for Ben Bulben and Knocknarea,' the rhyme goes, 'Many a poor sailor'd be cast away.'[57] This is from the early volume *The Celtic Twilight*, in which Yeats documents local beliefs linked with the supernatural. In several other texts of this volume, Ben Bulben is described as being a place redolent with faeries and mythological significance. Where the later poem 'Under Ben Bulben' will mention in passing the common people's faith in protective powers of nature in general, and of Ben Bulben in particular – 'ancient Ireland knew it all' (II, 4) – this dimension is spelled out in some detail in *The Celtic Twilight*. The latter volume also links the mountain with non-human horsemen who every night ride forth from an opening in the mountain:

> When the aged countrywoman stands at her door in the evening and, in her own words, 'looks at the mountains and thinks of the goodness of God,' God is all the nearer, because the pagan powers are not far: because northward in Ben Bulben, famous for hawks, the white square door swings open at sundown, and those wild unchristian riders rush forth upon the fields.[58]

These supernatural horsemen return at the beginning of 'Under Ben Bulben', riding 'the wintry dawn / Where Ben Bulben sets the scene' (I, 10–11). At this stage they are linked with 'superhuman' (I, 6) women. The horsemen – but not the women – recur in the finale of the poem, in the projected inscription to Yeats's grave: 'Cast a cold eye / On life, on death, / Horseman, pass by!' (VI, 8–10). Placed below his slab of stone, the poet claims a sense of community with the supernatural beings. His limestone grave reaches out to the limestone 'door of Faeryland' on the side of Ben Bulben.[59] Such is at least the implication of this poem, in which Yeats practically stages what one biographer, Brenda Maddox, has called his 'self-iconization'.[60]

Yeats thus speaks to us, as it were, from a mountaintop. The poem borrows the mountain's aura of supernatural revelation to refract its glories upon the speaker's own poetic persona, creating a commemorated self speaking with a bird's-eye view on mere mortality. It is by virtue of this aura, this force borrowed from the place, that he attains what Jahan Ramazani has called 'his by now disembodied but empowered voice, a voice from the timeless nowhere beyond the grave'.[61] In the process, Yeats draws upon the mythical authority of mountains, which he previously had noted in an introduction to Bhagwan Shri Hamsa's *The Holy Mountain*: 'To Indians, Chinese, and Mongols, mountains from the earliest times have been the dwelling-place of the Gods. Their kings before any great decision have climbed some mountain.'[62] Implicitly, the poet is laying claim to the authority of these mountain-climbing kings. He can also be compared to the goatherd of the poem 'Shepherd and Goatherd', of whom the Shepherd states:

> They say that on your barren mountain ridge
> You have measured out the road that the soul treads
> When it has vanished from our natural eyes;
> That you have talked with apparitions.
>
> (79–82)

'The Tower' makes more of a direct link between Yeats's poetical persona and Ben Bulben, since it includes lines celebrating a time 'in boyhood when with rod and fly, / Or the humbler worm, I climbed Ben Bulben's back / And had the livelong summer day to spend' (I, 8–10). As many of Yeats's texts point out, including the autobiographical *Reveries over Childhood and Youth*, the poet's very first memories are linked with Sligo, south of Ben Bulben: thus memory is here being linked to personal origins in a way not unlike what was the case with king Arthur in *Idylls of the King* and the beloved in 'Poems of 1912–13'.

Beyond such personal links, the introduction to *The Holy Mountain* insists there is a universal connection – embracing both East and West – between elevated sites and human revelation. 'We too,' Yeats writes, 'have learnt from Dante to imagine our Eden, or Earthly Paradise, upon a mountain, penitential rings upon the slope.'[63] The choice of a specific Irish locality for his own 'Earthly Paradise' is of course not coincidental. In a key anticipation of 'Under Ben Bulben', Yeats's autobiographical text *Four Years* (included in *The Trembling of the Veil*) celebrates how public spaces can function figuratively as unifying vehicles for both individuals and communities: 'a nation or an individual' will thus be endowed with some form of 'symbolical' or 'mythological coherence' with which to organize the 'separated elements' of their experience. This coherence must have some form of localized particularity:

> I would not endure, however, an international art, picking up stories and symbols where it pleased. Might I not, with health and good luck to aid me, create some new *Prometheus Unbound*; Patrick or Columbkil, or Oisin or Fion, in Prometheus' stead; and instead of Caucasus, Cro-Patrick or Ben Bulben? Have not all races had their first unity from a mythology, that marries them to rock and hill?[64]

Significantly, Yeats contrasts his own desire of creating such a cultural fulcrum with the endeavour of Shelley. Ben Bulben and Cro-Patrick are specifically Irish alternatives to the Caucasus landscape evoked by the author of *Prometheus Unbound*, just as Yeats understood Lady Gregory's collections of folklore to be an Irish equivalent to foreign anthologies of stories related to King Arthur.[65] 'Under Ben Bulben' is a text that has Ireland's troubled relationship to England at its wings, as the specific Irishness of the locality is chosen in postcolonial opposition to English precursors.[66]

The summoning of the more local and personal reference of Ben Bulben constitutes a typically symbolist manoeuvre, whereby a universal exigency is embodied in a local habitat. At the same time, the individual poet is being fixed as a national icon: individual memory is being transformed into collective memory. Both of these equations operate according to a synecdochic logic, where the part stands for the whole. There is something more than a little overweening about the result: 'By his command these words are cut,' the poem says, but Yeats is not Moses taking down divine dictation on top of Mount Sinai. There are at least a couple of acts of contextualization by which the poet can be brought back to earth. First, there are the curious events recently stressed (among other places) in Brenda Maddox's biography of Yeats. Maddox has pointed out that, for all the poet's plans, there seems to have been a considerable amount of confusion around the process of his burial. Yeats died in France just before the outbreak of World War II, and in order to fulfil his wish of a Sligo burial, his body had to be exhumed over nine years later. By then the French authorities had moved his remains to an ossuary, and it is quite possible that his bones were mixed with – or mistaken for – those of some other corpse. This dismemberment strikes an ironic light back on 'Under Ben Bulben', since the poem involves a celebration of bodily harmony. This is particularly evident in Yeats's address to Irish poets of the future, where he attempts to control how his own poetic memory is to be received by fellow practitioners. The poets in question are admonished to follow the example of Michelangelo's elevated bodies, and 'Scorn the shape now growing up / All out of shape from toe to top' (V, 3–4). An ideally unified body is thus linked closely to the poet's remains, even if those remains were in practice submitted to a haphazard rag-and-bone shop process of dismemberment and displacement.

Second, and more suggestively perhaps, there is the lack of identity between the poem 'Under Ben Bulben' and Yeats's actual gravestone. The Irish poet's stone is effectively broken apart, as the visitor to the Drumcliff Churchyard does not encounter the whole of the poem 'Under Ben Bulben', but rather an inscription which only includes its celebrated last three lines. Like Tennyson's 'Tears, Idle Tears' unmoored from *The Princess*, these lines acquire a different inflection when read in isolation: 'Cast a cold eye / On life, on death / Horseman, pass by!' What meaning do these lines have in isolation? How might they be modified through their extraction from the surrounding context of the larger poem? These questions concern nothing less than the entire legacy of Yeats – since *who* he is to be remembered by effectively frames any understanding of *how* he is remembered.

By linking the entire testamentary poem to these three lines, which also stand on their own, Yeats is once more linking part to whole. Here the logic of synecdoche works in a particularly risky way, exposing the poem to a multiplicity of metonymic connections rather than any simple, unified meaning.[67] Due to its semi-detached status, the epitaph on the tombstone submits the structures of meaning established in 'Under Ben Bulben' to a process of displacement. The process might be compared with that of Balin's sword, as the movement from inner-ness (or at least, in Yeats's case, the virtual status of a literary text) to an external memory object is fraught with difficulties and ambiva-lence. Certainly, Yeats's epitaph opens up several interpretive possi-bilities. According to one possible reading, the horseman in question becomes partially identified with the visitor or poetic pilgrim reading these lines, whoever this might be, and as a result the adjuration also acquires a subtly different value. The horseman is no longer identi-fied with supernatural beings, nor is he linked with the 'hard-riding country gentlemen' (V, 8) mentioned in passing in the fifth section of the poem,[68] nor can he be straightforwardly identified with the poets and artists referred to in its middle (poets being frequently linked with Pegasus – the horse of classical myth – in Yeats's verse).[69] The reader encountering the epitaph, and its traditional *Siste viator* adjuration, is cut off from such contexts and tempted to identify with the horse-man. As a result, Yeats's memory is also handed down to a more widely encompassing public: on its own, the epitaph is less selective, less elit-ist, in whom it designates as Yeats's inheritors, than the more specific 'Under Ben Bulben'.

A good parallel to the resulting open-endedness of this interpel-lation can be found in the epitaph of one of Yeats's contemporaries, Rainer Maria Rilke. It has long been known that Yeats wrote 'Under Ben Bulben' under the influence of Rilke, moved by a desire to oppose what he understood as the Austro-German poet's unappealingly quietist ver-sion of the process of dying. But there has been little interest in the formal relevance of Rilke's self-penned epitaph for Yeats. In many ways a more gnomic and challenging text than Yeats's, it nevertheless shares a certain sense of open-ended address:

> Rose, oh reiner Widerspruch, Lust,
> Niemandes Schlaf zu sein unter soviel
> Lidern.
>
> [Rose, o pure contradiction,
> desire to be no one's sleep
> under so many eyelids.][70]

The cryptic combination of the words 'Niemandes' (meaning 'no one's') and 'soviel Lidern' (meaning 'so many eyelids' – but also evocative of 'Lieder,' i.e., songs, and the petals of a rose) has taken centre stage in a large number of differing interpretations. The most relevant aspect in this context, though, is the way in which it can be said to stage an allegory of reading. Both this poem and poetry in general (in Rilke's symbolist conception of it) can be said to direct themselves towards an ideal reader, and this ideal reader is to be born as a form of absence (a 'no one') through the dispersed perceptions (the many eyes) of its actual readers. In short, Rilke's epitaph not only dramatizes the arbitrariness of its own reception – it actually embraces it.

In the case of Yeats's epitaph, matters are – despite the seemingly simpler tone of his text – less clear-cut. Suffice it to say that, where 'Under Ben Bulben' would seem to insist upon a mythological backdrop for its own reception, the epitaph has to fend its way without such a specification. The horseman's identity becomes open to various interpretations, although we have recourse to at least one way of limiting the field a little. In a reading of the various drafts of this poem, Jon Stallworthy has noted the general importance of horses for Yeats:

> the horse for Yeats was a symbol of spirited and courageous nobility, and time and again in his poems he refers to the good horsemanship of those whom he admires – such as Robert Gregory, Con Markiewicz, and George Pollexfen.[71]

All of these figures, and no doubt many more, can be said to lurk in the commemorative force field of the poem. Yet the second of these three names is particularly relevant. For there is one other instance, in Yeats's poetry, of a human rider passing through the same area close to Sligo. It is the only other occasion where the poet uses the very same words: 'Under Ben Bulben'. It takes place in the poem titled 'On a Political Prisoner', published in 1920 – one of a handful of poems by Yeats that celebrates the memory of Countess Markiewicz, born Constance Gore-Booth. A member of the Protestant Ascendancy of Sligo, Markiewicz would later become a revolutionary icon fighting against the class into which she was born. Yeats's vision of her riding by the mountain is a wistful one, evoking early promise and poise that would later be lost: 'When long ago I saw her ride / Under Ben Bulben to the meet, / The beauty of her country-side / With all youth's lonely wildness stirred' (13–16). The tone is not too far removed from that we came across when reading Hardy's speaker describing his beloved on horseback, in the

Cornish poems of 'Poems of 1912–13', but, as we shall see, the stakes are radically different.

The presence of Markiewicz under Ben Bulben, in these lines from 'On a Political Prisoner', is no accident. Like her sister, the radical mystic Eva Gore-Booth, Countess Markiewicz grew up in Lissadell; the Protestant Big House situated only a few miles away from Ben Bulben and even closer to Drumcliff churchyard. The grandfather of these sisters, Sir Robert Gore-Booth (1805–1876), not only had the mansion of Lissadell built, but also introduced hunting to the area and started a family obsession with riding that would culminate in Markiewicz being known as 'one of the finest horsewomen ever seen in the west of Ireland'.[72] It is instructive to note that, while Yeats chose to link his own legacy with the paternal Ben Bulben, the countess opted to name her daughter Maeve, in a gesture of homage and imitation with respect to the mythical queen Maeve, whose legendary grave is on Knocknarea – the mountain facing Sligo from the other, south side.[73] It is said that Countess Markiewicz used to quote poetry when she climbed Knocknarea – more specifically, the line 'Does the road wind up-hill all the way?' from Christina Rossetti's poem 'Up-Hill'. This does not, however, mean she did not have close links to Ben Bulben, too. Eva Gore-Booth consistently sent her own poetry volumes to Yeats, and in *Broken Glory* (1917) she included the poem 'To Constance – in Prison'. The latter anticipates a number of Yeatsian motifs, not only linking Eva's sister with the moment when the 'gods descend at twilight from the magic-hearted hills' (7), but also clearly identifying her with the landscape where Yeats would later be buried:

> Yours is that inner Ireland beyond green fields and brown,
> Where waves break dawn-enchanted on the haunted Rosses shore,
> And clouds above Ben Bulben fling their coloured shadows down,
> Whilst little rivers shine and sink in wet sands at Crushmor.
>
> (9–12)[74]

If these lines are at the back of Yeats's mind when he writes 'Under Ben Bulben', he does not let his audience know it. As his poem 'In Memory of Eva Gore-Booth and Con Markiewicz' makes clear, Yeats sees Markiewicz as a treasonous figure. Whereas Lady Gregory's Coole Park was threatened by an outside enemy – the new Catholic rule of Ireland – Markiewicz was a member of the Protestant Ascendancy who had denied her own birthright. As such, she was not a figure with whom Yeats would want his own memory intimately associated. If the subterranean geography of 'Under Ben Bulben' involves a triangulation between Lissadell, Drumcliff, and Ben Bulben, Yeats himself wished to establish a single, straight line from churchyard to transcendent mountain, comparably to what occurs in Hardy's 'Poems of 1912–13' – where the poet's soon-to-be wife, Florence Dugdale, doesn't get a look-in; the poet seeks to keep the troubling and inappropriate voice of a woman out of earshot.

Markiewicz's role in Yeats's poetry has been consistently downplayed in favour of Maud Gonne.[75] Like Markiewicz, Gonne was a beautiful woman who – in Yeats's eyes – had lost her grace due to a fanatical fervour for Irish nationalism. The poet also once told a friend that he wrote poems about Countess Markiewicz in order to work out arguments with Gonne. Critics have been quick to try to identify Maud Gonne as the underlying memory for many of the more important images of women in Yeats's poetry, allocating to her a kind of absolute presence in his work. Apparently desire suffers no detour or displacement (apart from that instigated by Gonne herself) in his poetry, but goes straight as an arrow to one single beloved. Yet, as Richard Ellmann once felicitously put it, Gonne is a 'symbol of a symbol'.[76] Not only does she frequently stand for Ireland, but she also stands in a secondary relation – as a kind of emblem or symbol – for the mythical female figures who previously had this role. In addition, of course, she is only one of many women who have had an impact on Yeats's life and writings. Yeats's cultivation of the myth of the overshadowing importance of the sole object of love is part of his conscious drive for simplicity and memorability in his verse. It can be compared to Dante's many stratagems in *Vita Nuova* (a text Yeats, like Eliot, studied carefully), where the poet's variegated love life is twisted and turned in order to present Beatrice as his true inspiration. More abstractly, it echoes the kind of stylistic revision that Yeats describes in *Dramatis Personae*:

> In later years, through much knowledge of the stage, through the exfoliation of my own style, I learnt that occasional prosaic words gave the impression of an active man speaking. In dream poetry, in 'Kubla Khan', in 'The Stream's Secret', every line, every word, can carry its unanalysable, rich associations; but if we dramatize some possible singer or speaker we remember that he is moved by one thing at the time, certain words must be dull and numb. Here and there in correcting my early poems I have introduced such numbness and dullness, turned, for instance, 'the curd-pale moon' into the

'brilliant moon', that all might seem, as it were, remembered with indifference, except some one vivid image.[77]

Yeats's editing of, and commenting upon, his own love poetry frequently has the same aim. Maud Gonne is to be the 'one vivid image' around which everything else must seem to be 'remembered with indifference' – or with a cold eye.

Yeats first raises the theme of covert expressions of his love for Maud Gonne in the poem 'The Old Age of Queen Maeve'. 'O unquiet heart,' the speaker of the poem asks himself, 'Why do you praise another praising her, / As if there were no tale but your own tale / Worth knitting to a measure of sweet sound?'[78] As has already been pointed out, Queen Maeve is a mythical figure intrinsically linked with Yeats's own Sligo background – specifically with her legendary burial site on Knocknarea. The whole cluster of memories and allusions becomes even more tangled when one brings into the equation the fact that Yeats's writings establish deep links between Knocknarea and supernatural horsemen of the kind encountered in 'Under Ben Bulben'. The autobiographical instalment titled *Hodos Chameliontos* makes this clear in a passage on Mary Battle, the servant of Yeats's uncle George Pollexfen:

> Mary Battle, looking out of the window at Rosses Point, saw coming from Knocknarea, where Queen Maeve, according to local folklore, is buried under a great heap of stones, 'The finest woman you ever saw travelling right across from the mountains and straight to there. ... The others ... are fine and dashing-looking, like the men one sees riding their horses in twos or threes on the slopes of the mountains with their swords swinging.'[79]

The allusion to an unearthly bodily beauty anticipates 'Under Ben Bulben', as do the supernatural horsemen, and as a result any decisive distinction between Ben Bulben and Knocknarea seems to be undercut. Certainly it seems clear that when Yeats, in 'The Old Age of Queen Maeve', draws – as a semi-covert screen for his love for Maud Gonne – upon a mythical backdrop linked with even earlier recollections from the mountainous landscape of Sligo, he is entering into a rather complex landscape of mutually contaminating memories.

Although he did not meet Countess Markiewicz in person until 1894, five years after his first encounter with Maud Gonne, he already knew of her family – and both she and Eva were part of the mythical landscape of his Sligo. In his *Memoirs*, Yeats thus recollects: 'all through my boyhood' she 'had been romantic to me. ... I heard now and then [of] some tom-boyish feat or of her reckless riding, but the general impression was always that she was respected and admired.'[80] All horse riding in the area was intimately linked with the Gore-Booth family, since it was their patronage that made it possible to stage horse races in sight of the 'enormous monster' of Ben Bulben, as one local journalist put it.[81] Yeats's memoirs also noted Constance's physical resemblance to Maud Gonne, a similarity which no doubt works both ways: as Markiewicz can evoke Gonne, the memory of Gonne arguably also summons that of Markiewicz.

But it is the countess, and not Maud Gonne, who will always be linked to the other mass of rock framing Yeats's hometown and facing Sligo Bay. It is a matter of poetical topography: as far as Yeats's poetry is linked to Sligo, and not just an abstract idea of revolutionary Ireland, the countess' place in his writings cannot be fully eradicated. Countess Markiewicz remains a disturbing presence – not a legendary figure of love, and not quite fitting in with the sanitized self-presentation of the poet's self-canonizing monument. His poem on Ben Bulben is meant to proffer – together with the gravestone – a symbol of a unified Ireland, but it is also a collective reminder of the divisions and differences of Irish culture. Like the old man in *Purgatory*, Yeats may have wished to 'Appease / The misery of the living and the remorse of the dead',[82] but any such reconciliation is imperilled by the imminent arrival of an unexpected – or at least unpredictable – rider of a horse. If 'Under Ben Bulben' aspires to weirdness in the sense of something supernatural, in its aim to make a decree from beyond the grave, it is also a 'weird' text in how its act of appropriation fails to control the disturbing memories it attempts to fend away.

If nostalgia is the attempt to make a safe enclosure for the self, often linked with a place of historical or personal memory, by bracketing out disturbing memories and conflicting narratives, then 'Under Ben Bulben' – despite its overt lack of sentimentality – is very much a nostalgic poem. In 'Under Ben Bulben', Yeats takes personal memories (of childhood and fairytale narratives), linked to one particular place, and tries to use them as building blocks in a commemorative project both national and universal in scope. As in what Linda M. Austin calls 'the recreational condition of nostalgia's modern and healthy form',[83] his poem seeks to achieve a state of health through purgation. But Yeats's catharsis of contesting national and individual narratives is too violent, too obviously exclusionary, to fully succeed. While Oona Frawley is quite correct in insisting that Yeats's nostalgia is not generally sentimental, but rather 'a pointed political tool that allows him to recover Irish trad-itions eclipsed by years of colonialism',[84] the sharpened point of his use of memory makes ruthless sacrifices of its own. Trying to implement what Nicholas Dames has called nostalgia's 'dilution and disconnection of the past in the service of an encroaching future',[85] Yeats makes use of a site – Ben Bulben and its environs – where the connoted mean-ings prove to be beyond control. The place itself displaces Yeats's poem from the sole control of its author's intentions. Where Hardy and (to a degree) Tennyson set aside nostalgia for less self-centred and exclusion-ary forms of memory, Yeats's strenuously controlled deployment of the past is upset by his chosen site rather than his own scruples.

  This chapter has inspected how three different poets in the Victorian and post-Victorian era addressed the issue of memory's materializa-tion. A common denominator has been how they have linked individ-ual memory – be it of king Arthur, the beloved of Hardy's 'Poems of 1912–13', or of Yeats's childhood – to western places bearing some col-lective significance of a 'weird' nature. In all three, individual memory is linked to collective memory, albeit in differing ways. Where Tennyson is ambivalent about the temporal investment of innerness in external and collective space, Hardy is more straightforwardly critical, trying to defend the beloved's memory against a more general indifference. Yet 'Poems of 1912–13' defend the beloved by supporting her memory on the basis of another, complex generality – that of the west of Romance. In Yeats, we find the strongest desire for a seamless fit between indi-vidual and collective memory. The Irish poet attempts to fully fuse the poet's own legacy with that of a locality which is to have a national significance. Yet even here ambivalence and multiplicity intrude, and can be exhumed by critical interrogation.

4
Modernism, Tradition, and Organicism in T. S. Eliot and Heaney

Modernism understood itself as a radical questioning of the pervading norms of art and literature. It was time to shake off the tired, dated idioms of the Victorians and Edwardians, and break new ground. As such, it was also time to free oneself of the shackles of the past. Thus Charles Baudelaire presented Constantin Guys as characterized by a 'modernity', which he identified with 'the ephemeral, the fugitive, the contingent, the half of art whose other half is the eternal and the immutable'.[1] Even that which appeared merely fashionable, or obsessed with the flickering moment, was infinitely preferable to the hackneyed, backward-looking traditions from which one was extricating oneself. On the British Isles, Ezra Pound became one of the most aggressive proponents of this tendency, asking nothing less from his colleagues than that they *make it new*. For Pound, the entire nineteenth century could be dismissed as 'a rather blurry, messy sort of a period, a rather sentimentalistic, mannerish sort of a period',[2] and it was vital to leave that disaster well behind.

Yet Pound did not simply ask modernism to take leave of the past, forgetting it entire. He himself not only entered into fruitful (if antagonistic) dialogue with a Victorian such as Robert Browning, but also dug deep in literary history in order to formulate a positive ideal for what modern poetry should be. According to Paul de Man, such returns to the past are characteristic of the very nature of modernity: 'The more radical the rejection of anything that came before, the greater the dependence on the past.'[3] Certainly, modernism could not deny the past wholesale, but rather had to make at least a selective appropriation of it. This theme is particularly clearly developed, of course, by Pound's friend and collaborator, T. S. Eliot. According to some estimates, Eliot's own interpretation of modernism led to a conservatism that has hindered British poetry ever since: even modernism itself is actually something nostalgic, it is held, obsessed with the past rather than dynamic and forward-looking. In this chapter, however, overly dismissive accounts of Eliot's essay 'Tradition and the Individual Talent' will be contradicted. This crucial and influential piece will be read as commenting, and putting its own stamp, upon the tradition of poetic use of memory established by Eliot's forerunners. By paying particular attention to the figures deployed in the essay, as well as reading it in the context of surrounding essays in *The Sacred Wood*, I will attempt to show that Eliot's understanding of poetic memory is more subtle and open-ended than critical consensus has tended to credit. I will, however, also demonstrate that the essay attempts almost the opposite of what Hardy does in 'Poems of 1912–13': rather than defending individual against collective memory, Eliot will seek, on the behalf of modernism, to challenge the former through the authority of a literary version of the latter. The rest of the chapter will show, in readings of *The Four Quartets* and of Seamus Heaney's poetry, how modernism's attempts to leave certain strands of poetic memory behind have – at least in these particular English and Irish versions – proved to be a passing, if instructive, experiment. Throughout, the abstract spatiality of organicism will be shown to be an important structuring device for the two authors concerned.

T. S. Eliot I: Figuring out 'Tradition and the Individual Talent'

T. S. Eliot's brand of modernism is of course far from renouncing the past. Without a historical sense, no formidable poetical career can be forged, Eliot tells us, and anyone who neglects this precept does so at his or her own peril. The second section of 'Tradition and the Individual Talent' is devoted to an impersonal theory of authorship, which might not immediately seem to have any relation to historicity. Eliot characterizes the poet as someone who creates a work of art, a poem, which is ultimately heterogeneous to whatever personal data were present at the start of the process. Literary writing is an essentially transformative act, where the result is inherently different from the raw matter with which the writer started. Towards the end of the essay, Eliot is keen to highlight how far he is removed from romanticism:

> The business of the poet is not to find new emotions, but to use the ordinary ones and, in working them up into poetry, to express

feelings which are not in actual emotions at all. And emotions which he has never experienced will serve his turn as well as those familiar to him. Consequently, we must believe that 'emotion recollected in tranquillity' is an inexact formula. For it is neither emotion, nor recollection, nor, without distortion of meaning, tranquillity. It is a concentration, and a new thing resulting from the concentration, of a very great number of experiences which to the practical and active person would not seem to be experiences at all; it is a concentration which does not happen consciously or of deliberation. These experiences are not 'recollected', and they finally unite in an atmosphere which is 'tranquil' only in that it is a passive attending upon the event. (48)

Here we find a significant criticism of Wordsworth's formula from the preface to the *Lyrical Ballads*. Yet not all of Eliot's points here are of the same weight or cogency. The distinction between 'emotion' and 'feeling' is not one he takes the trouble of establishing or defining: while Wordsworth's essay uses both terms, Eliot himself in fact seems to prefer 'emotion', so the actual use of words has no immediately obvious motivation. Perhaps Eliot wants to define the two terms differently here – presumably building on Remy de Gourmont's distinction between aesthetic emotions and other emotions – but no such definition is provided. Similarly, the opposition between Wordsworth's 'tranquillity' and 'a passive attending upon the event' is not clearly articulated. Only a few years later, Eliot will stress 'that intense and transitory relief which comes at the moment of completion and is the chief reward of creative work' – which indeed sounds like a heightened sense of tranquillity.[4] One might, however, argue that Eliot is describing a peaceful end to the poetical composition, while Wordsworth is claiming that the poet must compose him- or herself before commencing the process of writing.

Yet such *contretemps* are relatively small fry. The key difference between Wordsworth and Eliot lies neither in the beginning nor in the end of the process of composition: the two of them differ primarily with regard to how they account for the transformative process in between. 'Recollection' is, for Eliot here, precisely what the writing of poetry is *not*. Why not? Well, partly due to the fact that the recollective act is too deliberate. Poetical composition, he counters, 'is a concentration which does not happen consciously or of deliberation'. Here again, though, the difference from Wordsworth is arguably polemically exaggerated: romantic accounts of composition allow for an element of unconsciousness in the creative process, even if this is not as rigorously or as dogmatically expressed as among Freud's contemporaries.

More important for Eliot is the severance of the poem from its personal origins. By getting rid of 'recollection', he effectively wants to free the poem from being an act of private *mimesis*. Rather than express the poet's original emotions, the poem will mean and be in its own right. This does not mean that personal recollection is completely eradicated: Eliot does not deny that the poet fashions the finished work of art out of his or her personal givens,[5] only he adds that the distance from this origin is – in a certain sense – incalculable. No reader should attempt to calculate that origin, based on the data of the finished product.

Yet if Eliot effectively chastises Wordsworth with one hand for giving too much to memory, he returns a favour to memory with the other. 'Tradition and the Individual Talent' can be read in many different ways, but seen from the viewpoint of a poetics of memory it performs a complex act of reorganization. On the one hand, poetry's role as a carrier of individual memory is carefully and insistently circumscribed. On the other hand, though, the reader is left in no doubt that one of poetry's main responsibilities is as a form of collective memory. This collective memory is of a peculiarly literary kind: it is a memory of the literary tradition, and as such it is truly international rather than limited to the places of the nation. Yet it nevertheless constitutes a way, including both conscious and unconscious levels, of preserving the past in the poetical present. The argument presenting this kind of memory is not only circuitous and complicated, but has also attracted a great deal of critical comment of its own. A particularly trenchant critique has come from Richard Shusterman, who, in his comprehensive study *T. S. Eliot and the Philosophy of Criticism*, contrasts 'Tradition and the Individual Talent' unfavourably with how Eliot later articulates the concept of tradition. According to Shusterman, the early essay 'reflects his juvenile objectivism and literary purism',[6] and does not achieve the insight of Eliot's later work. In more mature texts, Shusterman claims, Eliot developed his theory to the point where he could proffer 'a more balanced and general account which no longer sought to erect tradition into an immutably absolute ideal and purely artistic standard of objectivity for judging the meaning and value of authors and their work'.[7]

Although 'Tradition and the Individual Talent' is by no means a faultless work of criticism, Shusterman is showing less fairness, and far more reductionism, here than he does with regard to Eliot's other critical work. Reacting against the 'literary' taint of this early essay, he effectively misrepresents the argument of what still remains a very important *précis* of

Eliot's view of collective and individual memory. Although 'Tradition and the Individual Talent' does have a specifically literary focus, this can be defended on several grounds. For not only does the subtitle of *The Sacred Wood* point out that these are *Essays on Poetry and Criticism* – making clear that this is indeed 'literary' – but the historical context of this work is relevant, too: Eliot's early work is preoccupied with correcting the imbalances of the biographical and impressionist approaches that were dominant at the time, and therefore the stress is necessarily on literary approaches and frames of reference. Shusterman's claim that the essay seeks to create an 'immutably absolute ideal' is, however, a far graver simplification of Eliot's argument. Shusterman's strongest evidence for the claim is Eliot's wording in this passage:

> The existing monuments form an ideal order among themselves, which is modified by the introduction of the new (the really new) work of art among them. The existing order is complete before the new work arrives; for order to persist after the supervention of novelty, the *whole* existing order must be, if ever so slightly, altered; and so the relations, proportions, values of each work of art toward the whole are readjusted; and this is conformity between the old and the new. (41)

Understandably, Shusterman finds the visual image of 'great and sturdy existing monuments ... shuffling and nudging each other about' less than elegant.[8] He goes even further, though, using this metaphor as key evidence in an argument for the basically flawed nature of Eliot's early conception of tradition:

> As the inherent flexibility of Eliot's concept of tradition is considerably contradicted and concealed by its metaphorical portrayal in terms of monuments and timeless orders, so the role of criticism in tradition is overshadowed by the suggestion (never explicitly stated) that within the literary past which includes both bad and good, there is embedded an 'ideal order', 'main current', or essence of tradition which is wholly good and calls for no criticism.[9]

Shusterman's indictment of what he calls 'a purified ideal literary tradition' bases itself on something 'never explicitly stated', as well as the extrapolation of one single metaphor from the surface text.[10] I propose that a fairer and more comprehensive account of Eliot's argument can be gleaned by showing how it deploys five other key metaphors. In a simplified form, these can be summarized as follows:

1. *Tradition is a gift.*
2. *Tradition is a process of self-sacrifice.*
3. *Tradition is a current.*
4. *Tradition is one memory.*
5. *Tradition is an organic body.*

These are five major figures of memory presented in the first section of 'Tradition and the Individual Talent'.[11] Any figuring out of the essay's argument is, arguably, dependent upon grasping both their individual contribution and interplay.

We learn that tradition is a gift only in passing, when Eliot states: 'Yet if the only form of tradition, of handing down, consisted in following the ways of the immediate generation before us in a blind or timid adherence to its successes, "tradition" should be positively discouraged' (40). Alerting the reader to the term's etymology, Eliot here alludes to the Latin *traditio*, meaning 'delivery, surrender, handing down, a saying handed down, instruction or doctrine delivered'. As something delivered or presented from one instance or individual to another, tradition involves the recipient in a process of bartering and mutual responsibility. Tradition's inheritors are granted the riches of the past, but those riches are accompanied by obligations that are far from negligible.

Eliot therefore stresses the 'great difficulties and responsibilities' of the poet (41). Literature is a craft that demands much patience and discipline, not only by being a search for formal perfection, but also in the tireless and understanding acquisition of a historical context. No responsibility is more difficult to yield to, though, than the call for the poet's self-sacrifice. This is the second of the five figures of tradition, presented towards the end of the first section of 'Tradition and the Individual Talent': 'What happens is a continual surrender of himself as he is at the moment to something which is more valuable. The progress of an artist is a continual self-sacrifice, a continual extinction of personality' (43–44). Eliot's lifelong fascination with asceticism and martyrs such as Thomas Becket and Saint Sebastian, as well as his interest (evident in *The Waste Land*) in anthropological and classical accounts of sacrifice, thus spills over into his poetics. If the poet receives the riches of tradition – not only the best that has been thought and expressed, but also much else – then there is a price to pay. As Eliot's theory of poetical composition makes clear, the poet cannot hope to salvage his or her personal emotions in the final work: confessionalism or expressivism is ruled out, as poetic labour yields something heterogeneous to its personal origins. But the alienation inherent in the individual creative process (whereby the poet is akin to the working-class artisan in Marxist philosophy) is coupled with, and perhaps even strengthened by, the way in which the poet must yield to a greater whole. Like a monk joining an order, or a believer joining a Church, the writer's contribution must find its meaning in the more encompassing context of tradition's 'ideal order' (41).

Later in this chapter, in a reading of *Four Quartets*, I will address the metaphorical nexus between memory and the sea. As Eliot's third figure of memory in 'Tradition and the Individual Talent', the same image – or at least images relating to moving waters – seems to enjoy only a minor and subterranean influence. According to Shusterman (cf. the reference to a 'main current' in the previously cited passage), it buttresses Eliot's construction of a purified literary tradition of perfected works. But this simplifies the deployment of this particular figure, since the latter serves several functions simultaneously. Eliot uses it to stress not only the magnitude of collective memory, but also its articulated structure. He grants that the poet may have certain favourite authors, and will probably also know some eras better than others. Yet none of this is enough: 'The poet must be very conscious of the main current, which does not all flow invariably through the most distinguished reputations' (42). This metaphor alludes back to Arnold's ideal, cited elsewhere in *The Sacred Wood*, of 'a current of ideas in the highest degree animating and nourishing to the creative power'.[12] In Eliot's usage, it highlights the dynamic nature of literary tradition, which he always is keen to portray as subject to flux and revision. But it has another role, too: instead of figuring tradition as the influence of certain elevated exemplars, fixed in the poetical firmament, the water metaphor moves horizontally rather than vertically. Since it highlights how 'the most distinguished reputations' are not the sole repositories of tradition's force, it actually deflects attention from the monuments favoured by orthodox accounts of history, and espouses a more widely encompassing approach.

Two later examples of this imagery are worth considering. The first is from the conclusion of the fourth Clark lecture, in 1926, where Eliot substantiates the variety of metaphysical poetry by claiming that the 'influence of Donne runs out in three channels,' and then adds 'We shall have to reascend these streams.'[13] This and other plural structures lead Eliot to 'suggest that "metaphysical poetry" in general, and "metaphysical poetry" of the seventeenth century in particular, has not one positive and unmoving centre upon which one can put the finger.'[14] Later, in *The Use of Criticism and the Use of Poetry*, Eliot defends his inter-pretation of the critical contribution of the circle of the Countess of Pembroke to Elizabethan literature by yet another deployment of this metaphor: 'I have wished to affirm that in looking at the period with an interest in the development of the critical consciousness in and towards poetry, you cannot dissociate one group of people from another; you cannot draw a line and say here is backwater, here is the main stream.'[15] Here the levelling tendency of the marine metaphor is being taken fur-ther than in 'Tradition and the Individual Talent': in the latter text, there is no doubt that there still is a 'main current' at the centre. But certainly other essays in *The Sacred Wood* corroborate that the dynamic nature of tradition makes it something both less placid and less easily surveyed than, say, a lake.

This can be seen, for instance, in how these other texts resist what Eliot calls a 'canonical' understanding of tradition. Despite the attrac-tions the concept of a 'canon' has had for recent critics, and the fact that one might expect the term's religious associations to be amenable to Eliot, the author of *The Sacred Wood* opposes what he understands to be a canonical reception of established authors. A first glimpse of this can be gleaned from a cryptic footnote in the introduction, where we are told: 'Arnold, it must be admitted, gives us often the impression of seeing the masters, whom he quotes, as canonical literature, rather than as masters' (xvii). The passage accompanying this note makes the point that it is the critic's 'business to see literature steadily and to see it whole; and this is eminently to see it *not* as consecrated by time, but to see it beyond time: to see the best work of our time and the best work of twenty-five hundred years ago with the same eyes' (ibid.). It is not quite clear what Eliot means with the phrase 'beyond time' here: this may be interpreted as either a remnant of a naïve attitude of ahistorical classicism, or as a rare lack of verbal precision, though it may also be an anticipation of the mystical transcendence of time later sought after in *Four Quartets*.[16] Be this as it may, Eliot's understanding of 'canonical' tradition as something static becomes clearer in the following essay, 'The Perfect Critic', when he claims that one 'must be firmly distrustful of accepting Aristotle in a canonical spirit; this is to lose the whole liv-ing force of him' (9).

A canonical understanding of the past would lead to a stemming of the current of tradition. Literature is only truly preserved, Eliot observes elsewhere in *The Sacred Wood*, when it survives as a 'living art' – when it has not 'lost its application', something which leads its recipients merely to indulge in 'a study of antiquities' (103). Thus Ben Jonson is said to be 'universally accepted', but 'read only by historians and antiquaries' who do not respond to his texts as works of art (88). His reputation is therefore 'of the most deadly kind that can be compelled upon the memory of a great poet' (ibid.). Such a reputation shows evidence not of what Eliot believes to be true criticism, but rather of an 'uncritical attitude', whereby literature is merely accepted as 'an institution – accepted, that is to say, with the same gravity as the establishments of Church and State' (33).

Gerald L. Bruns has derided what he calls 'the monumental idea of tradition that we get from T. S. Eliot, with his pantheon or five-foot shelf whose order is periodically adjusted to make room for new members'.[17] Dismissing what he calls Eliot's 'basic museum-piece theory of tradition', he basically restates Shusterman's view of 'Tradition and the Individual Talent', and is similarly seduced to misinterpret the whole text in light of one single trope. Such readings ignore that both this particular essay of Eliot's and the more general programme of *The Sacred Wood* are engaged in debunking a 'museum-piece' theory. The readings of Shakespeare included in *The Sacred Wood* are especially belligerent attempts to wilfully eschew any uncritical acceptance of the monuments of the past. The polemically iconoclastic analysis of what Eliot deems to be *Hamlet*'s 'artistic failure' in 'Hamlet and His Problems' is of course the most extensive and famous example of this (84). Irrespective of what one might think of Eliot's argument here, the essay itself remains a valid testimony to how he, at this time, precisely wants to resist reifying collective memory into a timeless order of static classics. By criticizing Shakespeare's perhaps most renowned play, Eliot is demonstrating that the best preservation of the past is something very different from a mere dusting and rearranging of already existing monuments. In related fashion, the essay on Marlowe is notable for how it objects to exaggerated, and imprecise, obsequies before Shakespeare. The latter's universality is cut down to size: 'one man cannot be more than one man; ... and to say that Shakespeare expressed nearly all human emotions, implying that he left very little for anyone else, is a radical misunderstanding of art and the artist' (73). One suspects that the argument made for Marlowe's rhetoric is primarily made in order to avoid misconstruction of the nature of the centrality of the more celebrated Elizabethan. Marlowe's primary asset is that he has a virtue that 'is quite un-Shakespearean' (80). Returning to the aquatic imagery, one might say that the current of tradition – as a confluence of several living streams – is never reducible to one simple position.

Nevertheless, even if it is not closed or excessively hierarchical, tradition is a whole. Indeed, it is – and here we come to the fourth of the operative figures in 'Tradition and the Individual Talent' – very much like one grand memory. It can include great variety, and it never loses that which it has gained. This point is made while Eliot is in the process of dismissing the transposition of facile notions of progress from the natural sciences to literary history. The poet, he insists,

> must be aware that the mind of Europe – the mind of his own country – a mind which he learns in time to be much more important than his own private mind – is a mind which changes, and that this change is a development which abandons nothing *en route*, which does not superannuate either Shakespeare, or Homer, or the rock drawing of the Magdalenian draughtsmen. (42–43)

There is a pronounced stress on comprehensiveness here, which obviously is meant to obviate the possibility of parochialism of any kind. The effective past of poetry is more than any narrow, localized tradition. A similar stress is to be found in a later text, when Eliot claims 'the great poet is, among other things, one who not merely restores a tradition which has been in abeyance, but one who in his poetry re-twines as many strands of tradition as possible.'[18] The main tradition actually comes about through a constructed interweaving of a plurality of more particular traditions. This not only contradicts Shusterman's account, discussed earlier, but also many other simplifications of Eliot's argument. Despite recent critiques of Eliot's understanding of tradition as constituting a closed, Eurocentric totality, a sense of fairness – and indeed tradition – demands that one should be alert to the generosity and inclusiveness of his ideal. These characteristics are particularly striking when his ideal is contrasted with nation-centred canons.

The open mind of tradition that embraces a plurality of figures and traditions is, of course, the memory of the individual writ large – a conception not unrelated to Yeats's *Anima Mundi*. The image of the mind as a kind of limitless receptacle preserving all its memories has attracted several twentieth century writers. If we are to follow Douwe Draaisma, figures like Eliot and Yeats may have been inspired by the feats of photography: 'As analogies for visual representations photographs particularly stress the *immutability* of what is stored as a memory: they suggest a memory that forgets nothing.'[19] Another source of inspiration may lie closer at hand, though; namely, Eliot's early interest in the philosophy of Henri Bergson. Unlike F. H. Bradley (who gave Eliot much else),

108 Figures of Memory

Bergson was a philosopher who could offer Eliot a comprehensive theory of memory. Bergson's theory can be glimpsed as a factor behind 'Tradition and the Individual Talent' in at least two different ways. The first has to do with the just discussed comprehensiveness of memory: the French philosopher's notion of a 'pure' or 'spontaneous' memory is precisely a dynamic conception of memory where nothing is lost. Like Eliot, Bergson believes the present is constituted on the basis of this totality: 'our character, always present in all our decisions, is indeed the synthesis of all our past states.'[20]

The second way in which Bergson's theory may have influenced Eliot – and certainly matches it – is in its vitalism. As Eliot's reference to Bergson in his third Clark lecture makes clear, the dynamic nature of this vitalism links it back to the water metaphor we encountered earlier: 'You know how the Absolute of Bergson is arrived at,' Eliot told his audience, 'by plunging into the flow of immediate experience.'[21] Although there are differences between Eliot and Bergson here, the latter's vitalism provides support for the fifth and final figure of memory, in this reading of 'Tradition and the Individual Talent': the comparison of memory to an organic body. This is arguably the master metaphor of Eliot's text, at least partially comprehending all the others. As Michael Levenson has pointed out, 'Eliot is engaged in nothing less than the task of spatializing time'[22] – but that spatialization takes a particular and indeed traditional form: that of an organically articulated whole. We have of course come across organic understandings of memory in the previous chapters of this book: even if his deployment of it is unique, Eliot's use of this metaphor is well prepared by his poetical predecessors.

Eliot alluded to the importance of organicism in 1923, in 'The Function of Criticism', when he took a backward glance and summarized the argument of the earlier essay as follows:

> I thought of literature then, as I think of it now, of the literature of the world, of the literature of Europe, of the literature of a single country, not as a collection of the writings of individuals, but *as 'organic wholes'*, as systems in relation to which, and only in relation to which, individual works of literary art, and the works of individual artists, have their significance.[23]

In Eliot's dismissal of antiquarianism and canonical approaches to the past, we have already come across his description of true tradition as being something 'living'. As when Nietzsche utilized the term in his

Untimely Meditations, the link with vitalist thought may be difficult to pick out at first sight, but it is not fortuitous. Tradition is living because it is a dynamic entity, ever developing and changing in time.

One of Eliot's most memorable and provocative pronouncements in 'Tradition and the Individual Talent' becomes self-evident and almost tautological, viewed in light of his organicism: 'Whoever has approved this idea of order, of the form of European, of English literature, will not find it preposterous that the past should be altered by the present as much as the present is directed by the past' (41). Although the relations between England, Europe, and the world are not clear here, the relations between the past and present are lucidly present – and are a logical consequence of organicism. For in an organic entity, all parts are like the members of a living body: they are interdependent, having – as Plato declared in *Phaedrus* – a fitting relation to each other.[24] They are mutually dependent upon one another, so that any change in one part will have ramifications across the board – or, as Eliot puts it, 'for order to persist after the supervention of novelty, the *whole* existing order must be, if ever so slightly, altered; and so the relations of each work of art toward the whole are readjusted' (41). If talk of monuments may seem to arrest tradition in a fixed order, Eliot's more pervasive and fundamental use of the figure of organicism compels past and present to engage in a continually developing process of interaction and change. The mutual relation between the gift of the past and the poet's responsibility, discussed earlier, is thus articulated within what Eliot calls 'the conception of poetry as a living whole of all the poetry that has ever been written' (44).

Organicism is, first and foremost, a form of holism. In 'Tradition and the Individual Talent', it provides a paradigm not only for Eliot's notion of tradition, but also for how he conceives of the work of art. For the notion of composition as a process that creates a 'fusion of elements' draws upon the idea that the organic structure not only is characterized by relations of internal interdependence (46), but also has a hierarchical centre. Here Eliot is echoing Coleridge. The most essential part of the creative act is the imagination, which – for Eliot as for Coleridge before him – is responsible for this act of gathering together. As Coleridge conceived of the imagination as a strongly inclusive faculty,[25] so Eliot too – if we move back to the theory of tradition, rather than the theory of composition – conceives of the collective mind as an unlimited and accepting receptacle.

Thus one can see an overlapping between the figure of the remembering 'one mind', on the one hand, and that of the organic body, on the other. But what of the metaphor of self-sacrifice? Is there any room for it in an organic conception of tradition? There is indeed: here too Eliot is elaborating on the idea that an organic unity is hierarchically organized – or, as Coleridge put it, how *'all* the parts of an organized whole must be assimilated to the more *important* and *essential* parts.'[26] For in hierarchy there is subjugation: the lower orders of the structure must serve the more elevated ones, just as all the single limbs of a body must serve the whole. On its own, a toe or an arm has no function: only by contributing to a whole, living body does such a body part have a role to play; this is in fact the only function it really has to serve. Similarly, Eliot's poet can only fulfil his own individual exigency through fitting in with the greater whole: 'not only the best, but the most individual parts of his work may be those in which the dead poets, his ancestors, assert their immortality most vigorously' (40).

In the context of this study, Eliot's essay comes across as a restraining influence on the poetics of individual memory that goes back to Wordsworth. A counter-reaction against the unrestrained individualism of some modernist tendencies – evident in the eschewing of traditional forms, coupled with the way in which Expressionism already was partly anticipating later confessionalism – is perhaps only to be expected.[27] Eliot not only restrains imagination and the self, though, but also seems to want to replace Wordsworth's individual memory with a collective memory containing the literary weight of ages. In light of this, and also in light of Eliot's many public endorsements of established forces of power, it is hard to dismiss accusations of authoritarianism out of hand. The way in which 'Tradition and the Individual Talent' finesses the distinction between a normative prescription (*the poet should be traditional*) and a more descriptive tone (*the poet is inevitably traditional*) is perhaps less of a shortcoming or sign of a neglect, in this respect, than a strategic muddying of the waters. The resulting lack of clarity does not deny Eliot access to a certain polemical power, while it at the same time forces critics like Shusterman to hold their horses somewhat: if Eliot seems to suggest to Shusterman that what survives as tradition is 'wholly good', this is nevertheless a position his modern critic must admit is 'never explicitly stated'.[28]

Can one derive a totalitarian form of political authoritarianism from a complex conception of the internal workings of literary tradition? We do know that Eliot was wary of how an internal structural logic could lead others into authoritarianism. In his essay on Bradley, a quotation where Bradley is concerned with the subjection of the private self to the divine ideal is followed by this remark from Eliot: 'There is one direction in which these words – and indeed, Bradley's philosophy as a whole – might be pushed, which would be dangerous; the direction of diminishing the value and dignity of the individual, of sacrificing him to a Church or State.'[29] Certainly Eliot, who criticized Hobbes and his followers for advocating an 'absolutist government' that displays a 'lack of balance',[30] is not as irredeemably bigoted on such matters as argued by his most vehement critics. Although he, like Coleridge, was not uncomfortable with abstract thought, and often found his most rewarding critical insights by transferring metaphors or conceptual schemes from one sphere to another, he was aware of the potential pitfalls. Thus in a later essay titled 'Catholicism and International Order' he warned against a too easy transfer of religious ideas into the political sphere: 'We are in danger always of translating notions too literally from one order to another. ... The ideas of authority, of hierarchy, of discipline and order, applied inappropriately in the temporal sphere, may lead us into some error of absolutism or impossible theocracy.'[31] Here, as elsewhere, little is gained by jumping to conclusions.

T. S. Eliot II: The Underground and *Four Quartets*

Moving away from 'Tradition and the Individual Talent', I want to address the development of Eliot's thought on memory from this early essay to *Four Quartets*. This process will involve a surprising, if oblique, reneging, on Eliot's part, of his earlier dismissal of personal memory. Even if the latter does not return in full Wordsworthian splendour, we shall see that a complex logic of spatiality – building on, but ultimately complicating his earlier organicism – will involve a subterranean survival of personal memory in the later Eliot.

   First of all, it is apposite to underline a point made by Erik Svarny, namely that 'in Eliot's early verse, culminating in *The Waste Land*, tradition has undergone a metamorphosis into fragments, which (intentionally) do not intellectually mediate between the poet and his audience.'[32] One might hesitate at the use of 'metamorphosis' here, though, as one might also at Svarny's claim that 'Eliot's specific employment of the literary past, "tradition", in his verse relates only tangentially to his employment of "tradition" as a critical category in his prose writings of the period.'[33] An important point for Eliot is that tradition without mediation or control will be as chaotic and incoherent as the present. Devoid of the gathering or collecting of recollection – without the unity that only a shaping of parts into an organic whole can provide – there will be either (1) an amorphous lack of structure or (2) a lifeless or 'canonical' quasi-structure. I differ from Svarny in claiming that these ideas are present in both the poetry and the prose.

Both the poetry and the prose of early Eliot portray how our shared memory is under threat and cannot be taken for granted. As Svarny points out, the role of the reader is different in the literary texts. Take *The Waste Land*, for instance: there it is an open question whether the viewpoint of Tiresias, as indicated by Eliot's footnote,[34] provides a redemptive unity to the text. Just as likely, the text presents us with a raw, poetical material that either awaits the unification granted by its reader, or actually highlights the impossibility of making such a unity. One is reminded of Eliot's description of *Kubla Khan* as a fragment where the 'imagery ... is not *used*: the poem has not been written'.[35] When the speaker, at the end of *The Waste Land*, tells us that 'These fragments I have shored against my ruins' (430), it is at least hard to escape the sense of a memory that has capsized in, and yet also somehow survived, the unmanageable waves of time.

If the latter reading is a valid one, it is in conformity with Eliot's 'Rhapsody on a Windy Night', which addresses how an individual memory, rather than a collective one, can become radically unhinged from its moorings. The first stanza of this poem shows how the speaker is forced to surrender the structural frame that keeps his memory in an orderly structure:

> Whispering lunar incantations
> Dissolve the floors of memory
> And all its clear relations,
> Its divisions and precisions.
> (4–7)

Devoid of any structuring 'floors' or organizing grid, the speaker suffers a form of maddening memory that is the associative process run wild. Since there is no base, this is a freely floating process, a metonymical plethora: 'The memory throws up high and dry / A crowd of twisted things' (23–24). Here a central mode of what Richard Terdiman has described as modernity's 'memory crisis' is insistently, overwhelmingly at work: through an 'eerie domination of *now* by *then*', memory loses its transparency and 'turns labyrinthine'.[36] Yet even if this midnight experience seems deranged and disturbing, the ironical ending of the poem alerts us to the fact that daytime order – where memory has 'floors' once more – provides no attractive alternative to the speaker returning from his nightly escapade:

> The lamp said,
> 'Four o'clock,
> Here is the number on the door.
> Memory!
> You have the key,
> The little lamp spreads a ring on the stair.
> Mount.
> The bed is open; the tooth-brush hangs on the wall,
> Put your shoes at the door, sleep, prepare for life.'
>
> The last twist of the knife.
>
> (69–78)

It is not quite clear whether the trenchant finale is due the unrewarding daily life of the main character, or whether the chaos of night-time memory is an escape from a particularly compelling and unhappy memory.

Despite the scepticism Eliot felt with regard to 'canonical' and 'antiquarian' orderings of history, the tendency of his critical writings after 'Tradition and the Individual Talent' is not, of course, towards a revolt against strict orderings of temporality. Indeed, one might see the early essay on tradition, and the poems of this period, as entailing an overly inclusive ideal from which the later Eliot would have to recoil. For 'Tradition and the Individual Talent' is less than clear on what should provide the centre of its living body of the past, while it also to a large degree sidesteps the issue of what is excluded from the structure. Organic thought has traditionally entailed a strict delineation of borders – an exclusion of what is beyond its confines, often (as in the romantics' dismissal of the machine) in the form of an anti-self or dismissed alternative. Although the (later renounced) opposition between classicism and romanticism contributes towards such a structure, neither it nor other conceptual oppositions utilized by the early Eliot have the precision necessary to clearly separate a totality from its outside: in his lectures on metaphysical poetry, he is thus forced to admit that 'as the frontiers are nowhere, even in the work of one man, clearly defined, we must be content to examine some poetry which is not, on the face it, metaphysical.'[37]

Without any clear demarcation of this sort between the inside and outside of his more comprehensive idea of tradition, Eliot's embraced order risks coming across as more than a little like the chaos that it is meant to counter. A truly living tradition tends towards the expansiveness and purposelessness of Donne's wit, as described by Eliot:

> In this elegy [i.e. 'Elegy I, Jealosie'] his wit is too lively to keep to the point; and indeed the peculiar fascination of Donne's verse resides in this curious trick of vagrant thought; or it is as if his theme picked up every possible felicity of image and oddity of thought in its neighborhood, and became as unrecognisable as the sea-god Glaucus.[38]

There can be too much life and liveliness: Donne creates a 'unity in flux' where there 'is no *structure* of thought'.[39] Eliot would like to distinguish the result from an organic totality – 'this spectacle of thought in dissolution produces colours and iridiscences never apparent in a living and organic system'[40] – but his conception of such a system lacks the kind of coherence that would be able to provide him with assurance on this matter. The appearing of the problem is not coincidental, stemming as it does from the fact that his ideal is of a wholeness of a particularly inclusive and challenging kind. As he puts it in the same Clark lectures, with a note of repeated hesitation which may indeed indicate the stakes involved: 'perhaps the highest unity of all' is constituted 'out of elements perhaps the most disparate and remote.'[41]

Overflowing with riches, the shared memory of tradition tends towards a state similar to that of Donne's 'vagrant thought' – as is made explicit in the nightmare vision of history presented in 'Gerontion':

> After such knowledge, what forgiveness? Think now
> History has many cunning passages, contrived corridors
> And issues, deceives with whispering ambitions,
> Guides us by vanities. Think now
> She gives when our attention is distracted
> And what she gives, gives with such supple confusions
> That the giving famishes the craving.
>
> (33–39)

The speaker of these lines cannot make sense of history: the inordinate gift of this *traditio* cannot yield any satisfactory transaction. This is due to its being embodied in a structure that leaves no room for redemption, with Piranesian subtleties only providing a form of amazement that stultifies and stuns its recipient. Commentators have shown how Gerontion's vision builds on *The Education of Henry Adams*, where we are told that the twentieth century historian 'entered a far vaster universe, where all the old roads ran about in every direction, overrunning, dividing, stopping abruptly, vanishing slowly, with side-paths that led nowhere, and sequences that could not be proved'.[42]

Spatial imagery plays an important role in 'Gerontion', where, time after time, the poem returns to emphasize the placing of the speaker: 'An old man in a draughty house' (31). There is the ending of the poem, where his thoughts are described as 'Tenants of the house' (74); there is the brief vision of Gerontion 'Stiffen[ing] in a rented house' (50); and there is the compressed evocation of the physical movements of characters such as Mr. Silvero and Fräulein von Kulp. The vacuity of the site where the poem takes place is, however, most forcefully raised in controversial lines at the beginning of the poem:

> My house is a decayed house,
> And the Jew squats on the window-sill, the owner,
> Spawned in some estaminet of Antwerp,
> Blistered in Brussels, patched and peeled in London.
>   (7–10)

Effectively, Gerontion's dilapidated home is a nightmare vision of tradition, presenting not an organic and vital site, but an empty maze. As such it is essentially related to the urban landscapes of early poems such as 'Prufrock', 'Preludes', and *The Waste Land*: the city streets are without goal, leading one 'like a tedious argument / Of insidious intent' ('The Love Song of J. Alfred Prufrock', 8–9) without any purpose or true issue. History is like a house, which again is like an urban sprawl: these figures are in close communication in Eliot, all communicating a dreaded lack of order, and all indeed providing something very different from the space of sacredness and overview we saw Yeats striving for in 'Under Ben Bulben'. Eliot's motive for writing 'Gerontion' would appear to be a desire to enact a decisive distancing that would hold the malevolent 'wilderness of mirrors' at an arm's length. Both the moneyed Jew and the lethargic sceptic are not representatives of the poet, but rather of all he wants to renounce.

The satiric energy of early poems such as 'Gerontion' and 'Burbank with a Baedeker: Bleistein with a Cigar' have led to criticism of Eliot's alleged anti-Semitism. Other poems from the same period – such as the compressed prose poem 'Hysteria' – have drawn the charge of misogyny. Such texts display a passionate exclusionary force at odds with Eliot's own ideals, as we have found them presented in 'Tradition and the Individual Talent'. Not only is the latter text's ideal of an inclusive and generous tradition contradicted, but such poems also arguably do not adhere to the critical essay's exacting theory of poetical composition. I do not want to be misunderstood as subscribing to what Jim McCue has called 'the widespread but absurd image' of Eliot 'as an anti-Semitic misogynist who should be read only as the supreme example of the unpalatable corruption of intellectual life in the first half of the last century'.[43] When Eliot writes 'The rats are underneath the piles. / The Jew is underneath the lot' ('Burbank', 22–23) the evident prejudice may be ascribed either to the implied author or merely to the speaker, but either way it is not enough to indict an entire career. What such passages do indicate, though, is a poetical practice not quite as Olympian as one might have expected after reading 'Tradition and the Individual Talent'.

Both the 'Jew ... underneath the lot' and the 'Jew [that] squats on the window-sill' ('Gerontion', 8) show a subterranean logic at work, which undermines the transparent lucidity of the ideal order. Not only in Eliot's imagery, but also in the very workings of his creative process a complex structure arises: rather than a complete transformation of personal emotion, we are given views that commentators have shown to be based on partisan, and indeed in some cases highly regrettable, beliefs. As Donald Davie has remarked: 'If Eliot enters his own poems only disguised as a persona, wearing a mask, at least he enters them. Reading a parody, we are inevitably aware (though as it were at one remove) of the parodist ... always tipping the wink.'[44] Drawing on Eliot's critique of *Hamlet*, one might say that these poems show a poet 'under compulsion' of his own emotions, producing an emotion which 'exceeded the facts'.[45] In light of Eliot's poetical prejudices, the intriguing, but arguably self-contradictory description of art as 'not the expression of personality, but an escape from personality' makes more sense.[46] Under the lot, or in the window-sill, of the poem, there are remnants of emotion – undercurrents bursting through the surface of his poems. Such undercurrent will, as we soon shall see, be given a peculiar prominence in *Four Quartets* and its dealings with memory.

Departing from the asceticism of individual memory prescribed by 'Tradition and the Individual Talent', *Four Quartets* is an intriguing and particularly compelling example of how personal memory can be linked to an encompassing collective memory in a single poem. By looking at the parerga and compositional genesis of the poem, I want to now address how Eliot created a complex textual structure in order to reconcile these contending exigencies. I will place some emphasis on this notion of structure, as it shows an interesting supplementation of the organicism of 'Tradition and the Individual Talent'. Critics such as Sean Lucy have pointed to the increasing allowance, through Eliot's career, for the role of individualism or personality in art.[47] But they have neither linked this to the roles of personal and collective memory, nor accounted for the resulting imbrication of surface and underground elements in *Four Quartets*.

Four Quartets is an articulated unity of four poems: *Burnt Norton* (1936), *East Coker* (1940), *The Dry Salvages* (1941), and *Little Gidding* (1943). Though they were first printed separately, structural effects – such as a shared, five-part structure, and a common thematic focus on the problem of finding redemption in time – bind them together in one composite work of art. The resulting sophistication of structure can make it difficult, at first, to find a way to the heart of the text. Early on in *Burnt Norton*, the reader will come across these inviting but enigmatic lines:

> Footfalls echo in the memory
> Down the passage which we did not take
> Towards the door we never opened
> Into the rose-garden. My words echo
> Thus, in your mind.
> But to what purpose
> Disturbing the dust on a bowl of rose-leaves
> I do not know.
> Other echoes
> Inhabit the garden. Shall we follow?
> (11–18)

The speaker does of course follow the echoes, which lead him on to 'our first world' and elusive childhood memories. But for the reader the injunction 'Shall we follow?' has other resonances, too, which are not so overtly developed. For Eliot's poem is – as is the entirety of *Four Quartets* – a veritable garden of delights of echoes and memories. The speaker's words 'echo / Thus, in your mind' to awake a plethora of recollections. Some of these may be personal to the reader, of course, reminiscent of the reader's own 'first world' – but many reach out not only to other passages in *Four Quartets*, or to other works by Eliot, but to a wide range of historical and literary precursors. Should the reader follow these? According to one of Eliot's most sensitive early readers, Helen Gardner, the answer is negative:

> If there are passages whose meaning seems elusive, where we feel we 'are missing the point', we should read on, preferably aloud; for the music and the meaning arise at 'a point of intersection', in the changes and movement of the whole. ... The sources are completely unimportant. No knowledge of the original context is required to give force to the new context.[48]

Despite such New Critical strictures, it is hard to escape a sense that *Four Quartets* is a text that, even while it invites an autonomous reading in terms of internal interrelations of meaning and music, also concomitantly frustrates such an approach. The reader is inevitably tempted to follow the text's allusive *largesse*, and to trace the words, events, and places that are evoked in its rich textures of sense and sound. As a result, any sense of *Four Quartets* being a circumscribed or closed entity is hard to countenance for long.

Instead of closing off the text in such a way, I want to engage with the complex structuring of temporality in the poem, and its relation to space. In an interpretation of *East Coker*, Edward Lobb has demonstrated how important structure – which he conceives of in terms of spatial forms or metaphors – is in *Four Quartets*. Looking at what he calls 'the closed-room motif' from the beginning of Eliot's career up to the latter work,[49] he demonstrates that closed rooms such as the 'thousand furnished rooms' of 'Preludes' are embodiments of Eliot's epistemological scepticism: like their bodies, the minds of these protagonists of these poems are decisively separated from an outside world. Lobb goes on to show how *East Coker* is structured around similar limited spaces in terms of temporality, ascetic discipline, and poetic form. Lobb convincingly argues for the spatiality of this poem, and goes on to show how *Four Quartets* inherits from Eliot's earlier work a desire to transcend limitations of closed space.

I would, however, argue that such a desire does not exclusively concern Eliot's poetry, as it also infuses his critical thought. As I showed earlier in this chapter, 'Tradition and the Individual Talent' is engaged with grasping time as an inclusive and unified space. In *Four Quartets*, though, Eliot develops his structural thought beyond the earlier articulations, developing a complexity of articulation that I believe transcends the simple opposition of closed or open spaces. Here I find some assistance in psychoanalytical notions of psychic structure, as these have been presented and elaborated by Jacques Derrida. In a preface to Nicholas Abraham and Maria Torok's *The Wolf Man's Magic Word*, Derrida discusses different ways of understanding the structuring of divided minds in terms of spatial analogies. He embraces a concept of the crypt which can be described as 'a kind of "false unconscious," an "artificial" unconscious lodged like prosthesis, a graft in the heat of an organ, within the *divided self*'.[50]

Now, it is my contention that *Four Quartets* is a complex, divided structure of a kind not entirely dissimilar to this. Yet I do not believe its depths are quite as unfathomable as those of Derrida's crypt.[51] The distinction can be approached via what will have to be a rather simplified account of the distinction between the terms 'introjection' and 'incorporation'. For Derrida, the crypt is the result of a psychological act of incorporation: incorporation seals an internal representation of a lost object within an ungraspable space within the self. It is a memory of loss, but one that is denied – and which therefore cannot be subjected to the cathartic process of mourning:

> the self recuperates its previous cathectic investments from the lost object, while waiting for a libidinal reorganization. Sealing the loss of the object, but also marking the refusal to mourn, such a maneuver is foreign to and actually opposed to the process of introjection. I pretend to keep the dead live, intact, *safe (save) inside me*, but it is only in order to refuse, in a necessarily equivocal way, to love the dead as a living part of me, dead *save in me*, through the process of introjection, as happens in so-called normal mourning.[52]

Introjection would not radically seal off the remembered representation, but rather provide it with an inner locality which is accessible but set apart: the representation would be localized inside the mind's space, and yet partially beyond it and on the verge to the outside. It would be – to link back to the imagery of Eliot's early poetry – like a window-sill or space underneath the lot of the house of the mind. Is the distinction between incorporation's crypt and the more accessible inner space of introjection a rigid one? Derrida addresses this question, and goes on to suggest that the self, when engaged in incorporation, '*mimes* introjection'.[53]

I would like to suggest that Eliot, in writing *Four Quartets*, actually *mimes incorporation*. The poem presents itself as a detached, impersonal object – as something approaching an autonomous whole. Yet it at the same time includes isolated fragments on the margins of this detached structure. The fragments in question are representations of memories, which can be located via the text – but which cannot fully be deciphered. The reason why these can be said to be introjected rather than incorporated is that Eliot was in fact fully conscious of placing them in the poem – or at least as fully conscious as anyone is in dealing with important personal memories. Furthermore, these representations are accessible in a manner the deeply unconscious contents of the crypt, as understood by Derrida, are not. Thus we can approach them by utilizing the kind of heuristic metaphors Derrida dismisses as unfitting for the crypt: the latter, he claims 'no longer rallies the easy metaphors of the Unconscious (hidden, secret, underground, latent, other, etc.)'.[54] Fastening on to the felicitous overlap of imagery in this passage and Eliot's poem, it is possible to say that *Four Quartets* is a structure that comes equipped with its own underground.

Most conspicuously, this underground can be localized in the names of the poem. Derrida has alerted us to the paradoxical position of titles, and how they are both within and without the borders of the text.[55] In *Four Quartets*, the separate titles of the quartets constitute a fold or junction, where their interior, public meaning abuts an inaccessible and private meaning submerged below the work's surface architecture. We are reminded of Eliot's humorous poem on 'The Naming of Cats', where every cat has three different names – one of which 'no human research can discover– / But THE CAT HIMSELF KNOWS, and never will confess' (23–24). The individual quartets have only one name each, but part of their significance is rooted in a congeries of memories that remains out of bounds for everyone but Old Possum himself. Thus early readers of *Burnt Norton* and *East Coker* were bemused by these poems' titles, not being familiar with the rather obscure place names. Reading an early draft of *The Dry Salvages*, Eliot's friend John Hayward mistook the title of that poem for a descriptive term – and in fact queried the wisdom of departing from the precedent of the two earlier titles. Eliot was forced to reply that:

'The Dry Salvages' *is* a place name (rhymes with 'rampages'). It is ('Les trois sauvages') the name of a group of three rocks off the eastern corner of Cape Ann, Massachusetts, with a beacon: convenient for laying a course to the eastward, Maine or Nova Scotia. It happens to have just the right denotation and association for my purpose; and therefore I am the more disturbed by your comment. It doesn't matter that it should be obscure, but if it is going to lead people quite on the wrong track, then something must be done. I don't like the idea of a note of explanation. Please advise.[56]

If the title might be obscure, but not 'lead people quite on the wrong track', this was because it could – indeed must, for important reasons – have a semi-autonomous detachment from the rest of the poem.

In the end, Eliot did opt for an explanatory note for this particular quartet, yet the obscurity remains – as does the 'association' that no doubt was an important motivation for Eliot's opting for this particular title. We know that Eliot had childhood memories linked to the Dry Salvages, from his many sailing trips on the coast of Massachusetts, but the precise details and their importance remain inaccessible. According to Hugh Kenner, the same goes for other titles of *Four Quartets*: 'each poem is named after some obscure place where the poet's personal history or that of his family makes contact with a more general Past.'[57] *Little Gidding* is partially exempt from this pattern, as this particular locality has an important historical pedigree – linked to Nicholas Ferrar's establishing a monastic community there in the seventeenth century – which almost completely overshadows Eliot's own visit there in May 1936. Perhaps this is the reason why Eliot felt troubled writing this particular poem. With such a public setting, the personal resonance was missing. As he wrote to Hayward: 'The defect of the whole poem, I feel, is the lack of some acute personal reminiscence (never to be explicated, of course, but to give power from well below the surface) and I can *perhaps* supply this in Part II.'[58] In the underground of *Four Quartets*, beyond any possible elucidation of its impersonal surface, personal memory was to function as a veritable motor of the poem's artistic force.

In the other quartets, it is less difficult to localize the subterranean depths. We certainly know that Burnt Norton and East Coker are places that Eliot visited in the 1930s, and that these were sites of considerable personal importance to him: East Coker due to its being the home of the Eliot family prior to Andrew Eliot's emigration to the United States around 1669, Burnt Norton for personal visits Eliot made there in the 1930s. The personal link in *East Coker* was further strengthened by Eliot's inclusion, in that poem, of quotations from his ancestor Sir Thomas Elyot's *The Boke of the Governour* (1531). Justifying his use of these quotations, Eliot once more distinguished between different levels of meaning: 'The public intention is to give an early Tudor setting, the private, that the author of The Governour sprang from E. Coker (apparently born in Wilts. but his father was the son of Simon E. of E. C.).'[59] As for Burnt

Norton, Lyndall Gordon has speculated at length about the circumstances of Eliot's visit there, and how this locality's obvious importance for him might be linked to a love affair with Emily Hale.[60]

The particular details of these memories need not concern us here. Suffice it to say that the poem opens up channels to a personal underground of recollections in their titles. The impact of these titles remains a difficult critical problem. As Helen Gardner points out, they do not function in any obvious denotative function: 'in *Four Quartets* the title of the whole poem tells us nothing of its subject, and the titles of the separate poems tell us very little. The poems are not "about places" though their subjects are bound up with particular places.'[61]

A title like *Burnt Norton* can be said to 'bind up' the poem with an actual locality, but it is neither obvious how such a binding takes place, nor self-evident what effects it might have. It is easy enough to identify some basic referential denotations – such as the 'drained pool' of *Burnt Norton*'s first section (33), which evidently had a counterpart in the place itself – but they are only of limited value. For the poem undermines simple referentiality through its own techniques. The vision of 'Midwinter Spring' at the beginning of *Little Gidding*; the evocation of the 'ragged rock in the restless waters' in *The Dry Salvages* (118); the allusion to 'the deep lane' that 'insists on the direction / Into the village' in *East Coker* (18–19): none of these is of the kind of specificity that might provide an informative description of place. These are sites that withdraw from full comprehension, like Michel De Certeau's conception of 'places' that are 'fragmentary and inward-turning histories, pasts that others are not allowed to read, accumulated times that can be unfolded but like stories held in reserve, remaining in an enigmatic state'.[62]

This reserve has complex ramifications for the poem's investment in nationalism. While Eliot's England might seem to lack the specificity and common appeal that might make it accessible to jingoism, the elusive nature of its placing nevertheless can be interpreted as amenable to an idealistic sense of national belonging. Even if the poem has been read as a defence of English values and traditions during wartime threat, one must not overlook the circumspection Eliot displays on this matter. Where Tennyson, in his concluding address 'To the Queen' in the *Idylls of the King*, went in search of a suitable 'tone of empire' (18), Eliot leaves us with nothing quite so worldly. When we are told, in the first section of *Little Gidding*, that 'Here, the intersection of the timeless moment / Is England and nowhere. Never and always' (52–53) the paradoxes should give us pause. Presumably, one of the meanings of these lines is that no place and no time can fully be said to represent the timeless: the divine is not to be identified with the transient or time-bound. Yet the temptation of a kind of ideological (and post-imperial) elevation of one particular nation to an absolute status is not obviously set aside in other passages. In the fifth section of *Little Gidding*, the idea that 'history is a pattern / Of timeless moments' (234–235) seems to elevate nationalism to a transcendental plane. It is difficult to dispel a suspicion that the Englishness of the origins of the Anglican Church is here tacitly being transmogrified into something which at least might be construed as a vision of one nation being God's chosen people: 'History is now and England' (237). The poem's reputation of providing a cherished insistence upon the values of England during a difficult time is not underserved.

Yet the deployment of place in *Four Quartets* has also been read as relating to Englishness in a particularly problematical way. Lyndall Gordon has shown conclusively not only that *The Dry Salvages* takes place in an American setting, and engages Eliot's own American background, but also that it is a poem that builds upon a panoply of literary sources from the United States.[63] Donald Davie made the very same point many years earlier – albeit in a less thorough manner. Yet for Davie the Americanness of *The Dry Salvages* indicates all that is wrong with this particular poem.[64] Eliot might here be compared to how the three poets scrutinized in the previous chapter related to liminal spaces on the very verge of the nation. In the case of both Tennyson and Yeats, national memory seems to be inexorably linked with marginal spaces tied to sacred origins. Nothing like this can be the rationale for how *Four Quartets* depicts the coastline of the American north-east: Eliot folds the borders of nationhood over onto an alien other, rather than just redirecting it to neglected or occluded origins.

Eliot's seemingly perverse resistance to fully rooting *Four Quartets* in an English sense of place has of course personal justification: the setting of *The Dry Salvages* is linked to the author's private memories. Would Eliot be using landscape, like Yeats in 'Under Ben Bulben', as a means to bolster authorial presence rather than disperse it into the anonymity of space? Answering such a question is not made any easier by the fact that Eliot himself seems to change his mind about the virtues of landscape. In *After Strange Gods* he ironically refers to what he calls Thomas Hardy's 'Wessex Staging' as 'the scenery dear to the Anglo-Saxon heart or the period peasants pleasing to the metropolitan imagination'.[65] The sentimentality of landscape seems to be under attack here. Furthermore, contradicting my own reading of how Hardy uses landscape in a complex and ambivalent way, Eliot writes: 'In consequence of his [i.e. Hardy's] self-absorption, he makes a great deal of landscape; landscape is a passive creature which lends itself to an author's mood.'[66] Combining sentimentality and egoism, landscape appears to be co-opted by nostalgia.

Whatever one might think of Eliot's interpretation of Hardy here, the absolute control of the subject watching over a landscape is also underlined in *The Use of Criticism and the Use of Poetry*. In order to exemplify his admittedly idealized portrait of a critic who can fully grasp and comprehend the entirety of literary tradition, Eliot there reaches out to natural landscape as a handy metaphor. Once 'every hundred years or so', a strong-minded critic will come and put the otherwise chaotic riches of the literary heritage into some sort of order. What the revaluating critic observes

> is partly the same scene, but in a different and more distant perspective; there are new and strange objects in the foreground, to be drawn accurately in proportion to the more familiar ones which now approach the horizon, where all but the most eminent become invisible to the naked eye. The exhaustive critic, armed with a powerful glass, will be able to sweep the distance and gain an acquaintance with minute objects in the landscape with which to compare minute objects close at hand; he will be able to gauge nicely the position and proportion of the objects surrounding us, in the whole of the vast panorama. This metaphorical fancy only represents the ideal; but Dryden, Johnson and Arnold have each performed the task as well as human frailty will allow.[67]

Here we encounter a striking overlap between the ideal of organic unity used in Eliot's criticism, on the one hand, and the seemingly so different workings of the crypt-like structure of *Four Quartets*, on the other. If landscape not only is a totalizing genre, providing an Olympian overview to its subject, but also is the way in which Eliot covertly preserves a personal presence in *Four Quartets*, what does this tell us about the latter work? Does this mean that not only parts of *Four Quartets*, but also the anticipatory landscape poems of the 1930s ('New Hampshire', 'Virginia', 'Usk', 'Rannoch, by Glencoe', and 'Cape Ann') have to be comprehended as essentially self-absorbed acts of Eliot's poetical imagination – contradicting not only the ideal of self-sacrifice he espoused in 'Tradition and the Individual Talent', but also the Christian ideal of self-renunciation evident in *Four Quartets*?

Perhaps one need not go quite so far. We might assume that there are different types of literary landscape. If important sites of Eliot's memory, such as Burnt Norton and the coast outside Cape Ann, are evoked in *Four Quartets*, it is with what is evidently only a limited amount of assurance and comprehension: the viewer of these landscapes does not evince the kind of *hubris* evident in the cited image of the ideal critic. A remembered landscape is something else than an aesthetically complete overview. Indeed, in *The Use of Criticism and the Use of Poetry* Eliot describes the workings of memory in a way that strikingly contradicts the subjective supremacy assumed by his ideal critic:

> Why, for all of us, out of all that we have heard, seen, felt, in a lifetime, do certain images recur, charged with emotion, rather than others? The song of one bird, the leap of one fish, at a particular place and time, the scent of one flower, an old woman on a German mountain path, six ruffians seen through an open window playing cards at night at a small French railway junction where there was a water-mill: such memories may have symbolic value, but of what we cannot tell, for they come to represent the depths of feeling into which we cannot peer. We might just as well ask why, when we try to recall visually some period in the past, we find in our memory just the few meagre arbitrarily chosen set of snapshots that we do find there, the faded poor souvenirs of passionate moments.[68]

While the 'six ruffians' appear in 'Journey of the Magi', the birds are of course familiar from references in *Burnt Norton* and many other poems. The conclusion of this passage indicates that memory is here understood via the metaphor of the photograph: like photographs, our personal memories have something mechanically dispossessing about them. Thus Barthes informs us that 'a photograph looks like anyone except the person it represents. For resemblance refers to the subject's identity, an absurd, purely legal, even penal affair.'[69] Eliot's stance signals a similarly uneasy sense of dissatisfaction. It is not only the meaning of the memories that perplexes Eliot, but also the way in which their ontological provenance – their status of being the property of the self – is deracinated. Such memories remain in the underground of the self, belonging as they do to 'the depths of feeling into which we cannot peer'.

If we are to believe this view, memory can be something suffered – a dispossessing passion – as much as a self-confirming action. Such an understanding is certainly one propounded in the *Four Quartets*, where Eliot consistently affirms that our being in time opens up to something beyond the self. In *The Dry Salvages*, the water imagery we pursued as one of the crucial figures of 'Tradition and the Individual

Talent' reappears as an image of the magnitude of time. Yet now it is compared to something untameable and totally beyond human subjectivity:

> a time
> Older than the time of chronometers, older
> Than time counted by anxious worried women
> Lying awake, calculating the future,
> Between midnight and dawn, when the past is all deception,
> The future futureless, before the morning watch
> When the time stops and time is never ending.
>
> (37–45)

The midnight anxiety of these 'worried women' is reminiscent of those of the speaker of 'Rhapsody on a Windy Night'. Where the latter figure was cast adrift through the discarding of the 'floors of memory' (5), the troubled women are here valiantly trying to resist the engulfment of a completely impersonal time stretching endlessly before and after. Forces of nature, such as the river at the opening of *The Dry Salvages*, are reminders 'Of what men choose to forget' (9). Does the distinction between the 'men' of this last quote and the 'worried women' of the previously cited passage indicate a statement about gender? Julia Kristeva has claimed that women are more receptive than men to a circular order of time,[70] and a similar position could be derived from Eliot's poem. Still, the anxious women of *The Dry Salvages* do resist the 'older' time, as its inhumanity – and perhaps also pagan origin – do not commend it to Eliot.

In *Four Quartets* Eliot cannot settle for this vision of time; such an impersonal *durée* cannot provide the final word. As in Hardy's 'Poems of 1912–13', the self must combat the impersonality of time. Already in *Ash-Wednesday*, Eliot had written of his Pauline desire to 'Redeem / The time' (IV, 18–19). In *The Dry Salvages*, the dynamism and impersonality of the current of time may be overwhelming, but such an understanding of temporality does not fully account for what might be contributed by the human grasp of time, however feeble or tenuous such a grasp might be. Eliot's speaker seeks to articulate a meaningful and coherent ordering of time:

> It seems, as one becomes older,
> That the past has another pattern, and ceases to be a mere sequence –
> Or even development: the latter a partial fallacy

Encouraged by superficial notions of evolution,
Which becomes, in the popular mind, a means of disowning the past.
(*The Dry Salvages*, 85–89)

In Memoriam provides a relevant precedent here, as Eliot's dryly discursive voice negotiates its way through a tradition of poetical meditations on time. Denying the comprehensive value of evolution as an explanatory scheme of understanding time, Eliot's allusive practice exemplifies his claim that 'the past experience revived in the meaning / Is not the experience of one life only / But of many generations' (*The Dry Salvages*, 97–99). If Tennyson resisted the domination of a temporality rooted in 'Nature, red in tooth and claw' (*In Memoriam*, lvi, 15), he was less inclined to oppose the conventional Victorian belief – dismissed by Eliot here as a 'partial fallacy' – in progress. Eliot's 1936 lecture on *In Memoriam* suggests, however, that Tennyson's 'feelings were more honest than his mind', and that 'he may have contemplated the future of England, as his years drew out, with increasing gloom.'[71] Writing in the shadow of World War II, Eliot himself, in *Four Quartets*, forcefully resists the secular optimism of that Victorian faith.

Eliot's lecture on Tennyson's poem points towards some general similarities between *Four Quartets* and the Victorian's great poem of mourning: both are 'a series of poems' that nevertheless must 'be comprehended as a whole'.[72] Like *In Memoriam*, Eliot's efforts have produced what can 'justly be called a religious poem',[73] even if it is religious in a different way. Eliot's poem also differs from Tennyson's in how it directly articulates an alternative to the Victorian notion of progress. Instead of a serial or successive temporality, *Four Quartets* meditates – from its very first lines – on the labyrinthine links between past, present, and future. These subtle meditations align Eliot closely with the phenomenological and hermeneutical traditions of philosophy, which have constantly sought to understand temporality on the basis of a everyday human consciousness – and the latter consciousness is indeed one in which the ecstasies of time present, past, and future interrelate.

Four Quartets seeks to gradually transcend the limitations of the quotidian, and one way in which it aspires to do so is by impregnating the everyday interaction of present, past, and future with a deeper meaning. As in Eliot's criticism, the notion of organic unity provides him with an invaluable instrument here. In Kant's third critique, it was shown how not only art but also nature could be understood in terms of organic structures presaging transcendence. As the harmonious interrelationship of the parts of the work of art make it a harmonious concord evocative of an ideal and free community (where all parts are not only means but also ends), so the teleology of nature can serve as an ideal model of time contradicting the mechanical and meaningless sequentiality of time in a world comprehended by the natural sciences.[74] Eliot makes use of both of these schemas, not only insisting upon the organicism of the literary work where the 'complete consort' of its language enacts a 'dancing together' (*Little Gidding*, 223), but also consistently returning to an understanding of time where 'In my end is my beginning' (*East Coker*, 209). Drawing upon different meanings and inflections of the word 'end', the poem stages a repeated transcending of terminating endings by purposeful ends. The organic notion of an inherent purpose only gradually unfolding itself, through a controlled temporal flowering that also is a consistent unearthing of an original impetus, legitimizes how the verbal repetition becomes a pervasive strategy in *Four Quartets*. Thus the reader is meant to identify with the speaker, when the latter ponders: 'We had the experience but missed the meaning, / And approach to the meaning restores the experience / In a different form' (*The Dry Salvages*, 93–95). This is recollection as revelation, as words and images amass new meaning through being repeated:

> We shall not cease from exploration
> And the end of all our exploring
> Will be to arrive where we started
> And know the place for the first time.
> (*Little Gidding*, 239–242)

In a poem full of paradoxes, this touches on what are perhaps two of the most fundamental ones. First, there is the conundrum, reminiscent of Tennyson again, that while Eliot seeks transcending natural being and the 'scheme of generation' (*Little Gidding*, 18), he still consistently deploys the paradigm of organicism. Second, though Eliot in *Four Quartets* is fully committed to the transcendence of time, this is also a poem that, to an almost unprecedented degree, is a poem of memory.

The latter paradox is certainly one insisted upon in the poem, most trenchantly when we are told in *Burnt Norton* that 'Only through time time is conquered' (89). Frequently Eliot will approach this problem in a Proustian way, by endowing particularly powerful memories with the ability to render the flux of time inoperable. A particularly striking generalization of memory's ability to free one from the fetters of transience is given in the third section of *Little Gidding*:

> This is the use of memory:
> For liberation – not less of love but expanding
> Of love beyond desire, and so liberation
> From the future as well as the past.
>
> (156–159)

This is an idiosyncratic twist on the idea that true memory (or tradition) is not only concerned with the past, but also empowers our future-oriented actions. Eliot's poem insists upon the same point, but with one important difference: rather than making us more engaged in our future, we are here told that memory detaches us from our own developing projects and affiliations. There is a parallel to Hazlitt's ethics of time, encountered in Chapter 2: as Hazlitt claims memory has the beneficial effect of loosening our emotional investments from the self, Eliot's lines show memory as further transcending any investment in particular beings.

Four Quartets is a poem that insists upon a collective dimension of memory, but not – as we have seen – to the point of engulfing or annihilating the personal dimension. Although Eliot's poem works in its own, subtle way, it is comparable to the texts scrutinized in the previous chapter, in how it insists upon collisions and interactions between the individual's past and more over-arching structures of memory. As a final example of this, I want to look at how the poem presents the London underground. In *Burnt Norton*, the subway is designated as a 'place of disaffection' (90) completely bereft of the revelatory potential of, say, the rose-garden or the church at Little Gidding. This is a place where pollution and technology combine to alienate the inhabitants of the city from any truthful comprehension of time. The 'bits of paper, whirled' (104) may refer to the litter of the city, though this could also allude to the distracting power of newspapers that divert the 'mind with shallow discussions of serious topics'.[75] We are given an unremittingly grim view of the deprivations of this urban *Inferno*:

> Neither plenitude nor vacancy. Only a flicker
> Over the strained time-ridden faces
> Distracted from distraction by distraction
> Filled with fancies and empty of meaning

> Tumid apathy with no concentration
> Men and bits of paper, whirled by the cold wind
> That blows before and after time,
> Wind in and out of unwholesome lungs
> Time before and time after.
>
> (99–107)

The meditative present is lost in this business that throws the restless city travellers from an arid past to an arid future. As in the first section of *The Waste Land*, death-in-life has undone so very many: both Dante and Eliot himself provide textual material that is being recalled here. Despite the artistry of these lines, though, it is tempting to agree with C. K. Stead, when he finds fault with Eliot's apparent lack of generosity towards the city-dwellers.[76] As the early Eliot satirically dismissed the denizens of the busy and smoky city streets, Stead believes the more mature author of *Four Quartets* is here distancing himself from the illusions of his fellows.

This is a seemingly plausible reading, but also – on consideration – somewhat unfair. For one thing, it overlooks that there is an 'underground logic' to Eliot's passage on the subway: as with the titles of the poems, and several unexplained references, there is a personal investment involved which complicates any idea of there being mere satire. Drawing on an unpublished personal material, other commentators have noted how the passage builds on Eliot's own daily routine, taking the tube from Gloucester Road Station to the Faber offices at Russell Square. The movement of section III, which first heads down to the underground and then 'Descend[s] lower' (114), echoes Eliot's own daily movement downwards (first by stairs, then by lift).[77] For Hugh Kenner, this throws a humorous sidelight on the apparent gloom of the episode: we can 'catch a glimpse of the author, sauntering through the crowd as Alfred Hitchcock does in each of his films'. This is to be interpreted as a 'private joke', giving off a 'whiff of the Possum's whimsy'.[78] It could also be construed as an indication of authorial identification with the distracted and anonymous urban crowd.

Stead's ethical strictures on this passage also seem to be based on a rather limited textual remit. For the quartets seldom approach any motif once without circling back to it at some later stage. The discussed passage in *Burnt Norton* is placed in a somewhat different light when one sets it beside these lines from the third section of the subsequent quartet:

> I said to my soul, be still, and let the dark come upon you
> Which shall be the darkness of God. As, in a theatre,

The lights are extinguished, for the scene to be changed
With a hollow rumble of wings, with a movement of darkness on
   darkness,
And we know that the hills and the trees, the distant panorama
And the bold imposing façade are all being rolled away –
Or as, when an underground train, in the tube, stops too long
   between stations
And the conversation rises and slowly fades into silence
And you see behind every face the mental emptiness deepen
Leaving only the growing terror of nothing to think about;
Or when, under ether, the mind is conscious but conscious of
   nothing –

                                   (*East Coker*, 112–122)

The first underground passage contrasted the deeper darkness of 'the world of perpetual solitude' (*Burnt Norton*, 115) with the neither fully dark nor fully light 'flicker / Over the strained time-ridden faces' (*Burnt Norton*, 99–100) of the travellers. Here in *East Coker*, however, the use of the underground is deployed as one of three everyday examples of a true, revelatory darkness. Though the emphasis is on the anxiety and meaninglessness of the city dwellers, this is nevertheless a limit experience of what Eliot elsewhere calls 'The point of intersection of the timeless / With time' (*The Dry Salvages*, 201–202). The first passage's disclaiming of any true darkness – 'Not here / Not here the darkness, in this twittering world' (*Burnt Norton*, 112–113) – is thus reassessed and opposed in *East Coker*.

As so many other times in *Four Quartets*, incidents and terms are given an added, and deeper, meaning through a doubling return: remembering is revaluation. Eliot's treatment of the underground motif is representative of the logic of the poem as a whole. It includes lines that gain added emotional power and significance from a hidden, subterranean context, only (partially) recoverable by the author. Writing of Virgil, Eliot pointed out that a poet's lines 'may be for him only a means of talking about himself without giving himself away; yet for his readers what he has written may come to be the expression of both their own secret feelings and of the exultation or despair of a generation'.[79] In *Four Quartets*, there is a covert expression of the personal self and its memories, but these coexist with a more general meaning (indeed expressing both the 'exultation' and 'despair' many felt during the war) in a way that is not accidental: both dimensions cooperate as essential parts of the poem's intentional structure. Under the influence of Yeats, but in a more covert and arguably less presumptuous manner, a place has been found for the kind of personal memory that was discounted in the conception of tradition offered in 'Tradition and the Individual Talent'. In the description of the underground in *Burnt Norton*, as in his use of titles, Eliot manages to give us both the surface world of a structure meaningful on its own, and a subterranean appendage that loads the rifts of the text with personal ore.

The description of the underground is representative of *Four Quartets* in that it gains added weight through its recollection of similar passages by Eliot and earlier writers from related traditions. Furthermore, as I also have shown, the description of the flickering half-light of the underground acquires depth, and perhaps even a new and more hopeful meaning, from Eliot's consequent return to the same motif in *East Coker*. But the layers of recollection and return do not stop there. While Donald Davie was engaged in separating out the Americanisms of the poem, he was also denying that the author of *Four Quartets* was contributing to any present, living tradition. Calling his essay 'T. S. Eliot: The end of an era', Davie declared a 'hope and ... confidence of something quite different in the offing'.[80] Impatient to usher in the dominance of the distinctively English contribution of the Movement, Davie was in a hurry to reduce Eliot's role to that of being a merely canonical author – a monument, in short. Fifty years later, though, it seems like this dismissal has only, at best, had a limited success. In the title poem of a recent collection, *District and Circle*, Seamus Heaney has returned to the London underground. Alluding to Eliot's poem, Heaney places us once more in a world of escalators and the thronging crowd. Similarly to Eliot, Heaney is worried by the dangers of 'succumbing to herd-quiet'.[81] Yet by the conclusion of the poem, hope is recovered as the speaker remembers both his own previous experiences of this place, and – implicitly – the precedent of not only Eliot's 'flicker' (*Burnt Norton*, 99), but also the latter's more generally allusive practice. Thus the traveller is jettisoned forward in the uncertain and mixed light of the underground:

> And so by night and day to be transported
> Through galleried earth with them, the only relict
> Of all that I belonged to, hurtled forward,
> Reflecting in a window mirror-backed
> By blasted weeping rock-walls.
>
> Flicker-lit.[82]

Seamus Heaney: from forgetting to perfect hindsight

It seems safe to say that Seamus Heaney is a man who has come through. Not only has he won the Nobel Prize for literature, but he is also a poet who has enjoyed a rare combination of critical acclaim and general popularity in his own lifetime. He has become a figure of memory while still very much alive and kicking. To a certain degree, his acceptance has been more of a constant presence than a gradual acquisition: as it has often been remarked, few poets have been so quickly and heartily embraced by the critical establishment as Heaney. Despite this – or maybe because of it – he has long struggled to attain a self-confident sense of mastery. In the final section of this chapter, I want to look into the formation of what this poet has called 'the fine surprising excess of poetic genius in full flight'.[83] As was the case with Eliot, it will become evident how Heaney's rebellion against memory is not only linked with modernism, but is also instructively followed by a return to the theme of the past. With particular emphasis on Heaney's prose and poetry from the mid-1980s to *Electric Light* (2001), the issue of authorial mastery or control of memory will be even more important than it was in the reading of Eliot. But, where our interpretation of the latter's *Four Quartets* focused on the role of concrete places, this reading of Heaney (on whose use of places much work has been done) will limit itself to showing how the underlying spatiality of organicism provides a rationale for the poet's dealings with temporality and memory.

Mastery and maturation have been constant themes of Heaney's verse: as Christopher Ricks's review of *Death of a Naturalist* (1966) pointed out, the 'central subject' of Heaney's first volume was the process of 'growing up'.[84] Its opening poem, 'Digging', famously balances the speaker's sense of his poetical vocation against a reverential *mimesis* of his forefathers' more earthy craftsmanship. A lifelong struggle between transgression and redressing is introduced by the poem's double bind, where the poet's metaphorical digging with his pen cannot fully repress the simple fact that 'I've no spade to follow men like them.'[85] Although Heaney from the very first makes claims for an achieved and fulfilled sense of adulthood, then, it is an accomplishment that is shadowed by indebtedness and a sense of ineptitude in relation to the claims of tradition and facticity. In another poem from *Death of a Naturalist*, though, the possibility of a different stance is broached. 'An Advancement of Learning' treats *paideia* not as an instance of precedent and respectful remembrance, but rather as one of forgetting. Walking alongside a river, the young protagonist of the poem is suddenly stopped short in his tracks by a rat. A moment of initiation occurs as the speaker musters up a new, resolute fearlessness:

> He trained on me. I stared him out
>
> Forgetting how I used to panic
> When his grey brothers scraped and fed
> Behind the hen-coop in our yard,
> On ceiling boards above my bed.
>
> This terror, cold, wet-furred, small-clawed,
> Retreated up a pipe for sewage.
> I stared a minute after him.
> Then I walked on and crossed the bridge.[86]

Crossing this bridge or frontier of maturity, the speaker does not flinch from his own feelings of aversion. As in traditional conceptions of the sublime, the experience of terror is only set aside once it is completely confronted and mastered. What the speaker has to forget is not the obstacle, not the actual rat, but rather his own condition prior to staring it down. For manhood to be achieved, weakness and immaturity must be swept aside by the erasing power of oblivion. Mastery is here presented as a forgetting of one's own limitations.

Compared to most of Heaney's early verse, 'An Advancement of Learning' is a rare expression of unqualified resolution and directedness towards the future. Not only does the early Heaney chew what he calls 'the cud of memory' with abandon,[87] shouldering the weight of both his personal past and the troubled, political past of Northern Ireland with obvious relish, but he is also very much a poet of New Critical ambiguity and balance. Yet the desire to leave behind weakness and uncertainty, and enter a state of full self-possession, never completely disappears. In the 1980s, the dream of a decisive and almost Nietzschean act of active forgetting, releasing the speaker into an unprecedented freedom and potency, becomes especially urgent. In Heaney's critical prose it surfaces as a call for a new modernism.

Heaney's relation to modernism is both complex and, it would seem, vexing. This is particularly evident around the time he publishes *Station Island* (1984) and *The Government of the Tongue* (1988). One moment he seems to be divesting himself of tradition, the next moment he affirms the continuity and necessity of the gifts of the past. His critical use of writers from beyond the Iron Curtain is of particular strategic importance at this juncture. When Heaney directs attention to the poetry of Eastern Europe in the 1980s, it is in order to find the seeds of fulfilment for what he calls 'the delayed promise ... of a native British modernism' – the tracks of 'a road not taken in the poetry in English in this century'.[88] Where some critics have claimed there to be two dominant traditions in twentieth century English poetry – a modernist one linked with Eliot, and a native, traditional one coming from Hardy – Heaney here makes no distinction. Even the most radical of the modernists were actually proponents of literary conservatism: 'Pound and Eliot and Joyce may have regarded themselves as demolitionists of sorts but from a later perspective they turned out to be conservationists, keeping open lines to the classical inheritance of European literature.'[89] As has been seen earlier in this chapter, a concern with memory and the past certainly is pervasive in Eliot's writings. In early Auden, however, Heaney believes – at this stage of his career – we find 'sketched out the possibilities'[90] of a less traditionalist alternative that the Irish poet now, with a little midwifery from the East, hopes to bring about.

In *A Season in Hell*, Rimbaud famously declared: 'One must be absolutely modern.'[91] Whether one calls this promised new departure of Heaney's a version of postmodernism or a revitalized modernism, there is in any case evidence here of a hunger for radical innovation that is rare for an acclaimed poet from the British Isles. It is as if Heaney is agreeing with Alvarez's scathing dismissal of both his own and much other British poetry as creating the 'comfortable prejudice that poetry, give or take a few quirks of style, has not changed essentially in the last hundred years'.[92] *Mea culpa*, Heaney seems to be saying, while he turns towards the east, spying for a new dawn. Yet this lookout does not live up to its promise: he ends up celebrating the religiosity of Osip Mandelstam's poetic faith and Czeslaw Milosz's 'impersonal, eschatological poetry',[93] as well as the tough-mindedness – bordering on a stiff upper lip – evident in the poetry of Zbigniew Herbert. A more radically innovative figure such as Paul Celan is not confronted.[94] It is tempting to claim that Alvarez got the dates about right: religious aestheticism and a quasi-Victorian, moral fortitude may have been important defining points a hundred years earlier, but this hardly strikes a challenging note towards the end of the twentieth century. We encounter a voice that is 'mired in attachment'[95] to well-known values and modes of locution rather than to any modernist embracing of newness. If modernism is a search for the strange – as in the *ostranenie* of Shklovsky,[96] or the *Entfremdung* of Brecht – then Heaney twists the trajectory of that strangeness back to the native past, just as Wordsworth's admonishment to 'show the ordinary in an unusual way' was at the behest of recollection. Nor is memory made strange through the depersonalizing filter of language: rather than seeking an impersonal, all-embracing memory in language (as Helen Vendler has claimed to be the case, and as happens in Rilke),[97] the Irish poet follows the Wordsworthian precedent. The latter affiliation is somewhat ironic, since Heaney's modernist flourish includes his mocking the 'cadences that drink at spots of time': in his critical prose of this time, he distances himself from poetry which, in this way, is cradled by what he calls the 'shelter' of a 'Romantic tradition' which no longer is apposite to the present.[98]

How does this simultaneous affirmation and foreclosure of the new display itself in Heaney's verse? Neil Corcoran has pointed out how *Seeing Things* 'is a volume that sees things with the pellucid clarity which turns them into something other than themselves'.[99] Published in 1991, *Seeing Things* might be taken as something of a new departure for Heaney, as he finally gives full attention to the plea voiced by the ghost of James Joyce in section XII of *Station Island* (1984): 'Let go, let fly, forget. / You've listened long enough. Now strike your note.'[100] Here at last the poet trusts himself, and gives free rein to his own imaginings. Indeed, the word 'free' crops up with unprecedented frequency in *Seeing Things*, as the giddy experience of passing beyond all limits of comprehension and calculation is repeatedly presented as something both sensual and unpremeditated. A childhood game of football, for instance, goes beyond its own boundaries once the sun goes down: 'Some limit had been passed, / There was fleetness, furtherance, untiredness / In time that was extra, unforeseen, and free.'[101] Not only is there what Heaney elsewhere calls 'an access of free power' here,[102] but we have also entered a temporal zone which is 'unforeseen', and therefore no longer under the dominion of the past. As Corcoran writes in connection with one of the 'Squarings' poems, there is celebration of 'an unlooked-for grace in the actuality of the moment'.[103]

This idea of breaking free from the past is given its most direct expression in the sonnet that ends the first part of *Seeing Things*, namely 'Fosterling'. Here Heaney signals what seems like a decisive break in his poetical career. Now he will leave behind all the heft and the backward-looking focus of a mainly empirical poetry. The precise delineation of passing facts and states of being is dismissed, and instead a more revelatory sense of inspiration is to be cultivated. Now, at the age of fifty, he is ready

> To credit marvels. Like the tree-clock of tin cans
> The tinkers made. So long for air to brighten,
> Time to be dazzled and the heart to lighten.[104]

The poet is ready to be swept up by dizzy raptures that will no longer adhere to the grounded nature of what is given by experience, or to the strict, sequential transience of a time that has not been 'dazzled'. No longer will he toil with the treasures of the deep bogs of self, language, and people; it is time to take flight. The arduous mourning of mother and father, so prominent in *Seeing Things* and the preceding volume *The Haw Lantern* (1987), seems at last to have released the poet into a full maturity, where he no longer is a 'fosterling' but rather a creative and moral force in his own right.

Nevertheless, there are important signs that this turning point – this moment one critic has called Heaney's 'escape from history'[105] – is neither as radical nor as straightforward as it has been made out to be. There is still a monkey – or is it a Daddy? – on his back.[106] It is as if Heaney catches sight of the potential nihilism of the 'empty transcendence' Hugo Friedrich has deemed characteristic of modernism – revelations of emptiness are rife in Heaney's poetry around *Station Island* – and decides to return to familiar strengths and responsibilities.[107] In effect, Heaney's self-liberating gestures in *Seeing Things* are more circumspect, and more anticipatory of what has been interpreted as a return to 'social, historical and political contingencies' in his subsequent volumes, than their critical reception has suggested.[108] Like Geoffrey Hartman's Wordsworth, the poet will not leave the nurturing origins of nature behind, just because he has discovered that his imagination is as autonomous as an unfathered vapour.[109]

The everyday will not be left behind. This is evident even in 'Fosterling', where the reference to the tinkers in the penultimate line can be read as implying that any future inspiration will have to be attuned to the heft and exigencies of gross matter. In the penultimate line, the words 'So long for air to brighten' can be read in two significantly differing ways. On the one hand, they might be taken as expressing a sense of surprise and dismay: 'It has lasted so long, far too long', or something along those lines. On the other hand, though, if 'long' is taken to be a verb, the meaning switches from the indicative to the optative: the poet is longing for inspiration, and his wings are the wings of desire rather than of fact.

The beginning of one of the so-called 'Squarings', which constitute the second part of *Seeing Things*, gives extreme expression to the reach and dominion of memory: 'Strange how things in the offing, once they're sensed, / Convert to things foreknown.'[110] That which appears, Heaney writes in the same poem, only does so 'in light of what has been gone through'.[111] One could hardly make a stronger case for the power of memory. Perception is here engulfed, and is presented as a subsidiary form of remembering, in a manner that is vaguely akin to Platonic *anamnesis*. In addition, these lines also make a simpler and more palatable claim on the behalf of memory: only in the light of the past, the hermeneutical poet tells us, does the present become present at all. Memories constitute a kind of inner home that you take with you wherever you may go. Thus the way forwards leads to a turning backwards, as Heaney indeed intimates in a later lecture, in 1992, when he expresses a hope for poetry to 'break through the glissando of post-modernism and get stuck in the mud of real imaginative haulage work'.[112] It is noticeable that Heaney here opts for a return to the concrete facticity – the rootedness in facts and the past – from which he earlier seemed to be taking off. There is a counter-flight, a recoiling from his flirtation with liberating release, taking place here.

Yet there is nevertheless a form of initiation, a growth of mastery, enacted in *Seeing Things*. It does not take quite the form propounded in 'Fosterling' – a poem that is perhaps more of a feint and a ritualized repetition of the modernist desire to constantly break one's style than a really decisive turning point.[113] Rather than providing a release from the earth and the past, Heaney's flight is the enactment of a new linguistic self-confidence. The past is not left behind – instead it is grasped and comprehended with invigorated relish. Indeed, it will not be long before Heaney is seeking an alignment between a 'literary deep past' and the 'historical present', which he admits 'sounds very Eliotesque, very un-post-modern'.[114] The rhetoric of *Seeing Things* contains the leftovers of Heaney's desire for a new modernism, but it actually signals a new assurance in dealing with the past.

From now on, Heaney finds a new lightness of being, a new level of spiritedness, which jettisons him to the airy status of something approaching an angel of history.[115] It is the culmination of a narrative of maturation that has deep roots in both his poetry and his prose. In the seventeenth of the 'Squarings' poems (in the second part of *Seeing Things*), the speaker experiences an 'unconstrained and spirited' feeling of lift-off, which provides him with access to the creative origins of the past – to what he calls 'the mud / Aristotle supposed all eels were sprung from'.[116] Aristotle is perhaps the greatest philosophical propounder of a kind of seamless development – the seed containing the final tree from the very beginning – which is to be taken as not only a natural but also a cultural, perhaps even cosmic, phenomenon. Heaney aspires to a mastery that is of this organic kind. 'If we call a writer a master,' he writes, 'it suggests an oeuvre with a kind of roundedness and finish,' and the ensuing masterwork stems from a unity in which a 'force evolves its form'.[117]

Thus organicism is no less at the heart of how Heaney's poetry approaches memory than it was for Eliot. The organic fusion of what Aristotle called *energeia* and *telos* lies at the root of how Heaney's poetry conceives of a number of different phenomena. It is also arguably the logic that facilitates the seemingly effortless mixing of those very same phenomena. The mastery of poetry not only overlaps with a form of ritual initiation characteristic of the sacred; it also crosses over into the mastery of craftsmanship (celebrated in Heaney's paeans to cairn-makers, thatchers, water-diviners, etc.), and the process of maturation which will be displayed by any informed recollection of a life. In all these spheres, Heaney operates on the basis of a teleology that believes that we can 'grow up to that which we stored up as we grew'.[118] Indeed, the ancient Greeks themselves were attuned to such parallels: their word *techne* had less to do with our word 'technology' and more to do with a form of practical know-how. Yet even such a word as 'know-how' is doubtless a bit too modern and, indeed, 'technological' to be fully attuned to the ancient mind. Heidegger's interpretation of *techne* iden-tifies it as a knowledge which brings 'forth beings ... *out of* concealed-ness and specifically *into* the unconcealedness of their appearance'.[119] Significantly, Heidegger ties this notion to a concept of truth – *aletheia* – which is also a form of remembering.

Heaney is of course neither a philosopher nor a scholar of the Greeks. Yet, in the important, early essay entitled 'Feeling into Words' (1974), he shows a far from fortuitous closeness to this way of looking at things when he makes a strong distinction between 'craft' and 'technique'. Interestingly, Heaney brings out the difference between the two by way of an example that draws metaphorically upon manual labour:

I think technique is different from craft. Craft is what you can learn from other verse. Craft is the skill of making. ... It can be deployed without reference to the feelings or the self. ... Learning the craft is learning to turn the windlass at the well of poetry. Usually you begin by dropping the bucket halfway down the shaft and winding up a taking of air. You are miming the real thing until one day the chain draws unexpectedly tight and you have dipped into waters that will continue to entice you back. You'll have broken the skin on the pool of yourself.[120]

Although this definition is actually only of craft and not of technique, it nevertheless exemplifies some general tendencies in Heaney's under-standing of poetry. The sense of release and freedom inherent in the description of the dropping bucket that brings up 'a taking of air' is one of many early passages that show that Heaney's flight in *Seeing Things* was well rehearsed. It is also interesting to note that the characteristic move of using the practical example of physical work to cast light on the practice of poetry, utilized here, does almost exactly the opposite of what Heidegger does in the famous discussion of Van Gogh's painting *Old Shoes with Laces* in *The Origin of the Work of Art*. Whereas Heidegger lets art find its source or origin in bringing to light the essential being of the workaday, for Heaney the windlass reveals the meaning of literature. Although these two figures are closely related in the way they uncover a common ground between these two spheres, there is arguably a subtle difference at work here. In Heaney's case, of course, the thinking of poetry in a practical horizon is cast in a strongly autobiographical light in such early poems as 'Digging' and 'Churning Day'. By rooting his vocation in the everyday struggle with the earth, and also by depicting that struggle as it unfolds in his childhood south Derry, Heaney is repaying his debt to his parents (particularly his father). Every act of poetry is a forgetting (a transgression) of his parental origins, a deviation that has to be twisted back into a form of remembering (through both the content and technical form of the poetic endeavour): the artist must, in short, follow the windlass.

In 'Feeling into Words', Heaney goes on to define how technique involves more than mere craft. Alluding to Eliot's definition of poetry as a 'raid on the articulate / With shabby equipment' (*East Coker*, 179–180), he claims that technique involves a 'raid [of] the inarticulate: a dynamic alertness that mediates between the origins of feeling in memory and experience and the formal ploys that express these in a work of art'.[121] We are presented with the kind of harmonizing of content (which is deeply rooted in remembered experience) and form which has been the hallmark, in varying ways, of the organic conception of art since romanticism. The desired fusion of lived experience and formal excellence is related to the way in which Heaney's critical writings tend to repeatedly come back to Yeats's dictum that 'The intellect of man is forced to choose / Perfection of the life or of the work,'[122] always quarrelling with and disputing this claim as if it haunted him like a malevolent spirit. Contrary to the Manichaeism inherent in Yeats's choice, Heaney would like to fuse the frontiers of writing with the republic of conscience – finding a golden mean between aestheticism and subjective responsibility. There is perhaps more than a little autobiographical resonance (a typical and self-admitted feature of Heaney's critical prose) in his description of 'Sylvia Plath's romantic ambition to bring expressive power and fully achieved selfhood into congruence'.[123] Certainly in Heaney's most recent poetry, and especially in *Electric Light*, the powerful deployment of memories from his own personal past can be seen as springing out of a similar ambition.

Electric Light (2001) also involves an attempt to bring past and present into congruence. The speaker's memories of childhood not only have to be unearthed – they have to be linked meaningfully to the present. In one account of this process, Heaney makes use of an analogy fairly close to the bucket image of 'Feeling into Words', comparing the process to fishing:

> Incidents from childhood and adolescence and the recent past swim up into memory: moments that were radiant or distressful at the time come back in the light of a more distanced and more informed consciousness.
>
> 'Informed consciousness'? Well, in the writing of any poem, there's usually being cast from the circumference of your whole understanding towards intuitions and images down there in the memory pool. If you're lucky, you feel life moving at the other end of the line; the remembered thing starts off a chain reaction of words and associations, and at that point what you need is the whole of your acquired knowledge and understanding, your cultural memory and literary awareness. You need them to come to your aid and throw a shape that will match and make sense of your excitement.[124]

Interestingly, the second paragraph seems to be reacting to a query (either imagined or actual) from an interlocutor: Why 'informed'? Heaney has introduced a typically Wordsworthian distinction between the maturity of the recollecting self and the more immediate participation of the recollected self. The two are divided by an advancement of learning, and the more 'distanced' experience of the former has to provide a holistic form or 'shape' to comprehend the data of the past. Through the strong stress on the aptitude and competence of the poet, Heaney is introducing a hierarchy between past and present, which could ultimately undermine all experiential continuity and lead to the severing of force from form. At the same time, though, the balancing stress on the passivity of the recollecting mind – the incidents 'swim up into memory' – gives a measure of validity to the claims of the past.

Heaney is somewhat worried by the potential arbitrariness of the resulting organic wholes, though. In the same account of his artistic practice in *Electric Light*, he goes on to stress how his recent poetry consciously strives towards providing some leeway in the structuring of his past experience, yet how this might lead to frustration on the reader's part:

> In many of the poems, however – 'Out of the Bag', 'The Loose Box', 'Known Word', 'The Real Names', the poem in memory of Ted Hughes, the title poem, and several others – it was not a single shape that was thrown, but several. Different sections of the poems represent the different casts made. The pleasure of doing it that way was in following each new impulse, finding and trusting approaches that allowed both oneself and the subject to stretch their wings. The risk was that the poem might then range too freely beyond the reader's ken – but it still seemed a risk worth taking.[125]

Both the poet and the subject will be allowed to take flight – they will 'stretch their wings' – yet there is some fear that, as in Icarus's case, too free a flight might prove disastrous. Both the reader and the remembering poet must make wholes: Heaney remains committed to an ideal of organic unity.

This is an organicism of juxtaposition rather than strict sequentiality. Although none of his groups of poems aspires to a rigorously mathematical or logical sense of sequentiality, Heaney's early sequences generally tend to evoke a sense of linear, univocal progression. They invite the reader to approach them in terms of an organic narrative: he calls his texts 'stepping stones' and publishes sequences titled 'Stations' and 'Station Island' where each separate poem is linked with a stage of initiation in an appropriation of a Catholic ritual of purification.[126] In his more recent output, though, a new and more complex aesthetic seems to be evolving. There is a looser configuration of the parts of single poems (as well as a profusion of fragments and shorts), which indicates a new departure. Heaney claims to have developed 'an opener, more indeterminate way of proceeding [where there are] Comings and goings around a central preoccupation'.[127] Strict sequentiality has been left behind, yet something 'central' still persists, an omphalos providing a sense of permeating wholeness and unity.

'Out of the Bag', from *Electric Light*, is a particularly rich and self-reflective illustration of this development. Divided into four sections, the poem takes off from the childhood experience of a Doctor Kerlin's repeated visits. Only through his assistance of the speaker's mother in childbirth does the doctor exist for the speaker: this is his sole mission, and it accrues an intangible mystique. The second and third sections of the poem swerve forward to a recent visit by the speaker to the remains of the ancient sanatorium of Epidaurus (linked with Asclepius), as well as his participation 'in an open-air procession / In Lourdes in '56'.[128] Thematically, the poem builds on a linking of associations around medicine, poetic inspiration, and childhood. A subtle intermingling of that which is 'technical and ritual' is conjured up,[129] which aligns crafts-manship, poetry, and the sacred in one and the same process. The poem does not overtly thematize what seems like a rather sinister male bias, inherent in how the bag of the masterful Doctor Kerlin – whose name is obviously meant to evoke Merlin – dispossesses the speaker's mother of all the responsibility and creativity of childbirth.[130] All the magic comes from the doctor, and the child's inability to fathom the mystery of generation. Many years later, this inability still has unforeseen ram-ifications: carrying the censer at Lourdes, the speaker has an important hallucination where the doctor's potency is given vivid expression:

> Doctor Kerlin at the steamed-up glass
> Of the scullery window, starting in to draw
> With his large pink index finger dot-faced men
>
> With button-holes in a straight line down their fronts
> And women with dot breasts, giving them all
> A set of droopy sausage-arms and legs
>
> That soon began to run. And then as he dipped and laved
> In the generous suds again, *miraculum*:
> The baby bits all came together swimming
>
> Into his soapy big hygienic hands
> And I myself came to, blinded with sweat,
> Blinking and shaky in the windless light.[131]

Earlier in the poem, the speaker has reminisced about the extremely fragmentary impressions he had of the bodies of his newborn broth-ers and sisters. Here the mastery of Dr. Kerlin brings it all miraculously together, refiguring the dismembered pieces into one organic whole. This is also an anticipatory image of the task of the reader, who must re-member all the pieces of 'Out of the Bag' – its diverse experiences and sections – into one textual body. Although there is no detailed specification of how the limbs of this body will become more closely linked than the arbitrary roll call of 'A toe, a foot and shin, an arm, a cock' evoked earlier in the poem,[132] it must nevertheless be assembled into one centred unity. Although memory is not presented as a coercive process, it does need its boundaries – it is, in Heaney's own agricultural image, something of a 'loose box'.[133]

Matthew Sweeney has called *Electric Light* 'a past-haunted book if there ever was one'.[134] The volume begins with a poem that recalls a number of important events that have happened 'At Toomebridge', and ends with a series of elegies to departed friends and fellow poets. In between, almost all of the poems make some or another reference to the unfathomably rich, electric light of memory, which allows a 'light that sparked' once to be sustained – to be kept – to the point where it 'has never stopped / Arriving ever since'.[135] As globalization and technology hurtle us through epoch-making changes at a steadily increasing speed, Heaney's chosen task is, it would seem, to redress the balance. Like the perch of the second poem of the collection, the onus is on him to resist transience in the very process of taking its measure: flowing with the current, even as he resists its pull, putting the fleeting destructiveness of time 'on hold / In the everything flows and steady go of the world'.[136] Where the temptation is to look one-sidedly to the future for the imminent realization of a new sense of community, a global village, Heaney implicitly admonishes us to look back. This point is made explicit in his prose, where he endorses Mandelstam's phrase 'nostalgia for world culture',[137] and its rather dubious projection of an ideal community onto the malleable past.

Heaney's embracing of the past is full of perils and temptations. The way he conceives of the past as his own possession is especially problematical. Despite his much repeated faith in Robert Frost's claim that poetic language can tap into preverbal depths and origins,[138] he seems to waver on the question of how poetic diction might refer to such depths in any way other than the purely acoustic. This affects Heaney's stagings of memory. For, while he often includes self-conscious allusions to how the riches of memory are organized and structured for the need of the present, the poetry is undecided whether these acts of organization are, after all, alien to the given of memory. How close is the form of memory to the force of the past? At one extreme of this problem, there is Heaney's frequent tendency – reminiscent of Yeats's 'All Souls' Night' – to treat the images and characters of his past almost like actors at the beck and call of his directing instructions. The passage in 'Two Lorries' where 'time fastforwards and a different lorry / Groans into shot' is a cinematic version of this.[139] On the other hand, though, there are passages like the following one from 'The Sharping Stone' (in *The Spirit Level*), where the free-flow of the remembered experience is marvellously mirrored by the flowing movement of time – a movement that will bring the datum to its long-awaited harbour in Heaney's recollective verse:

> The workers had gone home, saws fallen silent.
> And next thing down we lay, babes in the wood,
> Gazing up at the flood-face of the sky
> Until it seemed a flood was carrying us
> Out of the forest park, feet first, eyes front,
> Out of November, out of middle age,
> Together, out, across the Sea of Moyle.[140]

The Spirit Level is particularly full of such moments, where the medium of memory – time – seems to be fully at one with the passengers it ferries across the abysses of experience.

Part of the reason for this easy familiarity with the past lies, no doubt, in a sense of ethical responsibility. Heaney dons the mantle of poetical witness, attempting to become a medium for that which otherwise would disappear without a trace. The result is, though, that he does not square up to what Wordsworth – a far more sceptical figure here, by far – called that which was 'disowned by memory'.[141] Heaney may fit Thomas Docherty's definition of the postmodern, since he seeks 'to write in the interstices of history itself, to be historical and to be aware of the flow and movement of history, history as "becoming" even as he writes'.[142] Yet in this significant respect the romantic may indeed be less credulous than the putatively postmodern. For, far from being the 'finder and keeper of the self-as-subject' that Heaney has identified in him,[143] Wordsworth is first and foremost a seeker, and nothing else. As our reading of the Lake Poet at the beginning of this study demonstrated, his acts of remembrance are always embattled and tenuous forays into depths of experience, which provide no sure foundation. If the content of memory is an immediacy that is close to the sacred (and here Heaney seems to agree with the author of *The Prelude*), then the representations of the mediating poet still cannot ever hope to bring this numinous present fully to light.

In 'Feeling into Words', Heaney quotes a celebrated and, in this context, very significant passage in *The Prelude* where Wordsworth offers the following lament: 'I see by glimpses now; when age comes on, / May scarcely see at all.'[144] Heaney cannot see why this should be the case; he claims that the late Wordsworth 'lost the path that should have kept leading more confidently and deeply inward'.[145] Contrary to such a failure, the Heaney of *Electric Light* has problems neither in recalling the past nor in adjusting it to the kind of ordered 'measuredness' his imagination demands.[146] For instance, he remembers 'Nights of '57' with confident *élan*, in words that seem to be confidently upstaging and dismissing Wordsworth's scepticism: 'The older I get, the quicker and the closer / I hear those labouring breaths and feel the coolth.'[147]

To be sure, Heaney's latest poetry displays an impressively detailed and intense memory, where the normal depletions of time are offset by what seems like a surprisingly direct access to bygone experiences. If one of poetry's major responsibilities and virtues is to be a voice of memory, then Heaney's contribution in this regard is of great value and dignity. In addition, one should not overlook occasional tremors of doubt, which tend towards humanizing what otherwise might be construed as Heaney's superhuman acts of poetic recollection. The suggestive conclusion to 'Mint', for instance, can be read as implying that, even if the poet's gift of memory is awesome, this does not mean that it is always rightly applied. After declaring that his first memories will survive the longest in his mind, the last stanza goes on to show solicitude for, indeed almost bestowing a blessing upon, the smells of mint that are among the ignored and marginalized facets of life. In a powerful simile, which obviously also hearkens back to the Northern Irish Troubles, the speaker compares them to individuals to whom he has not been completely true:

> Let the smells of mint go heady and defenceless
> Like inmates liberated in that yard.
> Like the disregarded ones we turned against
> Because we'd failed them by our disregard.[148]

The 'disregard' evoked here shows that some parts of existence are not simply less dwelt upon than others – they are ignored altogether. A possible reading, even if it goes against the grain of practically all of Heaney's other poetry, is to interpret their freedom as *resulting* precisely from that act of omission. Yet, as we have pointed out earlier, the moment of freedom is usually related to the act of imagination for Heaney: he is far removed from any desire to pay his respects to any form of untouched nature or pristine recollective datum. In any case, the speaker here not only offers a blessing that goes beyond the admitted limits of his own recollection; he also implicitly seeks forgiveness for his own acts of neglect.

This liberating blessing of the 'defenceless' is evidence of a rare scruple with regard to Heaney's handling of memory. Yet ultimately it reduces memory to an ethical matter: he *could* surely have remembered these offerings of nature, yet he decided not to. The fault is one of the individual will, not an instance of a more fundamental limitation inherent in the temporality of human existence. The two final similes of the poem tend to strengthen the ethical bent of the poem, too, converting it to something more akin to a Christian instance of an intersubjective *mea culpa* than the kind of meditation on human responsibility to nature more characteristic of someone like John Clare. The ethical, humanistic bent on show here is characteristic of Heaney's acts of recollection, which try to be just either to friends or family or to an occluded potentiality or event constitutive of his own self. More often than not, memory seems to become a species of literary portraiture, and even – by extension – a form of autobiography.

Notwithstanding such exceptions, though, memory comes across as an almost infallible faculty in Heaney's poetry. He is constantly evincing what a recent poem, in *District and Circle*, calls 'pure hindsight'.[149] Whether it is in the name of the quickly disappearing traditions and crafts, long-gone friends and family members, or a more general responsibility for (and continuity with) the past, Heaney subjects the mists of memory to a strong, glaringly electric light. This is done with mastery – with clear signs of what Heaney (in a brief portrait of Auden) has called 'the definite growth rings of genius ... in his voice'.[150] Yet the organic, unbroken unity projected by the self-understanding of this genius is surely too insistent. Its shortcomings are too decisively dismissed by the kind of peremptory mastery that Heaney's early poem 'An Advancement of Learning' both celebrated and anticipated. One misses the sudden breaks, the humble interruptions, and the ineluctable lack of unity (whether loosely or strictly conceived) characteristic of all time-bound existence.

If Heaney is less than humble in how he presents the remembering self of his poems, there is nevertheless a sense of deference in his verse with regard to how he presents poetry as characterized by a sense of responsibility towards the past. In this regard, he is truly a follower of T. S. Eliot's example. Likewise, this chapter has revealed that both Heaney and Eliot rely on organic structurations of memory in order to achieve the temporal unities they desire. In my next chapter, three contemporary poets will be read in terms of how they seek ways to break, rather than comply, with the givens of tradition. In important respects, iconoclasm, rather than humility, will be shown to be the order of the day. In relation to this, the spatiality of organicism will make way for spatial structures that make for more broken figures of time, as the memory schemes of tradition and self will be set aside for other, less backward-looking temporalities.

5
Other Times: Contemporary Poetry's Breaks with the Past

What are the crucial issues concerning the use of memory in poetry today? What might be termed the mainstream of contemporary poetry, in England and Ireland, grants memory an important role both in terms of autobiographical exploration and in a questioning and supplementing of history (often in dialogue with more mythical approaches).[1] Yet this mainstream has come under considerable pressure in recent decades. If modernism, at its inception, challenged central tenets of the earlier nexus between poetry and recollection, the current state of affairs is no less combative. Old verities are consistently being questioned, as more and more voices are arguing that they represent strands that have been systematically marginalized throughout history. Some of these voices are not only making a claim for full access to, and inclusion in, the central alcoves of the canon and the institutions of power, but also insisting that the very nature of poetry is undergoing a radical transformation as a result of this ongoing process – one which Sean O'Brien has termed the 'deregulation' of contemporary poetry.[2]

The most public challenges to the mainstream have, among other issues, raised questions concerning identity politics: nationhood, class, ethnicity, and gender are all at the forefront. But there are also important tendencies that confront received notions concerning poetic form and our relation to the environment. This chapter will subject to close inspection the poetics and poetry of three contemporary poets, all of whom – in their individual ways – place the poetic tradition, and the concept of memory, under pressure. Even if the variety of contemporary poetry makes it impossible to even represent single tendencies in anything approaching full breadth, these three poets are at least partially representative of different challenges to poetic memory: Eavan Boland will be interpreted in the light of feminism, also standing as a representative for issues concerning identity politics in general. Further, J. H. Prynne will be read in terms of the temporality of the late modern avant-garde, and Alice Oswald as a representative of ecopoetry. In all three, the temporal ecstasies of past, present, and future interweave, to produce particular versions of temporality. These versions differ, and with some simplification one can identify each of them with an emphasis on a different vector of time: while Boland's resistance to patriarchal memory involves the discovering of another *past*, and Prynne's aversion to deterministic and teleologically determined time-schemes makes him search for an open *future*, Oswald's resistance to instrumental rationality leads her to embrace a spontaneous *present*. The given or conventional past is, for all of them, challenged by a time that is other – a temporal relation they believe can prove radically reinvigorating for poetry. On close inspection, though, it will be shown that, even if all three oppose simple confirmations or reifications of the past, each one of them develops an at least partially positive account of memory's role in poetry. Memory must be subjected to rethinking and realignment, but in various renewed forms it still has a crucial role to play.

Eavan Boland: the objection of woman

The Irish poet Eavan Boland's book *Object Lessons: The Life of the Woman and the Poet in Our Time* (1995) presents itself explicitly as a challenge to literary tradition. It demonstrates how a poet awoke to the fact that she was 'writing in a country where the word *woman* and the word *poet* were almost magnetically opposed'.[3] Boland's thesis is that this terminological conflict is symptomatic of a more encompassing malaise. Although some of her argument is specific to an Irish context, she argues that it nevertheless has a wider validity: it is 'rooted in one country and one poetic inheritance, and both of them mine. Yet if the names were changed, the issues might well be revealed as less parochial' (127).

Object Lessons is an unashamedly didactic book, weaving an autobiographical narrative into principled discussions of the stakes involved in, and the strategies needed for, the empowerment of the female poet. Unlike what was the case with earlier poets I've discussed, such as Eliot and Heaney, it transpires that she (as a young woman) felt a strong sense of alienation from the existing canon: 'the poetic tradition itself was a house which held out an uncertain welcome to me. And when I entered it ... it was as if one room remained shut, locked against the air and intrusion of newness' (109). At this juncture, she was presumably faced with the temptation of a radical forgetting – a feminist version of Nietzsche's injunction to leave the past behind. Yet as such the temptation remains largely without explicit formulation in *Object Lessons*, and is instead disguised and deflected. The reason for this is that Boland indeed wants to resist its siren call, and also to make quite sure the reader does so too. This becomes clear at the end of the book, where she spells out her opposition to a particular kind of feminism, which some 'would call separatist, but may more accurately be called antitraditional' (244). Against this tendency, she insists upon a more nuanced, critical negotiation with the existing tradition. This is in line with her understanding of high modernism as a positive phenomenon in its attempt 'to re-make the poem so that it could converse with the world it came from; and therefore with the past', but as a negative one insofar as it tried 'to pre-judge, re-make, re-train the poetry reader away from the old joys of memory and sentiment and song'.[4] For Boland, poetry's covenant with the past is unbreakable, if necessarily negotiable. As a result, she pits herself against some of the more outspoken or wholesale feminist attacks on literary tradition. Yet this does not mean that the urgency of the feminist present is in any means to be occluded by, or set aside for, reverence for the past of the canon: 'I believe that the past matters, yet I do not believe we will reach the future without living through the womanly angers which shadow the present' (254).

The result is a rich, broadly conceived act of mediation. The main forerunners for the arguments in *Object Lessons* are Virginia Woolf and Adrienne Rich. Boland also singles out Yeats and Patrick Kavanagh. The latter's turning against the objectification of, and stereotypes associated with, the peasant is said to provide an 'example of dissidence' (99) for Boland's own reworking of women's place with regard to poetry:

> To be politicized in a poetic tradition, without having powers of expression or intervention to change the interpretation, is an experience Irish woman poets share with Kavanagh. Like them, he was part of the iconic structure of the Irish poem long before he became its author. Like them, his authorship involved him in iconic reversals and important shifts of emphasis. (198)

The term 'iconic' points towards an important dimension of Boland's argument. Here it implies both the fact that Kavanagh and female poets have had to address 'iconic' structures in the sense of well-established conventions showing themselves in exemplary phenomena, and the way in which one of the most crucial of those phenomena was the image or icon itself. The act of remembering differently, of reconfiguring the existing tradition, has to go via readdressing the issue of representation.

Boland employs a series of concepts, which she uses with partially over-lapping meanings, in order to address this issue: not only icons, but also myths, legends, emblems, symbols, figures, images, and signs are at stake. Of these, the concept of the emblem takes upon particular importance for Boland, not only due to its Yeatsian echo,[5] but more importantly because of how it is obviously invested in the 'flags and songs and battle cries' (145) of political discourse. The goal of her argument is to arrive at the point where it becomes clear why 'the woman poet is now an emblematic figure in poetry' (xv). With this she means that the woman poet's project must be understood as being 'neither marginal nor specialist. It is a project which concerns all of poetry, all that leads into it in the past and everywhere it is going in the future' (235).

The emblem, then, goes to the very heart of the present, but also relates essentially to the past and future. Like the symbol, it articulates a movement in time, which may be rooted in the particular but that also points beyond itself to a more encompassing generality. Not all signs have this self-transcending dimension: in her reading of Francis Ledwidge's poem 'The Blackbirds', Boland deploys this conceptual distinction in order to contrast the poet's treatment of the Irish revolutionaries of 1916 with that of an old woman in the poem. Whereas the latter is merely a 'sign' due to excessive simplicity, the revolutionaries (figured by the blackbirds of the title) gain 'emblematic force' by virtue of how they 'have a life outside the poem' (143). As a result, they are 'effective images' (ibid.). This efficiency shows itself through a contrast between how mere signs quickly go 'out of our memory' and how emblems 'continue to be vital once the poem is over' (142). Self-transcendence, then, goes hand in hand with a performative power fundamentally linked to survival through memory.

This power is also the reason why one needs to address the emblem with care. It is seductive, like magic, which explains why Boland can refer to 'emblems and enchantments' in the same breath (136). In literary tradition, woman has been engaged in the structure of the emblem, but in a largely pernicious way. Boland's analysis is both astute and sustained on this particular point:

> The majority of Irish male poets depended on women as motifs in their poetry. They moved easily, deftly, as if by right among images of women in which I did not believe and of which I could not approve. The women in their poems were often passive, decorative, raised to emblematic status. This was especially true where the woman and the idea of the nation were mixed: where the nation became a woman and the woman took on a national posture. (134–135)

At this juncture, Boland draws a parallel between the emblematic and the mythical: 'Women in such poems were frequently referred to approvingly as mythic, emblematic' (135). The fact that she 'did not believe' in these images of women points to a slight deviation from the analysis of the Ledwidge poem: there 'emblematic' involved a referential richness, while in this instance the term signifies a 'simplified' phenomenon (135) – the mythical no doubt contributing to, or going along with, an attenuation of concreteness. At work here is the supplementary status of the emblem, which functions both as an elevating heightening of, and an abstracting sign for, experience.[6] The difficulty of controlling the emblem – of making sure that there is elevation rather than abstraction, and that one's own emblems clearly acquire a different validity than, for instance, 'the suspect emblems of harps and Celtic crosses' of Irish history (12) – provides an important challenge Boland does not significantly confront.

The nationalist use of images of women in Irish literature is present in proverbial characters such as Dark Rosaleen, Shan Van Vocht, and Cathleen ni Houlihan, as well as the *aisling* genre. For Boland, these figures are both valuable – insofar as they still have relevance for the post-colonial narrative of Irish history – and contentious: 'However distorted these images, they had their roots in a suffered truth. ... The wrath and grief of Irish history seemed to me, as it did to many, one of our true possessions. Women were part of that wrath, had endured that grief' (135). Boland identifies, however, three major problems with this state of affairs. First, emblematic representations of women are distorted due to their being bloodless abstractions, lacking the human vulnerability and everyday context that would make them believable. Second, the same images are typically eroticizing objectifications of women, rather than truthful representations. Third, an important reason for both of these distortions lies in the fact that these were images produced by male authors: the male gaze not only elides the lived context, but also converts the woman into a desired object.

Earlier readings in this study would seem to bear out Boland's analysis. The only female poet covered – Christina Rossetti – presented a self-abnegating gesture of a woman leaving the living behind. Male poets such as Hardy, Yeats, and Heaney were shown to either mourn or silence female figures, the latter only being present insofar as they were already lost or removed from the action. To readdress the ideological underpinnings of this state of affairs, Boland claims the female poet has to rework the tradition. She is adamant here: not only will she not jettison the existing tradition (seeking instead to subvert and reinterpret it), but she also understands her own role as that of a poet writing in a specifically Irish, nationalist tradition. She will take over the mantle of poets like Yeats and Mangan, but in doing so she will realign woman's role from being an 'image' to 'image maker' (140). Rather than continuing as mere objects or motifs, women must become poetic subjects with their own voices. Yet this is not enough: 'The emergence of women poets in Ireland guarantees nothing' (200). A woman poet may end up reproducing the structures and conventions of patriarchy, unless increased power is accompanied by substantial change. Thus, for instance, the young Boland's national and gendered identities were not enough to empower her or give her insight into her own position:

> I began to write poetry, in a serious way, in my late teens. I knew I was Irish. I knew I was a woman. But at the oilskin tablecloth where I laid out my books to work in the evening it sometimes seems to me, looking back, that I was, sexless, Victorian, a product of nineteenth-century ideas. (218)

Tradition can function as an alien and oppressive inheritance, which – if not subjected to severe scrutiny – can close down horizons rather than open them.

One important way in which Boland's emblematic woman poet can live up to her new role is by exhuming lost figures of the past. Although it has less obvious importance for her than the emblem, Boland actually uses the term 'figure' to cover a wider range of linguistic features in *Object Lessons*. The latter term might be said to synthesize the full range of operations projected for the woman poet. At the most basic level, it indicates raw material of poetry, the non-literal motifs on the basis of which patriarchy has distorted the reality of women's history: thus the traditional Irish poem includes 'tropes and figures' which are 'both persuasive and unsettling' (215). Boland uses the same term, too, to indicate the rhetorical efficacy of this kind of text: 'Yet I loved the poems of that past. Increasingly I had a sense of their force and effect, of the figure they made in the time they were able to rearrange and heal' (108).[7] More urgently, though, 'figure' also denotes the historical vitality of the concrete lives that she wants to unearth from the past:

> The past in which our grandmothers lived and where their lives burned through detail and daily incidence to become icons for our future is also a place where women and poetry remain far apart. What troubles me is not how difficult and deceptive my relation to this past – and to this figure within it – may be but that it might not have existed at all. (24)

The occluded figure, which here also is termed an icon, is not directly available for the poet. The latter's act of remembrance is not straightforward, for a number of reasons. One important reason is that of the constructed nature of our representations of the past: 'Memory is treacherous. It confers meanings which are not apparent at the time' (125).

Not only, then, is the scope of Boland's deployment of figural resources daunting, but it also deals with temporal relations that are fluctuating and unpredictable. Yet her engagement with memory does not stop here. Boland also stresses the necessity of making connections between different forms of memory. In *Object Lessons*, she insists on poetry's links with collective forms such as folk memory and oral history. Her grandmother, for instance, 'lived outside history' (68), but through the tales of her mother – which provide 'a small piece of an oral tradition' (67) – Boland can nevertheless bring her figure into view. Like collectors of folk tales, Boland's poet must occasionally seek out her informants in the most unlikely of places. Unlike Eliot's notion of tradition, this is one that perhaps primarily must seek outside the existing canon: this 'carries the risk of subjective codes and impressions. Yet in poetry in particular and women's writing in general, the private witness is often all there is to go on' (130–131).

In addition to bringing forward hidden figures from the margins of history, Boland's poet must also repossess the female body. Boland's autobiographical narrative is eloquent about how the literary tradition's deployment of it was alienating and distant: 'I began reading and writing poetry in a world where a woman's body was at a safe distance, was a motif and not a menace' (26). As a suburban mother, Boland's personal sense of her own body underwent an important change: a 'visionary landscape' unveiled itself, which was the result of 'the sight of my body' (219). Ultimately, Boland believes, the 'clear and different and intense' vision of this 'way of seeing' could be presented as an alternative to the male vision of tradition (ibid.). Where the latter eroticized the object, so that it became an index of the male poet's own verbal prowess, the female poet unearthed a less proprietary relation: 'whereas the erotic object inflected the power of expression and was fixed by the senses, these sensory objects revealed a world suffered by the senses but not owned by them' (220). If this might seem ingenuous (sidestepping, for instance, the way in which aesthetics long since has articulated similar relations), Boland nevertheless goes on to submit the claimed directness of this sensory experience to a complex act of negotiation:

> when she does enter upon this old territory where the erotic and sexual came together to inflect the tradition, the woman poet is in

that poignant place ... where the subject cannot forget her previous existence as object. There are aesthetic implications to this, but they are not separable from the ethical ones. And the chief ethical implication it seems to me is that when a woman poet deals with these issues of the sexual and the erotic, the poem she writes is likely to have a new dimension. It can be an act of rescue rather than a strategy of possession. ... The erotic object can be rescued and restored, from silence to expression, from the erotic to the sensory. When this happens, beautiful, disturbing tones are free to enter the poem. Poetry itself comes to the threshold of changes which need not exclude or diminish the past but are bound to reinterpret it. And the object she returns to rescue, with her newly made Orphic power and intelligence, would be herself: a fixed presence in the underworld of the traditional poem. (233)

Here Boland effectively undercuts her own notion of an unmediated access to sensory revelation, by saddling the woman poet with a more deliberate process of mediation with literary history. Although she glosses it here, Boland will later become more explicit about the potential conflict between aesthetics and ethics.

The notion that the female poet rescues the 'fixed presence' of 'herself' may for some strike a worryingly narcissistic note. Certainly, judged from the tenets of other feminist interventions – such as those of the French *ècriture feminine* – Boland may here be seen as investing the poet with too much rationality and linguistic control. In a reading that pits Boland against her contemporaries Medbh McGuckian and Eiléan Ní Chuilleanáin, Guinn Batten has recently argued along such lines. In the latter two poets, Batten claims,

we might find a surprising alternative to Boland's own insistence that the woman poet must cease to be an object in poems and become (in her words) a 'subject' who 'matters'. Contrary to Boland's extension of a secular and Enlightenment ideal of representative subjecthood to women, McGuckian and Ní Chuilleanáin have increasingly offered in their poems bodies that, as objects, become vehicles and even forms for the reincarnation of (in various senses) 'spirit'.[8]

According to Batten, Boland is here in line with 'Anglo-American feminist traditions', and the too subject-oriented nature of Boland's thought is evident in how she seeks 'to replace the male hero with the unsung Irish female'.[9] Batten also expresses concern about how Boland tends to elide the difference between the remembered (the marginalized women of the past) and she who remembers (the woman poet of today). For Batten, Boland is 'making herself a subject' at the 'expense' of 'Ireland's male heroes', and can therefore safely be contrasted, for instance, with Ní Chuilleanáin's view 'that the woman writer finds [her] voice *through* the objects of her poem who lead her from a hermit's estrangement into human connection'.[10]

In addition to *Object Lessons*, Batten's critique also bases itself on poems from Boland's 1998 poetry volume, *The Lost Land*. It claims to identify continuity between poetics and *praxis*: Boland practises what she preaches, but her ethics is, effectively, the wrong one. Rather than an ethics of alterity, Batten implies that both Boland's prose and verse instantiate an ethics of appropriation, serving the self. Clair Wills has previously made a not unrelated claim concerning the political slant underlying this ethics: 'Boland, in effect, is a suffragette. She seeks not to challenge the basis of the poet's authority, but to widen the political constituency, adding women to the electoral polls.'[11]

Such criticism is not entirely without grounds. Partially due to generic conventions inherent in its largely autobiographical mode, *Object Lessons* does at times come across as presenting an overly self-centred and self-serving version of the woman poet. Yet to elide the book's status into being solely a representative instance of second wave, Anglo-American feminism is perhaps to take its own deployment of emblematical figurality too seriously. I will return a little later to this particular text, but here – in line with Batten's critique – I want to broaden the scope a little, embracing some other texts by Boland. These will clearly indicate a more complex understanding of how the woman poet relates to the past, and also provide a more nuanced situating of Boland in relation to feminism.

Boland's relation to feminism is not straightforward. *Object Lessons* is arguably overly coy here, only directly addressing the issue in its final two essays, and effectively presenting Boland's self-awakening as a woman poet as only tangentially related to related processes that were going on simultaneously (and earlier) all over the world. In other contexts, she has been more forthcoming, affirming in a *Caffeine Destiny* interview (from 2001) that 'I've always been feminist, since I was a very young woman in Ireland, and at a time when women were very hampered by inequities there.'[12] In the same interview, however, a typical dislocation takes place. We saw, earlier on, that *Object Lessons* prescribed a fusion of the ethical and aesthetic, indicating that the directness of the woman poet's recourse to the immediacy of sensory perception was

mediated by a negotiation with the repressions of the past. In the interview, however, these two realms are held apart:

> feminism is a compelling ethic. But it's not an aesthetic. I've
> always been certain of its central value. But the truth is that poetry
> begins – as all art does – where certainties end. That's the departure
> point. It's rooted where the imagination is rooted: in ambiguities
> and darknesses and memory and obsessions that aren't available
> to ethics, but are capable of truth. So, even though the distinction
> seems too fine, it has meaning for me. Feminism has helped me
> see society differently, and define myself as a writer differently.
> But it stops at the margins of the poem, at the edge of the act of
> writing it.[13]

Here Boland questions some of the continuities she established earlier
in her career. Most importantly, she seems to be suggesting that her
poetry cannot be read simply as an exemplification of a prose narrative
or particular kind of feminism – as it arguably has been – and that its
inherent nuances are germane to this distinction.

If we turn to Boland's sequence of poems titled 'Outside History',
some of these nuances come to light.[14] This sequence appeared in the
volume of the same name in 1990, and was conceived of at the same
time – reflecting many of the same concerns – as *Object Lessons*. The
eighth of its twelve poems, 'An Old Steel Engraving', goes right to the
heart of the problem raised by Batten. As do many of Boland's poems
dealing with memory, this one confronts the past through an interpretation of an object handed over from the past. The old steel engraving
features a patriot who possibly has been wounded, with a river passing by in the background. As so many poets dealing with ekphrasis
before her, Boland presents this as a moment that is forever fixed. Yet
she insists on going beyond such stasis, identifying the reader – and
herself – with a passer-by who witnesses the soldier's predicament. The
imminent action of the passer-by is linked with the interpretive gesture
that will make sense of the otherwise mute image. Yet it is possible to
refuse the latter gesture:

> history
> is one of us who turns away
> while the other is
> turning the page.
>
> (20–23)

In this enigmatic formulation, Boland clearly identifies history as being a matter for interpretive responsibility. It remains unclear whether the poem insists – as an allegory of Irish history's many failed uprisings – that the patriot will not be helped, whatever stance is taken by the spectator. Nevertheless, she insists that there are two different responses, one of which is more solicitous of the soldier's predicament. The final stanza goes on to identify the other stance – which ignores or overlooks the historical weight of the engraving – with the anonymous, forward-driven impetus of the river.

Outside history, in the background of the picture as it were, there is myth. The concluding title poem of the sequence clearly declares how Boland herself – or at least her poetical persona – responds to this quandary: 'I have chosen // out of myth into history I move' (12–13). If we link this choice back to Guinn Batten's contrasting of Boland to McGuckian and Ní Chuilleanáin, some of the sting is taken out of that critique. 'An Old Steel Engraving' does allow a body to manifest itself through an object. As in so many of Boland's poems, the speaker is questioned by the object in question. It is true that she does not fully submerge herself in it, yet the reason for this also becomes clear: to completely surrender all that situates the speaker as a human being would be either to revert to the timelessness of myth or to abrogate the ethical responsibility involved here. It is because she is a humanist – not because she is a second-wave feminist of a particular generation – that Boland insists upon this. And it is, one might hazard, because she is compelled by the issue of memory and the way the past interrogates us that she insists upon the difference between agent and textual weave, between she who remembers and the past that is remembered.

As such, these observations do not acquit Boland of the accusation of a form of intellectual narcissism. Her defence of an ethical responsibility towards the powerless of the past does not in itself entail a questioning, or challenging, of the potency of the subject. As a consequence, a poem such as 'An Old Steel Engraving' does not submit its ethics to the uncertainties of aesthetics. In the second poem of the 'Outside History' sequence, 'A False Spring', one can, however, see both of these challenges entering into Boland's deployment of memory. This autobiographical text presents the poet as a young woman engaged in studying a passage from the sixth book of Virgil's *Aeneid*. She does not manage to fully engage with the text, though, and a group of flowers functions as an emblem of her failure: 'But narcissi, / opening too early, / are all I find' (21–23). Here the narcissi fill the poem with ambivalence. On the one hand, they can – if we read Boland's young self as identifying with the Echo that Narcissus jilts in the myth – signal towards a pristine callowness in the young woman, deriving from her victimization at the hands of men or patriarchy in general. On the other hand, though, these flowers may indict the poet's own attempt to forge an emblematic relation to her past self. In the complex, later poem 'The Art of Grief', Boland describes art's images as being inherently narcissistic:

> An object of the images we make is
> what we are and how we lean out and
> over the perfect surface where
> our features in water greet and save us.
>
> (45–48)

The flower's appearance in 'A False Spring' may thus be read as a tacit criticism of trying to use the past as a consoling self-image. Little wonder, then, that the final stanza concludes with ominous weather presaging an uncertain future. There may be connections between the self's past and present, but these connections do not provide a 'perfect surface' out of which a closed or predestined future can be constructed.

The sequence 'Outside History' is replete with such moments, where the remembering poet may feel responsibility for the wounded or helpless past, but still cannot come close to anything approaching transparent unity with it. In *Object Lessons*, Boland questions how poetry long has evinced 'the appropriation of the powerless by the powerful' (212), and in her verse we see how this questioning also involves revealing the fragility of art's power.[15] The past is not our possession: unlike those of Seamus Heaney, Boland's acts of recollection are, as a result, consistently presented as being tenuous or unsuccessful. In the words of the title of the tenth poem in 'Outside History': 'We Are Always Too Late'.

As a whole, the sequence amounts to a rich interrogation of history through not only instances of personal, autobiographical memory, but also myth, collective memory, and literary history. Together, its poems constitute a broken or punctuated arch, the distance or silences between each poem not easily resolved into chronology or any other order, making for an effect that might be compared to what 'The Art of Grief' presents as the structure of weeping:

> It is unrhythmical, unpredictable and
> the intake of breath one sob needs to

become another sob, so one tear can succeed
another, is unmusical: whoever the muse is
or was of weeping, she has put the sound of it
beyond the reach of the metric-makers, music-makers.
(17–22)

With this broken music, we are far removed from the ideal of harmonious organicism pursued by many of Boland's predecessors.

While the spaces between the poems unsettle the linear narratives
of life and history, the spaces of the poems themselves are equally
marked with loss. 'What We Lost', the penultimate poem of 'Outside
History', is more explicitly feminist than the poems we have looked at
so far. It argues that collective memory not only is embodied in stories passed down from mother to daughter, but also suffuses everyday
objects and locations. Implicitly, this female dimension seems to function as an alternative or hidden history, on the margins of patriarchy,
which cannot fully be recovered by Boland's backward-looking glance.
It is another time that will remain other. Breaking up the rigidly end-
stopped lines dominating the early stages of the poem, at the end
Boland moves towards a crescendo of lamentation. 'Who will know
that once,' she asks,

words were possibilities and disappointments,
were scented closets filled with love-letters
and memories and lavender hemmed into muslin,
stored in sachets, aired in bed-linen;

and travelled silks and tones of cotton
tautened into bodices, subtly shaped by breathing;
were the rooms of childhood with their griefless peace,
their hands and whispers, their candles weeping brightly?
(32–40)

Even though the question here is arguably not of a straightforwardly
rhetorical nature, the 'griefless peace' of the penultimate line might be
taken as indicating that Boland is slipping into a credulous form of nostalgia. Like much Irish literature dealing with nationalist ideas, 'Outside
History' does not hesitate to link the lost land of its desire with a current
location. Both 'White Hawthorn in the West of Ireland' and 'The Achill
Woman' negotiate with Irish nationalism's tradition of identifying the
nation's true origin in the far west.

All in all, though, Boland invests less in the importance of the mythical west for collective memory than did the poets we confronted in Chapter 3. This does not, however, mean that she opts for a virtual or free-ranging form of recollection. Most frequently, she clearly situates her poetry in autobiographically loaded sites in Dublin and its Dundrum suburb. As such, the topography of her poetry can be seen as confronting the spatiality of modernity head-on, where any remaining wildness of nature as sacred or original space is undermined by tourism and industry, and cities lose their role as places of habitation in order to become permeable sites of work, transit, and shopping. Although she shows some interest in the symbolic value of Dundrum's historical locality at the borderline of the Pale, Boland shows precious little nostalgia when addressing its current status as a residential area for Dublin's work force. It is a place of impurity, a 'space of truce', uneasily straddling town and country ('Suburban Woman', 2). It is distinguished from the city centre on two important and related accounts. First, it is unlike the monumental hub of a metropolis like Dublin in that it is devoid of the 'iron orators and granite patriots' ('Unheroic', 7) that signal permanence and power. It is 'fragile and transitory', and 'composed of lives in a state of process' (*Object Lessons*, 160). Although Boland's long poem 'Anna Liffey' (included in the 1994 volume, *In a Time of Violence*) displays some change in emphasis on this account, the city centre is largely seen as a patriarchal preserve in her writings: either as the playground of a male, political elite, or through its links with the masculine literati. This provides the rationale for the second major distinction between city and suburbia, whereby the latter is primarily defined by the figure of the housewife.

Boland's suburban realm belongs to the housewife – it is the latter's domestic role and mapping of space, and not that belonging to the commuter or the bird's-eye view of the town planner, which is explored in this poetry. As Oona Frawley has pointed out: 'The suburbs become the marginalized realm of the marginal within independent Ireland, housewives and mothers beyond the boundaries of the city, out of the reach of the countryside that governed so much of Irish ideology.'[16] Temporality is paradoxically both static and fleeting, as the impermanence of the suburban realm is intersected by the uniformity of the housewife's chores and weekly schedules. Neither of these two features would seem to provide much assistance for a poet seeking to find a dwelling place for memory: while change and reconfiguration of the streets and landscape tear down any would-be landmarks, the similarity of the passing days threatens to submerge everything in what Boland, in 'Monotony', calls 'brute routines' (42).

It would be easy, given such pressures, to take recourse in an idealized
past, either by dismissing suburbia for the pastoral pleasures of yore or
by projecting an idyllic vision of the Irish village onto it. Boland's poem
'Distances' clearly resists such temptations, as its speaker entertains but
ultimately rejects the lure opened up by the song of her significant other:
'Don't leave, I say. Don't go without telling me / the name of that song.
You call it back to me from the stairs– / "I Wish I Was in Carrickfergus"'
(4–6). Ian Davidson has accurately identified one level of this poem,
when he states that it has a 'message' that is 'straightforward; that it is
better to be at a distance to the unchanging of tradition than part of
it'.[17] Yet the desire to use Boland's poem as a simplistic mainstream foil
for a more avant-garde practice (exemplified, in Davidson's analysis, by
Catherine Walsh's 'from Pitch') leads him to unwarranted elisions and
simplifications. First, he does not dwell on the fact that Carrickfergus,
in this poem, becomes a closed space that is contrasted with the articulated span of a specific spatial phenomenon: namely, modern suburbia.
Not only is the latter a point of intersection between city and country,
but it also has a typical tension, in Boland's poem, between the more
reclusive upstairs working space of the poet and the downstairs level that
typically gives access, through the banging 'front door', to the outside
world of work, traffic, and children's play. In the poem, the spatial distance between upstairs and downstairs also becomes representative for
a difficult, but necessary, divide between husband and wife – an intersubjective border that is far too easily glossed, the speaker intimates, by
nostalgic yearnings. Davidson also claims that while Boland is limited to
'exploring, although not without doubts, the nature of an Irish identity
located in a specific place', the more questioning stance of Walsh involves
'interrogating the notion of identity and authority as expressed through
poetic language'.[18] This, too, unduly simplifies Boland's poem, since the
nostalgic song about Carrickfergus also plays the role of representing an
autonomous, and aestheticizing, approach to poetry that she claims –
most explicitly in *Object Lessons* – not only to be traditional, but also
one she herself has left behind. Thus the third of the poem's distances
(the plurality of which is indicated by the title) is between the mature
Boland's relatively unpolished, but experientially open idiom, on the one
hand, and the 'perfect / music' (16–17) that is created by 'the scentless
afternoon of a ballad measure' (19) on the other. Boland's poem is indeed
saying something about the identity and authority of what she sees as the
legacy of traditional poetical language: its music may be seductive, but it
does not open up for the intersubjective dialogism that has filtered into
her own poetry through the concrete experience of suburbia.

Such a dismissal of nostalgia and autonomy may appear to be brave, but it also leaves Boland's poetry vulnerable. Her often strident but seldom unheroic struggle against the ephemerality of suburbia frequently takes recourse in the political poem, in which she traces parallels and metonymies between everyday life and more publicized events (frequently those of the Northern Irish Troubles). Myth is also an important aid, as Boland makes typically feminist revisions of traditional Greco-Roman narratives, but with an added suburban inflection of her own. One might be tempted to think that the humdrum, everyday reality of Dundrum would be at complete loggerheads with the heroism of myth, but – in the words of Patricia L. Hagen and Thomas W. Zelman – in this poetry *'ordinary* is no longer pejorative, no longer synonymous with *simple* and *unimportant.'*[19] As Boland indicates in the *Object Lessons* essay titled 'The Woman, The Place, The Poet', myth may be born out of quotidian actions repeatedly carried out in a specific place:

> Is it true, as Patrick Kavanagh says in his beautiful poem, 'Epic', that 'gods make their own importance'? Is the origin, in other words, so restless in the outcome that the parish, the homestead, the place are powerful sources as well as practical locations? On those summer evenings, if my thoughts had not been full of details and children, I could have wondered where myth begins. ... Is there something about the repeated action – about lifting a child, clearing a dish, watching the seasons return to a tree and depart from a vista – which reveals a deeper meaning to existence and heals some of the worst abrasions of time? (168–169)

In the 'Outside History' sequence, 'The Making of an Irish Goddess' depicts a mother living at Boland's Dundrum residence 'at the foothills of the Dublin mountains / across which the lights have changed all day' (35–36). This woman's concern for her daughter, out in the neighbourhood, is presented as a modern-day parallel to Ceres' descent into the underworld to recover her daughter, Proserpine. It's a myth to which Boland has returned time and time again (most memorably, perhaps, in 'The Pomegranate') and it underlines the centrality of family relations – more specifically, mother–daughter relations – to her work.[20] In 'The Making of an Irish Goddess', the most arresting feature is the attempt at a gnomic summation of the modern-day role of myth: 'myth is the wound we leave / in the time we have' (31–32). For Boland, myth has to descend out of timelessness if it is going to have any relevance: to tell the truth about time, it has to be adjusted to 'a landscape in which you know you are mortal' ('Outside History', 10). Given these adjustments, myth still has relevance through its facilitating some kind of lasting duration. Effectively, one can read myth as providing a reversal of fate for the figures to whom the many hidden and lost histories explored elsewhere by Boland belong: whereas the concrete facticity of their lives is lost forever, their grievances nevertheless survive in a general and virtualized form, through myth. Such a reading implies, however, that the problem I noted earlier – concerning Boland's distinction, in *Object Lessons*, between pernicious and empowering emblems – is exacerbated, insofar as a major distinguishing feature of even beneficent emblems is their abstract quality. The emblem gives only by taking away.

Increasingly, Boland's recent volumes have seemed to signal a sense of futility and defeat with regard to her project of making suburbia memorable. Her investment in this kind of location has waned, as is particularly evident in the resolutely urban 'Anna Liffey'. In the recent volume *Domestic Violence* (2007),[21] the speaker's daughters have left the nest, with the result that her surroundings are now almost completely bereft of emotional resonance. In 'Inheritance' she resists leaving them the view from home 'between here and Three Rock Mountain, / the blueness in the hours before rain, the long haze afterwards. / The ground I stood on was never really mine. It might not ever be theirs' (3–5). Similarly, 'Falling Asleep to the Sound of Rain' declares: 'I know there never was / a single place for me. I never lost enough to have one' (32–33).

Dislocated, the poetical persona of Boland can, then, be seen as having tried and failed to strike roots in the postmodern quicksand of contemporary suburbia. As such, the problems hampering the use of the suburb are not unrelated to more general issues concerning the poet's imaginative deployment of emblems. Both the emblem and the suburbs (the latter itself being an emblem of sorts) provide freedom from prior determinations, but both are also so virtual and devoid of stable significance that they are hard to control over time. We are not too far away from *Idylls of the King*, and Balin's failed attempt to use the memory image on his shield as a means to forge a new identity. As in the latter case, Boland's investments of identity in place and language do not yield sure-fire returns: neither suburbia nor the figurative processes of poetry may provide the safest of foundations for identity politics. It is, significantly, thanks to the nuanced and perspicacious nature of Boland's poetry that one is able to see this. Yet something remains: not only the poems themselves, but also the example of the poet. As mentioned earlier, the strong degree of personal embodiment and recourse to autobiography in Boland's verse can be suspected of having its roots in a too simply politicized, or overly narcissistic, starting point. At the same time, there is little doubt that one of the major motivations for this strategy is the desire to provide a precedent for other female poets. If Boland does not survive in suburbia, or through her mythical or political poems, then her verse nevertheless promises to still have importance, within literary tradition, as that of an enabling forerunner. A short little poem titled 'Is It Still the Same' may seem portentous in envisaging that, in the future, when 'a young woman ... climbs the stairs' to write poetry after having closed 'a child's door' (1–2), she will find inspiration in that 'when she looks up, I will be there' (14). Yet it may prove to be accurate. For Boland's greatest gift of memory may not be her exhumations of the downtrodden and neglected, but the persuasive figure of the woman poet she presents to the female writers who follow in her footsteps. The future, rather than a different past, may be the other time that she most forcefully bequeaths to her readers.

J. H. Prynne: out of line

On the face of it, the contemporary avant-garde of British poetry would not seem an auspicious place to look for a complex engagement with memory, especially if one defines the latter term narrowly in terms of the individual mind's return to a surveyable unity of past perceptions. Seeking to challenge the reigning orthodoxy, the avant-garde might rather be seen as marking the end of the line for the humanism and nostalgia that provide ostensible bases for the mainstream. Certainly, the poet's own individual memory is relatively seldom in focus, as much alternative poetry chooses to jettison, or bracket out, the subjectivity of the writer, instead cultivating – in continuity with some strands of modernism – a more impersonal or objectivist stance. Furthermore, it also tends to embrace an experimental credo that is primarily forward-looking rather than retrospective. Thus Eric Mottram claims that the British poetry revival – a designation linked with the upsurge of the alternative scene from the 1960s onwards – has shown that poems 'need not illustrate dogmas but can enact with gestures flexible enough to hold potentiality as well as ascertained experience and prior formed knowledge'.[22] An audience encountering texts by poets such as Tom Raworth and Nathaniel Tarn, he claims, 'enjoy new encounters with form rather than a recovery of predetermined forms based on prejudice and habit. Their actions are not conservative but imaginative.'[23] The forms explored in such poetry are often of a spatial kind, involving typographical experiments that seem to insist upon the external, physical flatness of the written page rather than inner stretches of time. In this respect, the avant-garde is in line with the spatial turn recently identified with postmodernism.[24] Interpreting the fragmentation effected by Raworth's poetry, Ian Davidson has linked spatial indeterminacy in poetry to open-ended configurations of both identity and temporality:

> The mind begins to leap backwards and forwards between the verses, trying to make links and close them, but the poetry remains stubbornly open: each time an identity begins to be developed it is pushed aside or broken up in the movement of the poem. Raworth's point, of course, is that identity is not stable, and that a lyric poem which suggests a single perspective from a fixed identity is itself involved in the manipulation of embodied experience in order to produce a poem which may 'capture the moment' or 'make sense' out of a particular event.[25]

Space and change are embraced here, unleashing the reader into a seemingly unfettered realm of freedom and possibility, and eschewing old mainstays such as memory and the development of a unified account of an autobiographical self.

Yet perhaps one should beware of taking such generalizations too much at face value. According to Peter Middleton and Tim Woods, 'even avant-garde poetry, with little apparent interest in confessionalism, still devotes much of its inventive energy to rethinking the relations between poetic form, individual memory, history and temporality.'[26] Something similar is the case if one turns to the poetry and poetics of J. H. Prynne, an outstanding representative for the linguistically experimental avant-garde. On the surface, Prynne's notoriously challenging poetry would seem to be focused firmly on the present, and the possibility of freeing that present from subjection and ossification. As pointed out by N. H. Reeve and Richard Kerridge, the engagement with, and assimilation of, a wide range of existing discourses – including 'computer language, the languages of neurology, biochemistry and geology, and the language of the stock markets' – are an important reason for why Prynne's poetry can appear to be '*contemporary* in a way generally beyond the reach of literature now'.[27] Yet the dazzling interweaving of these discourses also threatens to sink the present under their weight: amid so much jargon, moulded and buffeted by the prescriptions of what Prynne has called 'the commodity spectacle and retail servitude of late-modern daily life',[28] where and when would there be time for an act – or even stray thought – of freedom? Enacting both the oppressive obliteration of the present and an avant-garde desire to liberate the here and now, Prynne's poetry is finely poised between sinking all in anonymous dejection and a more hopeful affirmation of the lyric moment.

At first sight, Prynne's concern with liberating the present would seem to be so fixed on the imperatives of the future, often criticizing the totalitarianism of utopian projection,[29] that memory and the past hardly get a look-in. As the early, angry poem 'Whose Dust Did You Say' indicates, the voluminous 'great palaces' (3) of Saint Augustine's inner recesses of memory may be where most of us dwell, but – given the choice – 'who can who would waste / his time who would fritter his time / away' (13–15) by lingering in those confines?[30] Rather than dwelling on history or tradition, this poetry would seem to be more obsessed with that which is to be done. Auden's humanist claim, in 'September 1, 1939', that 'We must love one another or die' is replaced by a more disenchanted mimicking of the market economy: 'Buy one / another or die' ('Questions for the Time Being', 53–54).[31] This kind of polemical stridency becomes increasingly rare, however, over the years. If the early Prynne is confrontational and frequently outspoken – vehemently asserting that 'No / poetic gabble will survive which fails / to collide head-on with the unwitty circus' ('L'Extase de M. Poher', 46–48) – his later approach is more cryptic, tending to mimic and unsettle rather than straightforwardly contradict the forces of circumstance.

In a reading of 'The Wound, Day and Night', Reeve and Kerridge point towards one of the more persistent formal features of Prynne's later style, noting how the verse calls

> the readers to order without telling them exactly how to proceed; in this way rhetorical authority is presented without an explicit or paraphrasable didactic purpose, since the responsibility for realigning oneself towards experience is transferred over to the reader. The desire on the poem's part is to restore the openness of relationship between human beings and their encounters.[32]

Often, however, Prynne throws out more pernicious, or at least ambiguous, imperatives at the reader. Thus one of the eight-line units of *Red D Gypsum* begins as follows: 'Address report under foot. Do the best one first. Get / quick subterfuge for the arm bent back' ('Address report under foot', 1–2). The combination of bureaucratic lingo with that of physical force makes it hard to read this in a fully benevolent light. The decontextualizing violence of forgetting that underlies such recommendations is spelled out in *For the Monogram*: 'Select an object with no predecessors. Clip off its / roots, reset to zero and remove its arrows' ('Select an object with no predecessors', 1–2). The subject is here commanded to sever an unnamed object's links with the past, in a procedure characterized by both arbitrariness and an insidious use of force.

Such sinister overtones should not, however, lead one to overlook Prynne's heavy investment in the future-oriented mindset of the avant-garde: he will not, in short, give up the future without a fight. His recent response to Ken Edwards's novel *Futures* indicates some of the stakes. The novel in question explores the various constrictions limiting its main character, Eye, in her daily life.[33] As she embarks on a journey in search of an open and untrammelled future, Eye's attempted transcendence of given time schemes is put into perspective by the fact that she's suffering retrograde amnesia, along with other side effects, subsequent to being raped. Prynne's response to the novel shows some impatience with how this explanatory context tends to reduce the reader's interpretive freedom:

> Also there were schemes for the exotic transformations within the dream-work which established in retrospect a real-time disposition for traumatic amnesia, making provision for memory loss and flicker in which the reading subject seems invited to know more about the links and boundaries than accepting their magic replacements to cover the suppression of violence; for some moments the implicit explanation for these blanks did seem in danger of overriding the direct experience of disconnection through narrative itself, suspending the value of suspensive frame by frame disclosure. ... no reader willing to travel like this wants also to hedge bets with a managed case-history of recaptured memory and recuperative overview. The flicker of free fall into shift after shift of figure has to somehow outlive a writing process in which the future of an unknown finale is increasingly devoured into a past of completion.[34]

For Prynne, the novel's archaeological unearthing of Eye's trauma is of less importance than how it disposes of its readers. In fact, the way in which the narrative threatens to limit the reader to a fully explicable and teleological narrative is deemed to be a problem insofar as it circumscribes the horizons of the reading process. The reader must not be forced to explicate through use of his or her memory, but should rather be enabled by the 'shift after shift of figure' to gaze ahead at the unfolding of an unobstructed future.

In addressing 'traumatic amnesia', Prynne's reading of *Futures* revisits a topic that his own poetry grappled with long ago. The 1974 collection *Wound Response* repeatedly returns to what appears to be the psychiatric treatment of a soldier suffering memory loss and other mental problems in the aftermath of some unidentified disaster. This is at least one possible reading: through a complex interlinking of different clusters of images,[35] Prynne characteristically makes any straightforward interpretation become questionable. But then this is not remarkable: Reeve and Kerridge have observed of another volume of Prynne's, *The Oval Window*, that 'Neither our memory, nor our capacity to predict what may come, seem able to provide a safe enough ground for the organizing of meaning, and the poem itself appears to look sardonically on our discomfort.'[36] In *Wound Response*, the sense of disorientation can be linked to the aforementioned war theme, as the text may be interpreted as exposing the reader to the bewildered thoughts and perceptions of the convalescing soldier. If the title *Wound Response* makes a characteristic nod towards terminology usually not prevalent in lyric poetry – its botanical vocabulary linking it closely to *The Plant Time Manifold Transcripts* – it does also have some human resonance. Kevin Nolan claims ' "wound response" was Pentagon cant during the Vietnam War for a successful strike' – if accurate, this identification would assist the reading of the volume in dialogue with its historical context.[37] The paucity of concrete references to Vietnam opens, however, for including other contexts, including both world wars.

What recollection or historical event of war might *Wound Response* respond to? However far afield speculation might take one, the poetry itself warns us that memory may always be inaccurate or manipulated. In 'The Blade Given Back', the reader's hunger for elucidation is frustrated, 'as the snow cruises / to the junctions of recall' (43–44). The reference to snow obviously links up with Prynne's use of landscape imagery in this collection: 'Treatment in the Field,' for instance, addresses 'the darker / folds of that guttural landscape which / lie drawn up under our touch' (10–12). Here, though, the drug-related slang meaning ('snow' signifying heroin or cocaine) is probably even more relevant, especially given how the beginning of 'The Blade Given Back' refers to 'snow crystals / in the blood / washing again' (2–4).[38] In 'Of Movement Towards a Natural Place', the patient does make a significant act of recollection that seems to revolt against the materialist reductionism of the surrounding discourse: 'See him recall the day by moral trace' (1). Yet soon enough his experience and its truth-value are addressed from an alienating and exterior perspective: 'His recall is false but the charge / is still there in neural space' (4–5). The concluding poem, 'Again in the Black Cloud', similarly tries to make amends for a damaged memory. Some kind of recourse to the past may be available, vaguely referred to in language that combines the legalistic, the scientific and the more straightforwardly phenomenological: 'the cells of the child line run back / through hope to the cause of it' (7–8).

I will return later to this resonant reference to a 'child line'. Suffice it to say, at this juncture, that it seems to indicate a trace of a distant, submerged memory. The earlier poem 'Chemins de Fer' (from *The White Stones*) uses similar imagery in a more clearly pessimistic vein:

> He goes
> slowly, her body
> fades into reason,
> the memory ever-
> green and planted,
> like a lost child.
>   (28–33)

While 'ever-/green' might seem to promise an unequivocal persistence to the memory of 'her body' here, the verb 'planted' nudges the imagery away from the unequivocally natural, and more in the direction of the manipulation of memory traces. Similarly, in 'Again in the Black Cloud', the tracing of the 'child line' back through hope to its cause may explain away the hope itself, and towards the end of the poem 'the reverse signs of memory and dream' (43) are not sufficient to free one from the alienating perspective and technically reductive lingo to which we are constantly returned. Whatever revelation may be hidden in the past, it amounts to no more than 'a pure joy at a feeble joke' (53).

In *Wound Response*, 'Treatment in the Field' may include a tacit allusion to the celebrated beginning of Eliot's 'The Love Song of J. Alfred Prufrock' ('the evening is spread out against the sky / Like a patient etherised upon a table'),[39] as the patient who's under 'basal narcosis' (16) is also identified as lying under a clear sky. If Eliot's modernist metaphor constituted an open guerrilla attack on the sensibilities of its readers, Prynne's audience are in for even more disorientation, as the spectacle of the operating table is compared to a battlefield, a natural landscape, an orchestral performance, and the origins of language. Typically for

Prynne, the resulting figural instability makes it hard to consistently affirm the bedrock of a metaphoric tenor under the rapid-fire procession of vehicles. Thus not only the content of memory is obfuscated; also the form of the poetry occludes any clear access to the past.

Arguably, the poem 'Thanks for the Memory', also included in *Wound Response*, exemplifies the alienation of memory on the level of discourse. Despite not including quotation marks, this poem is a verbatim transcription of a passage from Edward D. Kosower's 1972 article 'A Molecular Basis for Learning and Memory.'[40] The latter gives a neural account of recollection, focusing among other things on how short-term memory can be converted to long-term memory. Prynne's poem is based on the following passage, from one of the article's final paragraphs:

> The discussion given previously concerning the two types of ACh receptor allows a simple way of explaining how the postsynaptic receptor region can respond to an increase in the quantity of transmitter released by the presynaptic side of a synapse. An increase in the average quantity of transmitter (or other activating substance released from the VRS) arriving at the postsynaptic side over an extended period of time (minutes to days) should lead to an augmentation in the number of receptor sites and an expansion of the post-synaptic receptor region, through conversion of receptor monomers into receptor polymers and perhaps some increase in the synthesis of monomers. [None of these ideas bears upon the chemical basis for depolarization induced by acquisition of transmitter by receptor. There is evidence that disulfide links are near the receptor sites (51, 52).][41]

Prynne removes the opening sentence, which clearly reveals the summary nature of this discussion, thereby eschewing a cross-reference that would weaken the autonomy of his excerpt. On the other hand, by cutting off the poem after the words 'There is evidence', he highlights his own intervention into the found text. Apart from this interruption, and the title of the poem, the only other input coming from Prynne himself is the placing of the line-endings and the actual selection of the passage. As is often the case with found poetry, the author's actual intention – apart from the subversion of stereotypical conventions regarding poetic originality – is not immediately apparent. The poem's final words, 'There is evidence' (17), leave the specific nature of their evidence hanging; perhaps also making an allusion back to Prynne's 'Of Sanguine Fire': 'evidence hovers like biotic soup, all / transposable, all like' (5–6). The lyrics of the popular song 'Thanks for the Memory' look wistfully back at the brighter episodes of a failed marriage. Whether or not the reader is meant to recall this particular song, Prynne's poem might also be seen as being about a failed marriage: namely, the marriage of experience and discourse. Where the experience of memory is one of intimate interiority, the scientific terminology appropriated in this poem is insistently and obtusely reductive.

Is the poem a protest against such reductionism, in effect indicating that the workings of memory remain more mysterious than ever when exposed to such scientific terminology? In light of Prynne's general rebellion against the narrow discursive remit of lyric poetry, one might conceivably construct a reading of this poem as endorsing the reduction of subjectivity to a mercilessly material basis. The tradition of lyric celebrations, explorations, and defences of recollection traced in this study would seem to have been rudely interrupted by a disenchanted voiding of memory's inner spaces. Yet there are reasons to demur against such a reading. For one thing, Prynne himself has embraced phenomenology – in many ways a rearguard defence of the humanities against the perspective and concepts of positivism.[42] More directly relating to 'Thanks for the Memory', the title of Prynne's poem gives some grounds for irony (the expression 'Thanks for nothing' being a possible association),[43] and the actual content of the poem also links up with some of the more sinister passages of *Wound Response*. The epigraph for the volume as a whole (a quotation from the proceedings of a medical conference) deals with the possibility of medical manipulation of the brain. Although Kosower's article is based on experimental simulation of natural processes, his stating – in a smaller font, right at the foot of the article – that his work has been 'supported by the National Institutes of Health and the Army Research Office (Durham)' opens the possibility of disquieting uses of this research.[44] Although Kosower's passage actually details seemingly mundane issues concerning the possible neural underpinnings of the transformation of short-term to long-term memory, isolating it from its immediate context can provoke more suspicious or sinister interpretations. In Prynne's poem, 'activating substance / released from the VRS' (2–3) might suggest any range of substances and other active agents (since the reader presumably does not know that VRS stands for 'vesicle-release sites').[45] While the title might be read as referring to the patient's grateful acknowledgement of scientific assistance, other poems indicate a less benevolent context. The next poem of the collection, 'Pigment Depôt', apparently refers to the patient as a 'tenant' (1, 54) and 'hostage' (34). If Freud credited psychoanalysis with proving that the 'ego is not master in its own house',[46] Prynne's own analysis of memory and subjection would seem to indicate a similar displacement. In the metaphorical 'hostel' (7) of his own brain, the patient is 'already a victim' and 'does not / command the freehold' (21–22). Either despite, or as a result of, his treatment, the patient suffers from schizophrenia and (in the final poems) dissociation from his own emotions.

Even if it comes across as a somewhat despairing account of trauma and its effects, *Wound Response* thus insists that memory matters. Why does it do so, if Prynne elsewhere – for instance in his reading of Ken Edwards's novel *Futures*, addressed earlier – emphasizes how the past threatens to close down the horizon of the future? At one level, this is a question that concerns the preconditions of an open future. The latter cannot be a mere vacuousness at the mercy of various ideologies. Pure transcendence is unnervingly close to nihilism or, as Prynne puts it in 'The Common Gain, Reverted': 'the pure motion which has no track is / utterly lost' (40–41).

In order not to fall into line, the motion into the future must have amassed some inner impetus. Even if the 'track' into the future has to be left open, it does need a direction – and, to acquire the latter, the poet has to gain momentum from the past. Can memory, though, be made to work in this way, without foreclosing the openness of the future? When the early Prynne wrote of patiently waiting 'for the past to happen, which is to come into / the open' ('First Notes on Daylight', 2–3), was this a vain or ironic gesture? Is there another memory, apart from the teleological one dismissed in the response to Ken Edwards's novel? In another critical work, devoted to a reading of Wordsworth, Prynne insists upon precisely this. In *Field Notes: 'The Solitary Reaper' and Others*, he quotes Thomas Pfau's reading of 'Michael' as signifying

> how the lives of writers and readers – professionalized, sophisticated, and always forward-looking – had always been premised on their *not remembering* the affective, spiritual price exacted by the dramatic transformation of England's demographic and cultural landscape during the past two generations.[47]

What I've so far been presenting as a specifically avant-garde temporality of the future is here elided into a more general mode of modernity. Prynne's reading of 'The Solitary Reaper' frequently stops to question Wordsworth's own tendency to consign a particular history of suffering to obliviousness in the name of lyrical revelation. Yet even a poetry devoted to the present can be open to the future, through the way in which it one day will present to the future a liberating record of the past. Prynne's reading of Wordsworth's poem is acutely aware of this, using terms such as 'writerly memory', 'poet-memory', 'imaginative memory', and 'the enduring poetic record' to signify the phenomenon I have previously termed aesthetic memory: i.e., how poetry stores experience for generations to come.[48] Due to the force of history, even an art renouncing a direct or exhaustive commemoration of the given can one day become a testament to a particular past.

If this sounds a little constrictive, Prynne is alert to a more generous and open-ended understanding of the poetic afterlife. This becomes evident in his interpretation of Wordsworth's declaration that the solitary reaper 'sang / As if her song could have no ending'.[49] At first sight, nothing would prevent a reading of these lines in terms of a future-oriented infinity, with the young maiden unceasingly adding new notes to her song. Yet Prynne insists upon linking folksong with birdsong (evoked in earlier lines of 'The Solitary Reaper'), which he then associates with memory: 'Birdsong, too, has no ending in this sense, as also certain kinds of human feeling and memory that will not come to closure.'[50] He goes on to compare the phenomena in question to 'process music, with the sense of duration very vivid and immediate, articulated by repeated variations around a metrical beat or pulse but not by anticipations based on more extended structural memory and prediction'.[51] Memory, then, involves repetition, but those repetitions need not engulf one in a sense of predictability and closure. Repetition with a difference gives grounds for reinterpretation, the latter being a precondition for challenges to hegemonic distributions of power. For Prynne, the kind of backward-looking but open-ended duration that is in question is also characteristic of the aesthetic memory founded by Wordsworth's act of writing:

> The solitary poet-traveller in Wordsworth's poem knows, too, that his own song in part-imitation of hers is also a work-song, a part of the poet's work that can never be completed, and that his song will outlast his own life in the reception and memory of readers till to come: as indeed it has.[52]

Thus the poet becomes a figure of memory. In doing so, the poet also becomes comprehended by an alternative figurality of memory, as Prynne's contrast between a closed, teleological form of memory and a repetitive but open-ended one is linked to his understanding of language. Published twenty-four years prior to the reading of Wordsworth, his essay 'China Figures' – addressing the Penguin edition of translations of the ancient Chinese anthology *Yü-t' ai hsin-yung* (the English title is *New Songs from a Jade Terrace*) – shows that the two forms of memory intersect with two figural relations. In 'China Figures', Prynne defends the conventions of Chinese court poetry: where a modern reader might dismiss the tendency towards flatness and apparent cliché, he sees a 'subtlety of intelligible allusion, varied and superimposed, which here shews the power of metonymy both to support metaphor and to exceed it'.[53] Prynne's opposition between metaphor and metonymy builds explicitly on the work of literary theorists such as Roman Jakobson, David Lodge, and Jonathan Culler. Where metonymy builds on 'an established figural system', metaphor 'selects displaced or separated elements on the basis of a newly perceived relation which substitutes one element for another; it constitutes a new relation, rather than invoking one'.[54] Just as teleological memory anticipates the future, so does metaphor attempt to articulate the new; and, where the more open-ended form of memory is built on repetitions that do not clearly lead to a goal, so does metonymy deploy iteration in a manner that might seem to lack a clear direction. Yet Prynne defends metonymy (and its link with cliché) against the claims of metaphor.

The opposition to metaphor in 'China Figures' does not represent a new departure for Prynne: from early on in his career, he has had a bone to pick with this trope. In his 1971 lectures on Charles Olson's *Maximus* IV, V, and VI, Prynne belittles metaphor for not comprehending the encompassing relations aimed for in Olson's verse: 'the lyric relies on the gracious condition of metaphor, and metaphor transfers the small into the large, and the one thing into the other; and the lyric is not a condition of the whole, but a condition of the part.'[55] In these lectures, the isolated parts of metaphor are deemed inferior to a poetic approach that takes 'the whole condition of something called the cosmos into its aim'.[56] Prynne does not explicitly identify this approach as a metonymical one, but the part–whole relation it builds upon is, in point of fact, more characteristic of metonymy than the literalism cultivated at this stage of his career. What in the Olson lectures is described as obeying a logic where 'each of those little phrases has within it the curvature of the whole of the spatial condition'[57] becomes in 'China Figures', seventeen years later, a 'metonymic system [where] each local part of such a system [is] pre-implying the larger whole'.[58] The latter text's rather understated echoing of the totalizing systematics articulated by Jonathan Culler (already being challenged by post-structuralist thought in the early 1980s) is no mere slip of the pen;[59] it has its roots deep in Prynne's engagement in Olson and the poetics of the Black Mountain poets.

The 1971 lectures hedge their bets between memory and a more timeless, mythical participation in cosmic unity. For Prynne, Olson's sense of the cosmos 'comprises the rearward time vector, back to the past, and all the space vectors extended until they go circular, that is to say, until you reach the curvature of the whole, so that they solve themselves into myth'.[60] The lectures make much of the concept of a 'curvature', signifying an encompassing movement that gathers all particulars into unity even as it (due to its circularity) escapes the hierarchical quality of linear teleology. Prynne's closing statement calls it a 'noble arc' that extends 'from the land to the shore, from the shore to the sea, from the ocean to the void, from the void to the horizontal curve, which is love'.[61]

The dynamism of this vector is a persistent feature of Prynne's poetics. It appears even earlier, in a 1963 essay on modernism in German poetry, in a manner that anticipates much of his later work. The German poet Paul Celan, he notes,

> adopts Mallarmé's primary stratagem of purity, to set off the images that evolve from his thinly-populated poetic universe. His 'Kreuzmetapher', or combination of terms from different levels of discourse and abstraction, deploys a curious sense of imaginative dimensions almost empty of content.[62]

This description of Celan's poetical practice looks forward to the English poet's own, later interweaving of a variety of different discourses. It idiosyncratically misquotes the conclusion of Celan's 'Meridian' lecture, which described a search for 'something as immaterial as language, yet earthly, terrestrial, in the shape of a circle which, via both poles, rejoins itself and on the way serenely crosses even the tropics: I find ... a *meridian*'.[63] Prynne's allusion to Celan's meridian line is important, as it not only anticipates the 'curvature' of the Olson lecture, but also identifies it – through the reference to a *Kreuzmetapher* – with the disjointed tropology of his own later poetry: the curvature of the cosmos is intimated, one might say, by the crossing of metaphors and discourses.

Prynne's poetics can thus be exemplified through the meta-figure of a line. It is not a straightforwardly directed line – i.e., it is not 'linear' in a teleological sense – but one susceptible to erratic or eccentric swerves. Despite pretensions to totality, it does not circumscribe a larger whole through harmoniously delimiting the borders of a closed field. Rather, it sets off collisions and surprising intersections, combining more through breaks and collisions than through obvious coherency. One of the ways in which it can be identified as being metonymical is through its tendency to repeat, and return to, the same motifs. Generally, an important instance of the rebounding, returning dynamics of Prynne's poetry is its tendency to reflect on its own nature and operations.

An inspection of how Prynne's poetry inspects and exemplifies its own use of the line of the verse will make this apparent. By detailing some of the vicissitudes of self-reflective meditation on the 'line' in his poetry, I will try to gather up and link together the central findings of this reading of Prynne. At the same time, it will be shown how his poetry most clearly challenges memory, without dismissing it, on a micro-level through an encounter with the reader: this is a poetry where much of the drama concerns the interpretive challenges encountered by the reader in trying to establish sustained patterns of memory.

In 'The Western Gate', from *The White Stones*, 'lines' are presented as being a meeting place of physical and writerly dynamics:

> Write a letter, walk across the wet pavement,
>   the lines are taut with
>   strain, maybe they'll
>   snap soon.
>
>   (32–35)

Apart from implying the hermeneutical threat of an uncontrolled dispersal of meaning, this passage also exemplifies that threat with its use of suspended line-endings, leaving the anxious reader hanging mid-sentence. Although the line-breaks are not accompanied by a fully fledged break in the semantic continuity of the verse, a derailing of teleology – with its straightforward coherence between origin and aim – is presented as an ineluctable accompaniment to not only walking and writing, but also (by implication) reading. In later Prynne, the threatened rupture is occasionally made concrete, typographically, on the page. Here's the beginning of 'Write-Out':

> As a circumstantial infringement again loaned off
>
>   the said apart or   close by the index
>   by ill, sand given   longer marked on
>   object in sport   arranged dots: to.
>
>   (1–4)

After such disarray, what trust can the reader have in the author? Yet some trust the reader surely must have in the guidance of the poet, and the latter's imaginative ability to make the lines cohere in a fashion. More than most poetry, Prynne's makes it necessary, however, for the reader to make frequent rereadings: looping back to previous lines is often strictly necessary, in order to check the possible resonance of new lines with the connotations linked with those that have been left behind. Thus Prynne's interest in Kosower's article, which addresses the connection between long- and short-term memories, may have a further motivation: in reading this poetry, frequent acts of checking and reinforcing short-term memories become necessary in order to buttress any sense of cohesion and progression in the reader's interpretive process. These lines from 'Air Gap Song' can be read as dwelling upon the disarray into which the hapless reader can be thrown:

> the loop not connected
> but open & in-
>   duced to nothing. Here
> the guide falters.
> (21–25)

Without enough guidance, the reading experience is threatened by a breakdown, through which the temporality of the reading process is stopped short. Rather than a successive unfolding of interpretive gestures, combining with more holistic comprehension of the whole in accordance with the hermeneutic circle,[64] reading can become reduced to momentary experiences of isolated moments. This also risks undercutting temporality altogether, highlighting the immediate physical environment – a particular line or line-break on the flat page – to the detriment of any deep unfolding of semantic richness. When this occurs, the line-break can become an emblem of alienation, as in the beginning of a poem in *The Oval Window*, where 'Now the willows on the river are hazy like mist / and the end is hazy like the meaning / which bridges its frozen banks' ('Now the willows on the river', 1–3). Here the frozen banks of both river and text deny anything but a 'hazy' premonition of there being safe shores at the end. For the patient reader, however, some semblance of order never completely disappears for long. Thus the conclusion of 'If the day glow is mean' (in *Down Where Changed*) not only suspends its own impulse towards fragmentation by falling into line with a typical stanzaic grid (here a three-line stanza), but it also comments wryly on the apparent re-establishing of the given framework: 'the whole procession / reshuffles into line' (11–12). While the speaker of an early poem such as 'Smaller than the Radius of the Planet' could declare 'I lay out my / unrest like white lines on the slope' (3–4), the later, more stanzaically regular poet finds more grounds for order in poetic lineation. Yet, even as early as *Into the Day* (1972), the line seems to obey as merciless a logic as the waves of the sea. Crossing an unidentified 'shore', we follow

> the track
> of feet and spread
> to break, to wear
> the line, intact.
>
> ('This one is high in', 10–13)

Moving on regular feet (iambic metre), the poet's movement down the page may involve breaks and caesuras, but the line is – even if a little worse for wear after centuries of use – 'intact'. In the latter word, though, one might also hear an echo of the dissociation of feeling we encountered in *Wound Response*: 'intact' stems from the Latin *tactus* (from *tangere*, meaning 'touch'), and its use here probably signifies not merely that the line is untouched (in the sense of pristine innocence) but chillingly alien to touch.

The line is always a unit of exploration for Prynne. It is where recall and anticipation work together to trace an irregular, curving path. As such, it is not only figuratively related to the inescapable, fate-like repetition of the wave, but also to the errant itinerary of the nomad. Does the wanderer's journey – for instance that of Aristeas, in the early 'Aristeas, in Seven Years' – have a goal or final haven? If so, even that *telos* would have to obey the irregular logic of the line of wandering, being a beginning rather than an end. The ending of *Into the Day* indicates that even an apparent final destination leads but to a new journey: 'The ship steadies / and the bird also; from frenzy / to darker fields we go' ('After feints the heart steadies', 11–13).

The line is a place of transit, the intersection of various crossings in space and time. Much commented on by critics, the polysemic conclusion of 'Of Movement Towards a Natural Place' is also a celebration of the resources of the line. After three stanzas of ten lines each, a single line offers the following in gnomic solitude: 'Only at the rim does the day tremble and shine' (31). This line is itself 'only' and 'at the rim', in the sense of being both isolated (and different) from the other stanzaically organized lines of the poem. Ambivalently placed either beside or above the 'night lines above the cut' mentioned just before the line-break of the previous line (30), it can be read in terms of a traditional invocation of the revelatory power of dusk.[65] This is of course also reminiscent of the 'curvature of the limits', mentioned in Prynne's lecture on Olson as the place of revelation.[66] A privileged place, however, for such insight is provided by the boundary of the line itself, the transitions of the line-break providing the ever returning 'rim' by which a poem lives. Seen in this light, Prynne's citation of Anselm of Canterbury in lines 22–23 of the same poem (*'anima tota in singulis / membris sui corporis'*) would imply that not only in the human body, but also in the body of verse, is every individual unit suffused with spirit: even at the turning-place of every line-break does the poem speak its revelation. As it is put in 'As grazing the earth' in *Wound Response*: 'At the turning-places / of the sun the / head glistens, dew falls / from the apse line' (7–9).

In 'apse line', most readers will immediately pick up an allusion to the apses of Christian churches, and perhaps also presume a more sub-merged nod to the temporal line of the Church's history, for instance in the form of the apostolic succession. As so often with Prynne, a more technical term overlays such associations: in astrophysics, an 'apse line' relates to the imaginary or hypothetical line traced in an eccentric orbit.[67] Frequently, references to 'lines' in Prynne follow a similar procedure, whereby the tacitly self-reflective dimension is partially overlaid with more technical usages related to a variety of scientific and financial dis-courses. In a chemical experiment pursued in 'Nibble Song', 'the crystal tube / ploughs up thoughtful / acid lines, is cold' (7–9). Unsurprisingly perhaps, for a writer consistently critical of late modern capitalism, Prynne has also asked the reader to 'Read the lines of credit outsourced' ('Malicious rising sun fog plates', 4). Elsewhere, his characteristic sea-voyaging imagery intersects, for satiric purposes, with more commercial enterprises in several references to 'liners'. Thus in 'A New Tax on the Counter-Earth', a relatively straightforward criticism (by Prynne's stand-ards) of English politics from the Victorian age to the present, 'We move into sleep portioned / off in the restored liner, and the drowsy body / is closer to "nature"' (35–37). Certainly the line may go astray, as blood lines and shipping lines may issue into dangerous detours:

> As blood
> may track into a false channel,

> the small boat at sea a noted
> twist of cruelty.
> ('By leverage against the body', 3–6)

Does the poetic line necessarily buckle and lose its integrity under all the other lines in evidence, of which so many may be said to represent 'a false channel'? How can one distinguish the wayward line of Prynne's eccentric curvature from the mere lack of direction evinced by the late modern society that he criticizes? Certainly, without the lifeline of self-reflective guidance, the reader is in danger of losing his or her bearings completely, drowned in a sea of voices and impressions that cannot solidify into more long-term memories and structures of meaning. In a poem included in *The Oval Window*, the line is ignominiously swallowed up by the 'bin liner' of an imposed discipline that is one part financial, another part military force: 'That is the regimen, / the bin liner of the second subject, holding / our tongues like brevet clients on call' ('As what next if you can't', 12–14). But for Prynne 'Rubbish' is not only 'pertinent; essential', it is also 'the / most intricate presence in / our entire culture' ('L'Extase de M. Poher', 69–71). The waste dismissed by modern society may, in fact, open up a vantage point outside those under the regimen of its hegemonic forces.

This is where a particular 'line' of memory opens up, enabling a tracing of the curvature desired by Prynne's poetics. The 'line', in this sense, is a lineage, a chain of successive generations and the vital, generative principle underlying them all. This usage is active in Prynne's persistent exploration of the traditional link between poetry and agriculture, etymologically evident in how the word 'verse' has its origins in the Latin *versus*, meaning a turn of the plough or a furrow.[68] Prynne's lines are the furrows in which his poetry is sown. The lines physically split the poetic seed: 'From whose seed spread out / bend and cut, in the field, in far / rows sideways' ('From whose seed spread out', 1–3). Here self-reflection sends out tentative feelers to the world, rather than closing the poem in on itself, as the highly virtualized space of the poetic stanza becomes at least associatively linked with the concrete places of agricultural fields. In the same vein, Prynne's reading of 'A Solitary Reaper' expresses an intense fascination at the links between reaping and writing, actively pursuing both similarities and differences between Wordsworth's own acts of poetry and the young maiden's work in the fields. Even more than being a nod back to the field poetics of Charles Olson, Prynne's title for this work (*Field Notes*) can be taken as signalling towards the crucial importance, for him, of the common ground shared by poet and manual labourer. One of the more digressive passages surely says more about Prynne's own conception of poetry than anything specific about 'A Solitary Reaper':

> As he watches her singing at her work it is as if she directs her song specifically at what she does, not at or towards an auditor but into the work itself, at her moving blade: guiding the corn by melody onto the cutting edge. It is a most exquisite challenge to his own motives and his ability to control and overcome them, to cut and sever everything non-essential, to get in the seed, to apprehend how a true imagination is truly arduous and may not translate matter into spirit, which is the way that reality is lost by pursuit of factitious solace.[69]

The 'true imagination' knows, like the reaper, how to cut and sow, but has to be meet in everything. Removing that which is 'non-essential', it must nevertheless also be just as scrupulous in not excluding too much; most importantly, the particularity of 'matter' must not be bruised to pleasure the spirit.

Commodity capitalism would be the calculated use of not only material entities, but also lives, as disposable units in an ever-growing economy. In the second book of *Triodes*, Prynne envisions a mechanism 'ever disposed for a dip over countlines / boosting the birthrate, fits of / corrupted seed assault' ('Magpie target going in through the torus', 12–14). A 'countline' is a consumer product sold in bulk to a retailer, but even more relevant here is the link to brachytherapy, which uses radiation implants as a form of treatment for prostate cancer. A more heartening metamorphosis of the 'line', yet again related to the theme of generation, is envisaged in *High Pink on Chrome*, where 'Too far past the point / the seed splits / and saves its line' ('Too far past the point', 1–3). By breaking up, the seed sacrifices itself, as it were, for future life. We are very close here, thematically, to the 'child line' that gave tenuous – if obstructed – hope for memory in *Wound Response*. In both cases, the temporal continuity of a lineage is uncertain and threatened, yet some ground for resilience remains. The very links between generation, harvesting and literature are, of course, equally imperilled and tenuous, and the notions of originality and nature that have traditionally underpinned them are under considerable stress. As this reading has shown, however, Prynne's poetry and poetics would seem to declare that all is not lost. Breaking itself up, looping back, wandering nomadically on an erratic itinerary, the line persists. It does so not only by projecting itself forward into an indeterminate future, but also gaining impetus through an open-ended burrowing into the past.

Alice Oswald: giving pause

At certain historical junctures, unignorable crises have forced Western societies to radically re-evaluate their institutions and heritages. The ecological crisis can be understood as the last in a long line of such crises, but it is also, in one respect, vitally different from most of its predecessors. For it threatens, unless appropriate measures are taken, to end life as we know it. Civilization must, it seems, either change or suffer extinction. The thoroughness and depth of the needed changes are, however, up for debate – and so is the role literature might have in the process. If large-scale political reforms are needed, should an ecologically engaged poet embrace a didactic or polemical role? In a recent volume of essays titled *Ecopoetry: A Critical Introduction*, Roger Thompson suggests a direct approach:

> Ultimately, the ecopoet might be called cause-centered, declaring the natural world as center to societal reform. Ecopoets are, in fact, ecocritics themselves, shelving notions of nature as solely metaphoric divinity in favor of a conception of nature as potential action, possible location of human reform.[70]

At first sight, this makes perfect sense: if poets want to change the world, then they obviously need to step up on their rhetorical soap-boxes and tell their audience exactly how that change can come about. In the process, we are once again returned to the idea of poetry as oriented firmly, and almost exclusively, towards future action, which we encountered early in the reading of Prynne.

An influential alternative to the cause-related and rational form of environmentalism is, however, provided by a stance that questions the very nature of human subjectivity. According to the latter approach, a fundamental change in human attitudes to nature is exigent: only by leaving behind conceptions of nature being a pliable material or resource at the disposal of human technology will it be possible to avoid a potentially fatal destruction of nature. If large-scale change and ambitious technological projects are needed, they should nevertheless not be rashly pursued without taking pause in a very fundamental way. Jonathan Bate has articulated a particularly powerful account of ecopoetry on this basis, arguing that poetry is particularly well equipped to foster the necessary change of attitude. Departing from instances of ecocriticism that stress the necessity of rhetorical directness in environmental poetry, Bate insists that this is not a matter of propaganda: 'Ecopoetry is not synonymous with writing that is pragmatically green: a manifesto for ecological correctness will not be poetic because its language is bound to be instrumental, to address questions of doing rather than to "present" the experience of dwelling.'[71]

Building on the thought of Martin Heidegger, Bate suggests that the most important way we relate to the earth is through dwelling. For Heidegger, an authentic form of being in the world presupposes that one dwells in a way that does not entail reducing the earth to a disposable resource.[72] One must avoid the pitfalls of modern technology, through a radical reorientation that calls into question the essence of human-ity, thought, and action. Although Heidegger's understanding of this reorientation entails that it can only come about through a thorough interrogation of the history of thought itself, Bate is more attuned to the fruits of the process. Rather than implying historical consciousness, his notion of ecopoetry is primarily a matter of the present. Explicating Heidegger's understanding of the Greek term for truth, *aletheia*, he states that 'poetry is our way of stepping outside the frame of the tech-nological, of reawakening the momentary wonder of unconcealment.'[73] Bate's account thus sidesteps the fact that, for Heidegger, the isolated present – in opposition to the imbricated relating of the ecstases of past, present, and future to one another – is part of the heritage of a narrowly scientific world view. Furthermore, it also neglects the fact that *aletheia* not only means 'truth' and 'unconcealment', but also – as is made clear by Heidegger's rereading of Plato – 'remembering' (as the word has its root in *lethe*, meaning 'forgetting').[74]

Bate's account of ecopoetry provides a fruitful template for this final look at a contemporary poet challenging traditional poetic focus on memory with a forceful insistence upon an *other* time. Alice Oswald is, in many respects, an exemplary, contemporary exponent of ecopoetry as Bate conceives of it. Oswald's is a fresh voice, which builds on not only British but also American influences, and which – as a result – in many ways challenges the long-prevailing opposition between mainstream and alternative scenes in England. To date, she has published three main books of poetry: the collections *The Thing in the Gap-Stone Stile* (1996) and *Woods etc.* (2005), as well as the long poem *Dart* (2002).[75] Most of this work deals with the natural environment in one form or another. Oswald has spelled out the importance, as she sees it, of the nature poem:

We have a problem with our fields, with our weather, with our water, with the very air we breathe; but we can't quite react, we can't quite get our minds in gear. One reason perhaps is that our minds are conditioned by the wrong kind of nature poem, the kind that leaves us comfortable, melancholy, inert. Nostalgic. Dishonest.[76]

The following interpretations of Oswald's poetry will scrutinize how she seeks to avoid any vestige of a 'nostalgic' temporality in her dealings with nature, particularly by challenging the instrumental rationality of the subject. I will start off with her shorter, lyrical work, and only move over to *Dart* towards the end of this chapter.

The opening poem of *Woods etc.*, 'Sea Poem', presents a useful entry-point to both the ecological bent of Oswald's poetry and its distinct temporality. The opening line signals that what is aimed at, at least as an ideal, is a radical leave-taking with human subjectivity: 'what is water in the eyes of water' (1). Rather than presenting a personal vantage point, the speaker suggests that she might allow the sea itself to come into utterance. The absence of punctuation and capitals here can be read as a formal underlining of the poem's desire to transcend conventional framings of nature. Through its six stanzas, the poem highlights various features of the sea, such as its power and movement. The act of homing in on its pristine condition outside human cognition is compared to the sea's own washing itself clean 'of the world's increasing complexity' (7). The resulting condition also entails bracketing out the long vistas of human history:

> oscillation endlessly shaken
> into an entirely new structure
> what is the depth of water
> from which time has been rooted out.
> (9–12)

Traditional ideas of the circularity of nature (particularly of a seasonal kind), as well as pre-Socratic notions of the oppositions underlying existence, are carried over into the 'oscillation' of the first line here. Yet this pendular process is unceasingly interrupted, 'endlessly shaken', so that new formations and relations are constantly being formed. The resulting formation is unpredictable, severed from its antecedents by a brief but explosive hiatus. In this respect, no past causes, no layers of the sea's hidden history, have any importance: 'time has been rooted out'.

The phrase 'entirely new structure' brings together two important concerns for Oswald: I want to first focus on the temporal dimension of the 'entirely new', before subsequently focusing on how she confronts the articulated spatiality of a whole. Her poetry is obsessed with the fleeting instant, resolutely pursuing 'the clap of time' ('The Apple Shed', in *Thing*, 3) that vanishes as quickly as it is sensed. 'Otter Out and In' typically dwells upon the quick movement of an animal in its habitat: 'The whole river transforms upon an otter. / Now and gone, sometimes we see him / swimming above the fish' (in *Thing*, 9–11). Here the overarching structure is the river, while the otter is a dynamic principle subjecting the whole to metamorphosis through its movement. Always alert to the vital movement of small creatures, Oswald may here be read as exemplifying Bate's claim that 'if you don't have what Edward Wilson calls "keystone species", such as the sea otter, a site once destroyed may remain barren.'[77] The existence of such species is essential to the prolonged life of ecosystems. Oswald's poem goes on to compare the otter's transient appearance with that of its spectators, as they too end the poem going 'out and in and disappear in darkness ...' (20). At the most immediate level, this can be read as indicating that the human observers are marginalized, and lose their vision of ecological wholeness, once the transitory epiphany of the otter has vanished. On a second level, the poem may be interpreted as hinting at the possible consequences of the extinction of further natural species: lose the cornerstones of the ecosystem, and human life, too, will 'disappear in darkness'. At a third level, Oswald may also be writing an allegory of her own kind of brief, transitory poem. Bate makes a similar connection: 'Could the poet be a keystone sub-species of *Homo sapiens*? The poet: an apparently useless creature, but potentially the saviour of ecosystems.'[78]

D. H. Lawrence recommended that poets should slough off the dead weight of the past and the future, and instead embrace 'the moment, the immediate present, the Now'.[79] Oswald is following not only in his footsteps, but also in those of Ted Hughes, whose poetry she has described as having an 'imaginative grasp of the present – that ability to speak strictly within one moment and not through a misted screen of remembered moments'.[80] Timothy Morton has articulated the obvious objection to ecopoetry's desire for immediacy:

> Ecological writing may want to drag us into the here and now, in a mystical or primitivist or exoticist gesture that seeks to sweep away bad Western cunning. The past is just an illusion. The future is yet to come. Dig the present! But when we get there, we discover that the here and now does not exist either.[81]

Close attention reveals, however, that Oswald shows if not 'cunning', then at least considerable sophistication – both in terms of how she tries to set to work a poetics of ecological immediacy, and in the way she recoils from, and questions, her own approach. She is fascinated by the beginnings of nature – what one might call its rooted newness or, to use Heidegger's Greek, *phusis*. Poems such as 'Leaf', 'A Winged Seed' and 'Ideogram for Green' all circle around spots where life bursts into being: 'the invisible places / Where the first leaves start' ('Ideogram for Green', in *Woods etc.*, 1–2). 'Head of a Dandelion', in *Woods etc.*, envisages an entity in which such beginnings would be a constant phenomenon. A 'flower of no property' (17), the dandelion would instantly surrender its possessions. Nothing is kept, nothing is stored for future disposal: 'This is the flower of amnesia. / It has opened its head to the wind, all havoc and weakness' (5–7). As in 'Sea Poem', the sedimented riches of time are once more being denied. The more personalized form of temporality in 'Head of a Dandelion' – dealing, as it does, with 'amnesia' rather than the absence of the more abstract 'time' – is in tune with the latter poem's metaphors: the dandelion is compared to both an old woman and a wooden man. Implicitly, something of a poetical *ethos* is being intimated: just as Keats (more directly) asked whether the poet should not be more like a flower than a bee,[82] Oswald is proffering the dandelion as something of an imitable exemplar. At the same time, the destructive nature of the similes (the old woman is falling apart, while the wooden man walks through fire) hints towards ambivalence: if impersonality involves an Eliotic sacrifice of the self, it is a sacrifice that may have a catastrophic issue.

To be open to nature amounts to not dominating it, not subjecting it to the 'hyperrationality' that J. Scott Bryson has identified to be the enemy of contemporary ecopoetry,[83] but rather putting one's senses and being in a state of acute receptivity. Oswald eschews an 'art of thinking' that presents itself as 'a pommel / to pound the world into conformity' ('The Three Wise Men of Gotham Who Set Out to Catch the Moon in a Net', in *Thing*, 8–9), and instead seeks a more passive approach. In the words of a line that functions as a semi-autonomous section in 'A Greyhound in the Evening after a Long Day of Rain', the imperative is straightforward, if relentlessly demanding: 'Listen Listen Listen Listen' (in *Thing*, 13). Who is doing the listening here? Unlike what is the case with 'Sea Poem', some sense of human identity is inescapable in this context.

Morton claims that the 'ultimate fantasy' of a particular mode of ecological writing is the achievement of 'ecology without a subject'.[84] Yet even if Oswald may generally eschew autobiographical detail, instead opting to write an 'Autobiography of a Stone' (in *Woods etc.*), this does not remove certain fundamental givens from her poetry. While 'Sea Poem' desired the transcendence of all human subjectivity, 'Head of a Dandelion' is more forthright in owning up that this remains a desire rather than an accomplishment. Of course, a subject devoid of memory would also, if we are to follow traditional accounts, be one stripped of any identity. How can one know who one is – let alone contribute to changing the world – if one does not have a narrative of the past upon which to build? Oswald is in proximity to the postmodern critique of identity and authorial presence, yet seldom pretends to attain an absence of intention or state of free, subjectless play. Some poems dwell upon a subject gaining access, through subterfuge, to a kind of unadorned presence of nature. In 'Wood Not Yet Out', in *Woods etc.*, the speaker listens 'to the releasing branches where I've been – / the rain, thinking I've gone, crackles the air / and calls by name the leaves that aren't yet there' (12–14). In the same volume, 'Tree Ghosts' plays with the possibility of capturing the sound of 'Whatever the wind says when there's no one there' (44), while 'Excursion to the Planet Mercury' describes a planet that is 'a mystery / without I without air, / without you without sound' (6–8).

Such imaginings might be dismissed as insignificant instances of the pathetic fallacy. A more generous reading would, however, make allowances for the validity of these thought experiments, conceived of as either (impossible but not unproductive) challenges to the poetic imagination or testaments to the weight of the ethical demands compelling the ecological poet. Oswald is caught in the oscillation between differing pulls, differing pressures, which Bate explicates as follows:

> The poetic is ontologically double because it may be thought of as ecological in two senses: it is either (both?) a language (*logos*) that restores us to our home (*oikos*) or (and?) a melancholy recognizing that our only home (*oikos*) is language (*logos*).[85]

Far from being a straightforwardly naive poet, Oswald is deliberate and supple in her use of language – frequently to the point of acute self-consciousness. Nature is always being nudged against and into language, as she explores what Bate identifies as 'the problem of writing', namely 'the gap between "presence" and "representation"'.[86] She often presents – in concordance with post-structuralist theory – the earth as always-already imbricated in language.

Once there is language, there is no longer pure immediacy, but rather articulation and retrieval. If Oswald's poet, then, does not deal with, or depend upon, her long-term memories, the intensity of the lyric moment is nevertheless dependent upon something like short-term memory for the sake of the struggle with interpreting and deciphering the given of nature. What presents itself as, to all intents and purposes, a poetry of the present is, on closer scrutiny, a poetry of that which quite recently has been. Rather than instantiating the present, pure and simple, her poetry would commemorate a past experience of a present. Alternatively, one might identify this as an exploration of the very hinge between the present that has been and the past that is coming to be – the gap, or pause, that wedges itself in between not only presence and representation, but also the successive, 'entirely new' structures of nature.

The title poem of *The Thing in the Gap-Stone Stile* approaches this issue via legend. The speaker of the poem is an enigmatic, seemingly all-powerful being, portrayed in an offhand yet wily manner that might bring to mind Jo Shapcott's humorous dramatic monologues. Towards the end of the poem this speaker identifies herself as a personification of interstices: 'I am a gap' (13). Due to her powers of generating space, she is the occasion of wonder: 'I certainly intended / anyone to be almost / abstracted on a gap-stone between fields' (18–20). Generating the very spatiality that can be filled by objects, the speaker is, one might say, difference itself. She is the articulator of spaces, herself devoid of any concrete form; hence explaining the absence of specification in the 'thing' of the title of the poem. In the same volume, 'Mountains' pursues a similar effect through its use of the indeterminate noun 'Something'. The latter text describes its elusive object as being at work not only in spatial gaps such as those 'between two horses' (8) and in 'a holey stone' (9), but also operative in the temporal articulation that 'inslides itself between moments' (15).

Here Oswald is in close proximity to Jacques Derrida's notion of 'diferánce' as the non-metaphysical grounding of spatial articulation and temporal deferment.[87] It is not impossible to see her as more of a post-structuralist, or even a postmodernist, than a conventional ecopoet. Her figure of the dandelion – which we encountered earlier, in 'Head of a Dandelion' – is not, for instance, very unlike Roland Barthes's conception of the ideal reader. In *S/Z*, Barthes identifies this reader as someone who disseminates the text in 'a perpetual present, upon which no *consequent* language (which would inevitably make it past) can be superimposed', gladly surrendering meanings to oblivion.[88] Is Oswald really more of a ludic poet who articulates the coming into presence of momentary singularities, of any kind, rather than an earnest pursuer of natural essence? In a comment on her first volume, Oswald claimed 'you could mistake the book for something polished or earnest or quaint or nature-ish,' insisting: 'I'm not a nature poet, though I do write about the special nature of what happens to exist.'[89]

As was the case with the reading of Prynne, considerable insight can be gained into both the temporality and spatiality of Oswald's verse, by an inspection of how she self-consciously uses, and thematically addresses, the poetic line. In the opening line of 'Mountains' – 'Something is in the line and air along ledges' (1) – Oswald's typically self-reflective use of 'line' hints that the effects of this 'Something' can be felt in the actual lineation of her own verse. The form of poetry itself is constituted through such articulation, as Oswald points out in a short introduction to the poetry of Sir Thomas Wyatt:

> the important question (for me) is whether you hear in Wyatt a hurrying, incremental kind of music or whether you hear something more to and fro and rewinding, like birdsong – in which case the poem's overall effect is mainly made of the turnings and spaces between phrases. I think these two ways of reading are radically, even metaphysically different. ... The second way of reading is to do with the echo and opposition of real sounds within one line. It needs to proceed much more slowly, because the centre upon which the meanings converge lies outside the language, in the pauses.[90]

Oswald has frequently tended to mark such pauses in her texts, either by adding extra spaces between words (in a manner reminiscent of modern American poetry) or – as in the recent 'Fragment of an Unfinished Morning' – by the marked use of the word 'pause' itself.[91] In 'The Thing in the Gap-Stone Stile', the penultimate stanza indicates that the generative gap of Oswald's poetry is not only one of external spaces, but also the formal grounds, within poetry, for such articulation: the personified gap identifies her position as being 'before behind antiphonal, my cavity the chord' (17). Similarly, 'Another Westminster Bridge' (from *Woods etc.*) identifies the moment of revelation as being 'a breath-width instant' (6).

If Oswald's ideal poetic line is marked by an internal break, or shaking, that causes new structures to come into being, it also aspires (to use her own words from the quotation above) to be a place of convergence of 'meanings', coming from a 'centre' that 'lies outside language'. The ideal event of her poem is an extralinguistic one. Furthermore, the convergence of meanings is not a matter solely of difference, but also of likeness. 'Hymn to Iris', from *Woods etc.*, involves an ambiguous linking of poetic language's figurative resources to the interplay between difference and unity. The opening addresses the rainbow goddess, 'whose being is only an afterglow of a passing-through' (2), thus indicating that temporal movement is one of the traits of the being in question. The subsequent imagery develops the idea of Iris being a goddess of bridges: where the opening constituted her as a goddess of the bridge between moments, much of the remainder of the poem celebrates the spatial connections made by various bridges. There is a nod back to Oswald's earlier treatment of such issues in the plea 'May two fields be bridged by a stile' (16), and also an indication that differences between human individuals need bridging. All of this might lead one to anticipate a rounding off that celebrates organic unity, but the two final lines come up with a surprise: 'And may I often wake on the broken bridge of a word, / Like in the wind the trace of a web. Tethered to nothing' (18–19). There is no full stop after the final 'nothing', leaving the poem hanging, as it were, between nihilism and an incomplete pursuit after articulation. Timothy Morton's conception of a more sceptical form of ecology, an ecology without nature that entails 'a relentless questioning of essence',[92] provides one feasible way of reading this ending.

Oswald may be a poet who celebrates marriages and the unifications made by bridges, but she is also very aware, then, of the differences and gaps that predate any such mediation. Poetry does forge links through use of figurative language, yet it also lays bare the gaps and pauses – or broken bridges – that lie in between. In her remarkable long poem, *Dart*, Oswald exemplifies this by including a central pause that constitutes something of a hinge around which the whole poem revolves. This occurs immediately following lines that seek to portray the final thoughts of a historical figure, John Edmunds, before he drowned at Staverton Ford in 1840. After the words 'the silence pouring into what's left maybe eighty seconds',[93] Oswald leaves a large empty space, which is only tenuously broken by the word 'silence' in the right-hand margin. Like Oswald's ideal poetic line, then, *Dart* is broken in two by a central, spatial interruption.

The poem as a whole follows the Devon river from its source in Cranmere Pool, on Dartmoor, all the way down to the sea. It is site-specific, using the geographical make-up of the river as its prime mode of organization. In what might sound like an overly submissive response to the world of cartographers, word follows place. Has not

Eavan Boland, for instance, told us 'That the Science of Cartography Is Limited', inferior as it is, in some respects, to poetry's ability to capture the historical imbrication of pain and place?[94] Yet an excess of subjectivity can also be censured for its overly selective consequences. As in Elizabeth Bishop's poem 'Map', a levelling gesture underpins the use of geography in Oswald's poem: the small, seemingly insignificant spots are not neglected for the haunts of tourist or local historian.[95] The figure or schema of the map – the importance of which is hinted at by an old man who 'consults his map' (1) at the very beginning – eradicates the hierarchies of mind and history.

Indeed, history itself might, at first sight, seem to be completely absent in *Dart*. As the poet's short prose introduction points out, the text 'is made from the language of people who live and work on the Dart. Over the past two years I've been recording conversations with people who know the river' (unnumbered). Although the poem is far from being a straightforward reproduction of these interviews, these sources give the text something of the feel of an anthropological field report. We are provided, as it were, with a synthesis of the voices and activities of the present users of the river, rather than any wider sweep or explicit contextualization. As the river is in a constant state of passing by, so life itself is just a matter of one moment – 'thrown into this agony of being swept away' (7).

Read this way, *Dart* can be interpreted as expressing much the same negation of memory and time as is attempted, at least partially, in Oswald's shorter poems. A closer look, however, indicates that the long poem in some ways transcends the aesthetics of her other texts. Most obviously, the use of several different voices undermines the solitary lyric voice typical of her shorter work. Although *Dart* frequently attains a hauntingly lyric voice – particularly in its central dream song (cf. 27–28) – there is a wide range of registers and tones present, something which is underlined by the alternation between various lyric forms and short prose monologues. While we on one extreme have the river itself muttering the traditional sounds of 'come tongue-in-skull, come drinketh, come sleepeth' (15), on the other we have the dairy worker dryly informing us about his daily routines (cf. 29). Capturing not only the voices of water nymphs and other fictional *genius loci*, the poem also allows naturalists, fishermen, oyster gatherers, crabbers, tinners, boatbuilders, bailiffs, ferrymen, sealwatchers, foresters, wool workers, and dairy workers, as well as various tourists and day-trippers, to have their say. The poem is also broad in its sweep regarding other forms of life, including lists of the birds present on the river (11), types of water (17),

varieties of stone (33), and names of boats (34–36). Despite moderniza-
tion, there is biodiversity: even in the twenty-first century, the river is
solicitous of a teeming manifold of existence. As such it is like a tree
in the poem, which we are told will 'stand getting slowly thicker and
taller, taking care of its surroundings, full of birds and moss and cavities
where the bats'll roost and fly out when you work into dusk' (12).

The poem's rich panoply of daily life undermines the solitary nature
of the lyric form, thus conforming to Jonathan Bate's claim that the
'ecopoetic vision is inclusive, not exclusionary'.[96] It also frames the
voices in practical, everyday tasks, in a way that can be contrasted with
the more freely floating and disembodied voice of the traditional lyric.
If the activities mentioned bring with them a closer intimacy with the
earth and elements, they also imply a temporality of their own. Rather
than the isolated moment of the vision, the speakers of *Dart* are engaged
in the ongoing, and iterative, temporality of work. As Oswald interprets
it, work involves a physical engagement with matter. It reconfigures
subjectivity, rooting it more firmly in the body.

Not only the individual, bodily experience of work, but also the
large-scale operations of plants and factories are included in *Dart*. In
The Song of the Earth, Jonathan Bate endorses Heidegger's exemplifying
of the overly dominating way of interacting of a river with the use of
the Rhine for a power plant.[97] Treating nature as an object, rather than
a dwelling place, is, in Bate's view, an important cause of the ecological
crisis. On this point, Oswald comes across as more inclusive than the
ecological theorist, however. *Dart* includes important passages giving
voice to workers at an alluvial plant (17–18), a woollen mill (20), a water
abstractor (24–26), and a milk factory (29–30). Not all of these are without satirical or critical nuances of tone, yet generally the poem shows a
delight in how the river has important uses far beyond its own shores.
It does not constitute a delimited, idyllic place, but is the point of intersection for a variety of spatial relations of trade and traffic.

One example of this is when the tin-extractor accounts for the beginnings of his present occupation in his first findings, quite some time
ago, in his own fields. He then 'began to work slowly upriver looking for
the shodes, the bigger tin-stones that lie close to the source. I followed
it up a brook of the Dart and built my own alluvial plant with a pump
re-circulating the water' (17). Another genesis narrative is provided by
the ballad rendering of the myth concerning Brutus's landing on the
Dart, after the Trojan war, as the origin of Britain: in Oswald's version,
it's emphasized that these founding fathers were marginal figures, 'out-
casts of the earth' (31), rather than pillars of society. Generally, though,

Dart tends to shy away not only from the kind of 'history-through-topography' that Bate traces from William Camden to Wordsworth,[98] but also from all narratives of origin. We are fairly far removed from the linking of place and collective memory to nationhood characteristic of *Idylls of a King*, or even the more tenuous tendencies in *Four Quartets*.

Still, the past makes itself felt in other, less teleological ways: not only through the ongoing, institutional work of power plants and factories, but even more through the ghostly voices of the many individuals who have died on the river. Deryn Rees-Jones has claimed that, in *Dart*,

> Oswald seems to be offering the lives of those who live and work alongside the River Dart as a collective version of a historical moment in which biography and autobiography, which become our histories, are scrutinised in relation to nature and thus redefine it as they coalesce into a dramatised autobiography of place.[99]

This elegantly dovetails several important themes in the text, emphasizing the work of those who interact with the river as well as the way in which several individual voices together create a fragmented collective utterance. As a 'collective version of a historical moment', *Dart* takes more the form of a construction of a collective memory than any form of institutionalized history. The obsessive way in which the poem returns to the dead of the river draws attention to another important distinction, glossed over by Rees-Jones's use of the term 'autobiography'. For *Dart* does not so much retell the lives of these figures, i.e., present their autobiographies, as dwell on the circumstances of their demises. Apart from the archive the poem itself produces of the various places of, and events that have taken place on, the river, *Dart* is not concerned with using memory as a means of storing the past in anything resembling a total or surveyable form. Rather, it deploys the past as an intimation of our own mortality, a natural *memento mori*, manifesting that, before long, we will all be as long gone as the mythical figure Jan Coo, who is said to haunt the Dart (cf. 4).

Death is presented as a limit-experience that constantly impinges upon our own lives, a state that is impossible to fathom but that nevertheless can be approached from afar as a metaphor for a deeper, less self-bound involvement in being. In this respect, Oswald is not far removed from Maurice Blanchot's understanding of dying as a paradoxical step beyond the limitations of empirical selfhood.[100] While Oswald says of the dead tinners of the West Dart that 'Some are photos, others dust' (10), she is generally more fascinated by the very moment where one passes beyond integral subjectivity than interested in reflecting upon death from a distance. Thus a canoeist is 'pinioned by the pressure, the whole river-power of Dartmoor', to the point that he becomes 'a tattered shape in a perilous relationship with time' (15). Drowning, John Edmunds experiences that his 'voice is being washed away / out of a lapse in my throat' (20). The river takes over his voice, appropriating it to itself, as it does later with that of a sealwatcher: 'Self-maker, speaking its meaning over mine' (48).

Ultimately, Oswald would want us to recognize that all of the voices of the poem are appropriated in such a manner. Her introductory note puts this bluntly: 'All voices should be read as the river's mutterings' (unnumbered). The ending of *Dart* also makes a similar point, subsuming all the speakers to the river's own self:

> This is me, anonymous, water's soliloquy,
>
> all names, all voices, Slip-Shape, this is Proteus,
> whoever that is, the shepherd of the seals,
> driving my many selves from cave to cave.
>
> (48)

We are, then, returned to the kind of poetics we encountered earlier, in Oswald's 'Sea Poem'. But *Dart* is not simply an attempt to capture the element of water in its very being, somehow divested of an external, human perspective. It presents a more differential structure than that: allowing the many human voices (both dead and alive) of a river to be heard in their own right, the poem would finally appropriate all of these to the river's own self-expression. Through its inclusiveness, the achieved voice is impure and multifarious; a 'jabber of pidgin-river' (15). In retrospect, Oswald has admitted that this is a simulacrum: 'Ideally I'd create water, but I've had to make do with mimicking it – a rush of selves, a stronghold of other life-forms.'[101] Such an admission should be taken as a salutary sign of forthrightness rather than as an instance of simple self-contradiction. As Timothy Morton points out, the 'best environmental art is deconstructed from the inside'.[102] As such, *Dart* remains a compelling testament to a profoundly ecological exigency, one that twists poetry into fascinating new shapes. This newness comes about through various constructed transcendences of the givens of a traditional poetic idiom, yet the resulting poetry operates in productive tension with – rather than complete obliviousness to – the subjectivity and memory of that idiom.

In this respect, my reading of Alice Oswald's poetry has some similarity to those made, earlier in this chapter, of the poetics and poetry
of Eavan Boland and J. H. Prynne. Through more or less representative figures, feminism, late modernism and ecopoetry would seem to
have been exposed to what might be construed as a deconstruction
of mystified attempts not only to renounce oppressive pasts, but also
to unlink poetry from memory itself. In Boland's case, of course, the
poet would herself be an accomplice to this gesture, having distanced
herself throughout *Object Lessons* from the more radical form of forgetting embraced by some feminists. Hopefully, though, the itineraries of
these readings have been more nuanced than this. The ways in which
these poets have embraced not only various forms of spatiality (in concordance with a general spatial emphasis in postmodernism), but also
other times – another past for Boland, an embattled future for Prynne,
an impossible present for Oswald – cannot be said to be ingenuous or
misguided. If memory and a general orientation towards the past are
an inescapable fact of not only poetry but human existence *per se*, so is
a passionate engagement with the present and a hopeful, desiring, and
at times despairing impetus towards the future. Like several other contemporary poets – and other movements and schools – not addressed
here, Boland, Prynne, and Oswald not only provide good reasons to
rethink how we engage with the past, but also force us to reconsider
the fundamentals underlying the constitution of a poetic canon. Most
clearly, perhaps, their poetry has tended to critically challenge the
subject-oriented and holistic nature of memory characteristic of most
of the preceding readings in this book. If the present point in history
constitutes a unique time for poetic memory, it is mainly due to these
two specific challenges.

6
Conclusion: Imperfect Hindsight

Some poets have a distinguished afterlife thrust upon them; others achieve it after extensive preparation. The latter, more often than not, involves spending significant amounts of time during the later parts of a career either revising old texts or making sure that the correct account (often in the form of a biographical narrative) is handed down to future generations. For figures such as Tennyson, Hardy, and Yeats, the legacy of the poet – his or her memory in years to come – is something to be carefully moulded in one's own lifetime, with an eye to future audiences. As a result, the afterlife of the poet is to have something of a monument's solidity and majesty. What would Yeats have made of the Dutch novelist Cees Nooteboom's memorable comparison of memory to a dog that lies down where it pleases?[1] Most likely, he would have been no more impressed than he would have been by my attempt, in Chapter 3, to bring the stray, suppressed memories surrounding his self-commemorative effort in 'Under Ben Bulben' into the light. The contemporary view on memory is more sceptical, or less credulous, than the one Yeats cultivated. If there was already at his time (to use Richard Terdiman's phrase) a 'memory crisis',[2] scepticism regarding memory's powers and persistence is even more pronounced now.

This study has, then, been in line with a *Zeitgeist* that declares that grand narratives are difficult, if not impossible, to uphold, and that memory is more characteristically a faculty that stalls or misfires than a deliverer of perfect hindsight. With regard to the study of poetry, being attuned to variations and problems regarding memory arguably has beneficent consequences. It is not a case of crudely transforming the poet's 'priceless things' into 'a post the passing dogs defile' (Yeats, 'While I from that reed-throated whisperer', 13–14): rather than being reduced, poetry's riches become all the more apparent when one does not flatten out memory's work as something simple or straightforwardly monumental. Ethically, too, an understanding of the limitations and situated nature of the remembering subject may have the salutary effect of preventing *hubris*. In this respect, the tenor of this book has been broadly informed by Heideggerian and post-Heideggerian thought, a heritage that consistently challenges the overweening subject and its use of instrumental rationality.

Yet the bravado of the craftsmanship and system-building procliv-ities of a poet such as W. B. Yeats still compels fascination. If it is easier to tear down than to build up, and if the deconstructive and sceptical gestures of post-structuralism and its sequels have gained a measure of predictability with their widespread acceptance (albeit more often than not in a more historicized form), then the real challenge, at this junc-ture, may be to construct and conjoin rather than to keep niggling away at insufficiencies. Certainly, poetry that does not simply surrender to the quandaries and pressures of memory can both prove empowering and help our understanding of how recollection works. As a result, this book has tried to combine a questioning approach with a patiently reconstructive one in tracing the complex and elaborate architectures of memory – frequently rooted in organic structures – underlying the poetry of writers such as Tennyson and T. S. Eliot.

A similar point may be made with regard to literary history. In an astute article on literary memory from George Eliot to T. S. Eliot, Rick Rylance has asserted: 'Real histories, like memories, are not processional. Nor are they stories of deliverance. They are convoluted and dispersed like experience itself, and the contexts we attribute in them are often sinewy and contingent.'[3] Rylance's point is well taken: it is harder than ever, today, to give credence to teleological narratives of the past. At the same time, too prolonged or too automatically applied forms of scepti-cism degenerate into complacency. A critical understanding of memory involves not merely picking to pieces whatever models and narratives are already out there, but also trying to establish new ones – however tentative and vulnerable the new suspects may be.

If there has been an underlying, historical narrative in this book, it has been one dominated by precisely such a critical conception of memory. Each poet and each era has, in individual fashion, skirted or dismissed a conception of memory that was felt to be unhelpful or inaccurate. In Wordsworth, we see a dismissal of the idea of memory as a mechanical assemblage of past impressions, and instead an embracing of the idea of an organically unified self bolstered by certain privileged spots of time. Later nineteenth century poetry feels that the resulting conception of the poetic subject is too tenuous, or too isolated, and it therefore seeks mediation for the self through investment of its resources in outer places and objects. Yet even here the Victorian tendency towards nostalgia's closure and stasis is a dangerous temptation, which poets such as Hardy and Tennyson have to work hard to circumnavigate. Investment in the memories of place is, for Tennyson and Yeats, interlinked with the politics of nationalism. Seeking a truly international art, modernism subsequently unchains the forces of memory from particular places. Also severing its connection with the personal, remembering self, the idea of a collective, aesthetic memory called 'tradition' takes hold – as has been shown in the reading of Eliot's 'Tradition and the Individual Talent'. Similarly to the earlier conception of individual memory, the modernist alternative may suffer from its own too rarefied nature: in a poem such as *Four Quartets*, both self and place again accrue important roles in the deployment of poetic memory, and the ambitious extremism of modernism appears to have capsized.

For some, this is the reigning state of affairs in British and Irish poetry today: modernism itself appears to have become a distant memory, and poets such as Thomas Hardy or Robert Frost are to be considered more truly our contemporaries than any radically experimenting avant-gardist.[4] Yet, as my previous chapter demonstrated, there are strands of contemporary poetry that rebel against drawing such a conclusion. In Eavan Boland, I identified a politically oriented, revisionary form of memory, preoccupied with going beyond the established bounds of history and literary tradition. The readings of J. H. Prynne and Alice Oswald revealed even more iconoclastic questionings of the very idea of poetical memory: where the former questioned the backward glance on the grounds of its tending to foreclose an unfettered exploration of the future, the latter's ecopoetry eschewed not only poetic nostalgia but all memory in order to transcend the technical rationality of the subject–object dichotomy. Both of the latter rebellions appeared to be in line with a postmodern emphasis on spatiality, reacting against what Edward S. Casey has called 'the continuing miasma of temporocentrism'.[5] But both also seemed, on closer inspection, to opt for revised forms of memory rather than downright dismissals of the value of the past. Prynne's insistent challenges to the reader's teleological schemas were supported by a recourse to an open-ended, metonymical kind of memory, while Oswald's *Dart* went beyond lyrical subjectivity in order to present an inclusive account of collective memory (as well as reminders of individual finitude) in a given, but not delimited, place.

The historical figure – in the sense of a delineated pattern – traced by this study can be summarized in such a manner. Yet neither a rage for order nor an impatience with mere incoherence can hide that the actual itinerary of this book has been more subject to variation and unpredictability than the prescribed motions of a figure skater. Where particularly Chapters 3 and 4 seemed to tend to a certain uniformity of narrative, the final readings of Boland, Prynne, and Oswald revealed a splitting into a variety of differing tendencies. Evidently, the present poetry of England and Ireland constitutes less of a unified tradition than a plurality of approaches and projects. Obviously, scrutiny of the many notable poems and important poets not addressed in this study would most likely reveal an even more complicated and nuanced image of poetry's engagement with memory. Furthermore, the rather simplified overview just presented cannot hide the fact that there has been much, in the preceding readings of this book, which militates against any overly streamlined notion of tradition. Certainly, the Irish poets addressed can only be partially understood in light of British literary history, and Irish responses to its postcolonial quandaries represent a forceful and instructive anticipation of the way in which British poetry today is exposed to, and interwoven with, traditions heterogeneous to established narratives of 'Britishness'. The political situation of Ireland also presents one plausible explanation for why, in poets such Yeats and Boland, collective and individual forms of memory are linked closer together than in comparable, English figures.

In addition, the multiplicity of memory revealed in Chapter 2 opens for a variety of narratives, rather than one 'processional' (to use Rylance's term) unfolding. For instance, the historical role of Christina Rossetti's 'Song' appears radically different, whether one sees it primarily as (1) an example of the kind of victimization of woman criticized by Eavan Boland's feminist revision of literary history, (2) a *reductio ad absurdum* of the subject's implosive flight into romantic isolation, or (3) a proto-modernist embracing of literary autonomy. Similarly, Wordsworth's role cannot be circumscribed to some form of straightforward embrace of romantic innerness: my reading showed not only that his conception of poetry transcended the self (thus anticipating later movements beyond subject-centred forms of memory), but also that it suspended the question of memory's nature in a open-ended force field of poetic figures. J. H. Prynne's account of 'The Solitary Reaper' confirmed this, and simultaneously threw a spanner into the works for any too tidy or monological account of literary history: here a politically radical exponent of late modernism found common ground with a poet who has (in some accounts) been presented as a reactive Tory engaged in shoring up an isolated, introspective self. Apparently Wordsworth constitutes something more than a monumental and fixed figure of memory, and even one of the most radical instances of contemporary poetry can draw sustenance from a critical engagement with his heritage.

Privileging a metonymical conception of poetry, Prynne's poetics embraces one of the recurring figures of this book. It has been consistently shown that the poetic use of memory is neither reducible to the closed, self-centred relations of nostalgia, nor adequately described in terms of a literal imitation of perception's data. Poetic memory is better captured in terms of a productive exploration in and through the figurative resources of language. The result may be overwhelming and it may also in some cases be disconcertingly various. Certainly, rather than ordered revelations of essences, this book has not only offered, but also to a large degree championed, rather imperfect forms of hindsight. Far from the exemplary perfection that Yeats, for instance, envisaged as his poetical legacy, it has at least in part been a case of looking at what the dog has dragged in. Hopefully, though, the resulting richness has had the compensating virtue of revealing something of poetry's persistent, critical, and imaginative engagement with the past.

Notes

1 Introduction: The Returns of the Past

1. Richard Terdiman, *Present Past: Modernity and the Memory Crisis* (Ithaca, NY, and London: Cornell University Press, 1993). Through readings of Musset, Baudelaire, Proust, and Freud, Terdiman articulates 'the distress engendered by the memory crisis, by modernity's experience of an uncertain and tense relation to the past' (ibid., 316). The main causes, in Terdiman's account, of this crisis are (1) the oppressive weight of the sheer mass of available memories, and (2) the fracturing of the self through the separation of its present identity from those of its past. The latter feature is particularly relevant to my own study. Another significant forerunner to my own study is Philip Davis's more autobiographically slanted work on memory and writing in English literature. His book *Memory and Writing: From Wordsworth to Lawrence* (Liverpool: Liverpool University Press, 1983) shows how writing undermines any pure naturalness in literature's acts of memory.
2. Terdiman, *Present Past*, 19.
3. David Farrell Krell, *Of Memory, Reminiscence, and Writing: On the Verge* (Bloomington: Indiana University Press, 1990), 14–15. Unless otherwise mentioned emphases found in quoted material are found in the original.
4. Saint Augustine, *Confessions*, translated by R. S. Pine-Coffin (London: Penguin, 1961), 223.
5. See for instance 'The Return to Philology', in Paul de Man, *The Resistance to Theory* (Minneapolis: University of Minnesota Press, 1986). Recently, cognitive theories of metaphor have tended to stress the epistemological value of figurative language (see for instance George Lakoff and Mark Johnson, *Metaphors We Live By* (Chicago: University of Chicago Press, 1980)). In doing so, they have confirmed and buttressed positions presented by I. A. Richards, particularly in *The Philosophy of Rhetoric* (Oxford: Oxford University Press, 1965 (1936)).
6. Nicholas Dames, *Amnesiac Selves: Nostalgia, Forgetting, and British Fiction, 1810–1870* (Oxford: Oxford University Press, 2001), 14.
7. Paul Ricoeur, *Memory, History, Forgetting*, translated by Kathleen Balmey and David Pellauer (Chicago: University of Chicago Press, 2004).
8. Pierre Nora, 'General Introduction: Between Memory and History', in Nora (ed.), *Realms of Memory: Rethinking the French Past*, volume I, edited by Lawrence D. Kritzman, translated by Arthur Goldhammer (New York: Columbia University Press, 1996), 18.
9. Ibid., 15.
10. Excluded fragment no. viii ('He was too good and kind and sweet'), line 8, included in Alfred, Lord Tennyson, *In Memoriam*, edited by Susan Shatto and Marion Shaw (Oxford: Clarendon Press, 1982), 152–153.

2 Multiplicity and Mourning: Wordsworth, Christina Rossetti, Tennyson

1. Cf. Fredric Jameson, *The Political Unconscious: Narrative as a Socially Symbolic Act* (London: Methuen, 1981). For evidence of Jameson's crucial influence on historicist interpretations of Wordsworth, see pages 127 and 129–130 of Marjorie Levinson's *Wordsworth's Great Period Poems: Four Essays* (Cambridge: Cambridge University Press, 1986) and page 50 of Alan Liu's *Wordsworth: The Sense of History* (Stanford: Stanford University Press, 1989).
2. Kenneth R. Johnston, *The Hidden Wordsworth: Poet, Lover, Rebel, Spy* (New York: W. W. Norton & Company, 1998), 8.
3. Jerome McGann, *The Romantic Ideology: A Critical Investigation* (Chicago: University of Chicago Press, 1983).
4. John Locke, *An Essay Concerning Human Understanding*, volume I, edited by Alexander Campbell Fraser (New York: Dover, 1959), 449.
5. Jorge Luis Borges, *Labyrinths: Selected Stories and Other Writings*, edited by Donald A. Yates and James E. Irby (London: Penguin, 1970), 94.
6. 'My heart leaps up', lines 8–9. All references to Wordworth's poetry, apart from *The Prelude*, refer to William Wordsworth, *The Poems*, volume I, edited by John O. Hayden (Harmondsworth: Penguin, 1977).
7. All quotations from *The Prelude* given directly in the body of the text refer, unless stated otherwise, to book and line number of the 1805 version of *The Prelude*. All citations use the following edition: William Wordsworth, *The Prelude: The Four Texts (1798, 1799, 1805, 1850)*, edited by Jonathan Wordsworth (London: Penguin, 1995).
8. For the much-cited description of the function of the 'spots of time', see the passage in *The Prelude*, book XI, beginning with line 257.
9. 'Preface to *Lyrical Ballads*', in Wordsworth, *The Poems*, I, 886.
10. Wordsworth, *The Poems*, I, 979.
11. Robert Langbaum, 'The Evolution of Soul in Wordsworth's Poetry', 226, in W. J. Harvey and Richard Gravil (eds), *Wordsworth: The Prelude. A Casebook* (London: Macmillan, 1972).
12. Geoffrey H. Hartman, *The Fate of Reading and Other Essays* (Chicago: University of Chicago Press, 1975), 292.
13. Paul de Man's reading of the 'Boy of Winander' episode concurs with Hartman's in that it interprets the mourning of the boy as evincing a problem of the self: it is 'the epitaph written by the poet for himself' (Paul de Man, *Romanticism and Contemporary Criticism: The Gauss Seminar and Other Papers*, edited by E. S. Burt, Kevin Newmark, and Andrzej Warminski (Baltimore, MD: Johns Hopkins University Press, 1993), 82).
14. See especially Emmanuel Levinas, *Time and the Other*, translated by Richard A. Cohen (Pittsburgh: Duquesne University Press, 1987).
15. William Hazlitt, *The Complete Works*, volume I (London: J. M. Dent & Sons, 1930), 9.
16. Ibid., 11.
17. On Wordsworth's familiarity with this essay, see note 34 on page 286 of James K. Chandler, *Wordsworth's Second Nature: A Study of the Poetry and Politics* (Chicago: University of Chicago Press, 1984).

18. Michael H. Friedman, *The Makings of a Tory Humanist: William Wordsworth and the Idea of Community* (New York: Columbia University Press, 1979), 10.
19. 1799 *Prelude*, line 3 (line 273 of book I in the 1805 version).
20. Paul de Man, *The Rhetoric of Romanticism* (New York: Columbia University Press, 1984), 91.
21. Geoffrey H. Hartman, *The Fateful Question of Culture* (New York: Columbia University Press, 1997), 70.
22. On this theme, see Krell, *Of Memory, Reminiscence, and Writing*.
23. 'Tintern Abbey', lines 65–66.
24. Ibid., lines 138–142.
25. David Bromwich, *Disowned by Memory: Wordsworth's Poetry of the 1790s* (Chicago: University of Chicago Press, 1998), 175.
26. See Bromwich's 'biographical surmise' in ibid., 17.
27. 1850 *Prelude*, I, 613–615.
28. See Friedrich Nietzsche, *Also Sprach Zarathustra* in *Werke in drei Bänden*, volume 2, edited by Karl Schlechta (Darmstadt: Wissenschaftliche Buchgesellschaft, 1997 (1955)), 394.
29. Harold Bloom, *The Western Canon: The Books and School of the Ages* (London: Papermac, 1995), 253.
30. Martin Heidegger, *Being and Time: A Translation of 'Sein und Zeit'*, translated by Joan Stambaugh (New York: State University of New York Press, 1996).
31. Recent scholarship has provided a nuanced understanding of nineteenth century nostalgia. For three complementing, but also in some ways conflicting, accounts, see Ann C. Colley's *Nostalgia and Recollection in Victorian Culture* (Basingstoke: Palgrave, 1998), Nicholas Dames's *Amnesiac Selves: Nostalgia, Forgetting, and British Fiction, 1810–1870*, and Linda M. Austin's *Nostalgia in Transition, 1780–1917* (Charlottesville and London: University of Virginia Press, 2007). I return to nostalgia in more detail in Chapter 3.
32. Lines 200–207 of book V of Elizabeth Barrett Browning, *Aurora Leigh*, edited by Kerry McSweeney (Oxford: Oxford University Press, 1993), 152–153.
33. All references to this and other poems by Christina Rossetti draw upon the following edition of her work: Christina Rossetti, *The Complete Poems*, with text by R. W. Crump, notes and introduction by Betty S. Flowers (London: Penguin, 2001).
34. See Gilles Deleuze, *Nietzsche and Philosophy*, translated by Janis A. Tomlinson and Hugh Tomlinson (New York: Columbia University Press, 1985).
35. Rossetti, *The Complete Poems*, 294.
36. Eric Griffiths, 'The Disappointment of Christina G. Rossetti', in *Essays in Criticism*, 1997, vol. XLVII(2), 121–122.
37. Angela Leighton, '"When I Am Dead, My Dearest": The Secret of Christina Rossetti', in *Modern Philology*, 1990, vol. 87(4), 380.
38. Betty S. Flowers, 'Notes', in Christina Rossetti, *The Complete Poems*, text by R. W. Crump, notes and introduction by Betty S. Flowers (London: Penguin, 2001), 889.
39. Leighton, '"When I Am Dead, My Dearest": The Secret of Christina Rossetti', 375.
40. Ibid.
41. Without making the link to the Sappho poems, Constance W. Hassett makes a similar reading of 'Song', insisting that the mood of the poem's

final lines 'can be read in any number of ways *except* as straightforward disinterest' (Constance W. Hassett, *Christina Rossetti: The Patience of Style* (Charlottesville and London: University of Virginia Press, 2005), 31).

42. Sandra M. Gilbert and Susan Gubar, *The Madwoman in the Attic: The Woman Writer and the Nineteenth-Century Literary Imagination* (New Haven, CT, and London: Yale University Press, 1984), 564.

43. Hassett, *Christina Rossetti*, 57.

44. Jan Marsh, *Christina Rossetti: A Literary Biography* (London: Jonathan Cape, 1994), 96. See ibid., 101, for speculation about a link between the poem and the engagement.

45. See Lawrence Lipking, *Abandoned Women and Poetic Tradition* (Chicago: Chicago University Press, 1988).

46. Jerome J. McGann, 'Christina Rossetti's Poems', in Angela Leighton (ed.), *Victorian Women Poets: A Critical Reader* (Oxford: Blackwell, 1996), 97.

47. Ibid., 100.

48. Isobel Armstrong, *Victorian Poetry: Poetry, Poetics and Politics* (London and New York: Routledge, 1993), 351.

49. Hassett, *Christina Rossetti*, 37.

50. Cf. J. Hillis Miller, *The Linguistic Moment: From Wordsworth to Stevens* (Princeton: Princeton University Press, 1985).

51. W. H. Auden, 'Introduction', x, in Alfred, Lord Tennyson, *Tennyson: A Selection and an Introduction*, edited by W. H. Auden (London: Phoenix House, 1946).

52. Although Ann C. Colley complicates our understanding of Victorian nostalgia, she allows that it can involve 'a genuine impulse to discover refuge from the vicissitudes of time and to nestle in an environment where one's being is confirmed rather than always doubted. It is a way of closing the question of identity' (*Nostalgia and Recollection in Victorian Culture*, 77).

53. Cited in Hallam T. Tennyson, *Alfred Lord Tennyson: A Memoir by His Son*, volume I (Bridgewater: Baker & Taylor, 1989), 81; emphasis added.

54. 'He said that "The passion of the past, the abiding in the transient, was expressed in 'Tears, Idle Tears', which was written in the yellowing autumn-tide at Tintern Abbey, full for me of its bygone memories"' (cited in Hallam T. Tennyson, *A Memoir*, I, 253).

55. Antonio Negri, *Time for Revolution*, translated by Matteo Mandarini (New York: Continuum, 2003), 165.

56. See Sigmund Freud, 'Mourning and Melancholia' in Freud, *General Psychological Theory: Papers on Metapsychology*, edited by Philip Rieff (New York: Collier, 1963); Peter M. Sacks, *The English Elegy: Studies in the Genre from Spenser to Yeats* (Baltimore, MD: Johns Hopkins University Press, 1985).

57. For quotation of poems by Tennyson other than *In Memoriam* and *Idylls of the King*, I refer to the following source: Alfred, Lord Tennyson, *Tennyson: A Selected Edition*, edited by Christopher Ricks (Harlow: Longman, 1989 (1969)).

58. Seamus Perry, for instance, reads these poems in roughly similar ways. See *Alfred Tennyson* (Tavistock: Northcote, 2005), 33–35 and 127–152.

59. Angela Leighton, 'Touching Forms: Tennyson and Aestheticism', in *The Tennyson Research Bulletin*, 2001, vol. 7(5), 230.

60. Robert Douglas-Fairhurst, *Victorian Afterlives: The Shaping of Influence in Nineteenth-Century Literature* (Oxford: Oxford University Press, 2002), 252.

61. Excluded fragment no. viii ('He was too good and kind and sweet'), line 8.
62. For a discussion of the role of this image, see Leighton, 'Touching Forms: Tennyson and Aestheticism'.
63. Maurice Blanchot, *The Space of Literature*, translated by Ann Smock (Lincoln: University of Nebraska Press, 1982), 149.
64. See the essays 'The Image of Proust' and 'The Work of Art in the Age of Mechanical Reproduction', in Walter Benjamin, *Illuminations: Essays and Reflections*, edited by Hannah Arendt, translated by Harry Zohn (New York: Schocken, 1968).
65. See Ricks's editorial comments in *Tennyson: A Selected Edition*, edited by Christopher Ricks (Harlow: Longman, 1989 (1969)), 984.
66. Dames, *Amnesiac Selves*, 6.
67. Hallam T. Tennyson, *A Memoir*, I, 252.
68. Tennyson's jewel image does not, on the immediate surface, involve any explicit reference to waste or idle ostentatiousness. The reworking of the same image in *Maud* might, however, be said to uncover the covert presence of such associations: 'barbarous opulence jewel-thick / Sunned itself on his breast and his hands' (I, 455–456).
69. Ibid., II, 203.
70. *Princess Ida*, section IV, lines 58, 51, and 55–56.
71. Edward S. Casey, *Remembering: A Phenomenological Study*, second edition (Bloomington: Indiana University Press, 2000 (1987)), 218.
72. Timothy Peltason, *Reading 'In Memoriam'* (Princeton: Princeton University Press, 1985), 15.
73. Stéphane Mallarmé, *A Tomb for Anatole*, translated by Paul Auster (San Francisco: North Point Press, 1983), 183.
74. Stéphane Mallarmé, 'Tennyson, Seen from Here', translated by Mary Ann Caws, 257, in *The Tennyson Research Bulletin*, 2001, vol. 7(7).
75. James Stevens Curl, *The Victorian Celebration of Death* (Stroud: Sutton Publishing, 2000), 176–177.

3   Weird Wests: Victorian and Post-Victorian Displacements of Nostalgia

1. Austin, *Nostalgia in Transition*, 19. Austin is not alone in tracing links between literary memory and nineteenth century science. For an intriguing account, see Rick Rylance, 'Twisting: Memory from Eliot to Eliot', in Matthew Campbell, Jacqueline M. Labbe, and Sally Shuttleworth (eds), *Memory and Memorials, 1789–1914: Literary and Cultural Perspectives* (London: Routledge, 2000).
2. Austin, *Nostalgia in Transition*, 58.
3. Ibid., 81.
4. Ibid., 199.
5. Ibid., 61.
6. The term 'displacement' has entered literary studies via psychoanalysis, as a translation of Freud's *Verschiebung*. Jacques Lacan links the concept with metonymy in 'Agency of the Letter in the Unconscious' in *Écrits: A Selection*, translated by Alan Sheridan (New York: Norton, 1977). My own usage not

208 *Notes*

      only makes use of this link, but also plays on the fact that the poets in question encounter displacements of meaning via the issue of place.

7. Norman Malcolm, 'Memory and Representation', in *Noûs*, 1970, vol. 4(1), 63.
8. Hallam T. Tennyson, *Alfred Lord Tennyson: A Memoir by His Son*, vol. II (Bridgewater: Baker & Taylor, 1989), 127.
9. Quotation of particular books and line numbers from *Idylls of the King* will make reference to the following edition: Alfred, Lord Tennyson, *Idylls of the King*, edited by J. M. Gray (London: Penguin, 1983).
10. For the concept of mimetic desire, see René Girard, *Deceit, Desire and the Novel: Self and Other in Literary Structure*, translated by Yvonne Freccero (Baltimore, MD: Johns Hopkins University Press, 1966).
11. A number of recent studies have investigated the virtualities involved in Victorian uses of ghosts. See for instance Robert Douglas-Fairhurst's *Victorian Afterlives*, Julian Wolfreys's *Victorian Hauntings: Spectrality, Gothic, the Uncanny and Literature* (Basingstoke: Palgrave Macmillan, 2002) and Tim Armstrong's *Haunted Hardy: Poetry, History, Memory* (Basingstoke: Palgrave Macmillan, 2000).
12. Hallam T. Tennyson, *A Memoir*, II, 127.
13. On these stances with regard to history, see 'On the Uses and Disadvantages of History for Life' in Friedrich Nietzsche, *Untimely Meditations*, edited by Daniel Breazeale, translated by R. J. Hollingdale (Cambridge: Cambridge University Press, 1997).
14. Roger Simpson, *Camelot Regained: The Arthurian Revival and Tennyson, 1800–1849* (Cambridge: D. S. Brewer, 1990), 220.
15. Peter Ackroyd, *Albion: The Origins of the English Imagination* (London: Chatto & Windus, 2002), 118.
16. Hallam T. Tennyson, *A Memoir*, II, 123.
17. Ibid., 202–203.
18. See 'Tennyson's Faith: *In Memoriam A. H. H.*', in Wolfreys, *Victorian Hauntings*, 54–73.
19. Paul Ricoeur, *Memory, History, Forgetting*, 7.
20. All references to Hardy's poetry in this chapter make use of the following edition: Thomas Hardy, *The Complete Poems*, edited by James Gibson (Basingstoke: Palgrave, 2001).
21. Paul Zietlow, *Moments of Vision: The Poetry of Thomas Hardy* (Cambridge, MA: Harvard University Press, 1974), 161.
22. Donald Davie, 'Hardy's Virgilian Purples', in *Agenda*, 1972, vol. 10(2–3), 156.
23. M. L. Rosenthal and Sally M. Gall, *The Modern Poetic Sequence: The Genius of Modern Poetry* (New York and Oxford: Oxford University Press, 1983), 83.
24. Ibid., 84.
25. Casey, *Remembering*, 182.
26. Ibid., 183.
27. J. Hillis Miller, *Thomas Hardy: Distance and Desire* (London: Oxford University Press, 1970), 250.
28. Philip Davis, 'Memory through the Looking Glass: Ruskin Versus Hardy', 91, in Matthew Campbell, Jacqueline M. Labbe, and Sally Shuttleworth (eds), *Memory and Memorials, 1789–1914: Literary and Cultural Perspectives* (London: Routledge, 2000).

29. David Farrell Krell glosses Aristotle's argument on this issue as follows: 'Remembrance instigates a peculiar kind of presence. It "has" an object of perception or knowledge without activating perception or knowledge as such and without confusing past and present. For while remembering, a man tells himself that he is now present to something that was earlier' (Krell, *Of Memory, Reminiscence, and Writing*, 15). Tom Paulin argues that Hardy wants to transcend memory in *Thomas Hardy: The Poetry of Perception*, second edition (Basingstoke: Macmillan, 1986), 59.
30. Colley, *Nostalgia and Recollection in Victorian Culture*, 120.
31. For a Derridean reading of ashes in Hardy's poems for Emma, see Armstrong, *Haunted Hardy*, chapter 6.
32. Ellen Anne Lanzano, *Hardy: The Temporal Poetics* (New York: Peter Lang, 1999), 47.
33. Davie, 'Hardy's Virgilian Purples', 150.
34. Lanzano, *Hardy*, 77.
35. Ibid., 80.
36. Ibid., 85.
37. Ibid., 106.
38. Ibid., 89.
39. Casey, *Remembering*, 189.
40. Armstrong, *Haunted Hardy*, 138.
41. Thomas Hardy, *A Pair of Blue Eyes* (Oxford: Oxford University Press, 2005), 3, 208, and 199.
42. Thomas Hardy, *The Dynasts* and *the Famous Tragedy of the Queen of Cornwall* (London: Macmillan, 1931), 533.
43. Matthew Campbell, *Rhythm and Will in Victorian Poetry* (Cambridge: Cambridge University Press, 1999), 229.
44. Casey, *Remembering*, 195.
45. Claire Tomalin, *Thomas Hardy: The Time-Torn Man* (London: Viking, 2006), xix.
46. Gillian Beer, *Darwin's Plots: Evolutionary Narrative in Darwin, George Eliot and Nineteenth-Century Fiction* (London: Routledge & Kegan Paul, 1983), 254.
47. Thomas Hardy, *Tess of the D'Urbervilles* (Oxford: Oxford University Press, 1983), 142.
48. On memory and World War I, see Paul Fussell's classic study, *The Great War and Modern Memory* (Oxford: Oxford University Press, 2000 (1975)).
49. Mary Jacobus, 'Hardy's Magian Retrospect', in *Essays in Criticism*, 1982, vol. 32, 275.
50. Ibid., 261.
51. All quotations from Yeats's poetry refer to the following edition: W. B. Yeats, *The Poems*, edited by Daniel Albright (London: Everyman, 1990).
52. A. N. Wilson, *The Victorians* (London: Hutchinson, 2002), 539.
53. See the discussion of Sade's will in Philippe Ariès, *The Hour of Our Death*, translated by Helen Weaver (Oxford: Oxford University Press, 1981), 351–352.
54. See Robert Macfarlane, *Mountains of the Mind: A History of a Fascination* (London: Granta, 2003).
55. W. B. Yeats, *A Vision* (London: Papermac, 1981 (1937)), 7. On page 54 of the same book, in a different context, Yeats states: 'I recall what Plato said of memory.'

56. Thus the mountain is not a natural image, but rather akin to what Paul de Man has called an 'emblem'. See 'Image and Emblem in Yeats', in de Man, *The Rhetoric of Romanticism*.
57. W. B. Yeats, *Mythologies* (London: Papermac, 1989 (1959)), 89.
58. Ibid., 90.
59. Ibid., 70.
60. Brenda Maddox, *George's Ghosts: A New Life of W. B. Yeats* (London: Picador, 1999), 364.
61. Jahan Ramazani, *Yeats and the Poetry of Death: Elegy, Self-Elegy, and the Sublime* (New Haven, CT: Yale University Press, 1990), 148. See also Jahan Ramazani, *Poetry of Mourning: The Modern Elegy from Hardy to Heaney* (Chicago and London: University of Chicago Press, 1994), 213.
62. William Butler Yeats, *Later Essays*, edited by William H. O'Donnell, with assistance from Elizabeth Bermann Loizeaux (New York: Scribner, 1994), 143–144.
63. Ibid., 144.
64. William Butler Yeats, *Autobiographies*, edited by William H. O'Donnell and Douglas N. Archibald (New York: Scribner, 1999 (1965)), 166–167.
65. In *Four Years*, in a passage preceding the one just quoted, Yeats singles out the setting of Shelley's poem for some criticism: 'I believed that if Morris had set his stories amid the scenery of his own Wales, for I knew him to be of Welsh extraction and supposed wrongly that he had spent his childhood there, that if Shelley had nailed his Prometheus, or some equal symbol, upon some Welsh or Scottish rock, their art would have entered more intimately, more microscopically, as it were, into our thought given perhaps to modern poetry a breadth and stability like that of ancient poetry' (ibid., 137). On Lady Gregory's stories and King Arthur, see ibid., 285 and 335–336.
66. For postcolonial readings of Yeats's appropriation of space, see pages 807–808 of Jahan Ramazani's 'Is Yeats a Postcolonial Poet?' (in David Pierce (ed.), *W. B. Yeats. Critical Assessments: Volume IV, Assessments: 1980–2000* (Mountfield: Helm Information, 2000)) and chapter 3 of Oona Frawley, *Irish Pastoral: Nostalgia and Twentieth-Century Irish Literature* (Dublin: Irish Academic Press, 2005).
67. Compare Michel de Certeau on tactical memory, which he describes as 'composed of individual bits and fragments. One detail, many details, are memories. Each of them, when it emerges in a shadowy setting, is relative to an ensemble that lacks it. Each memory shines like a metonymy in relation to this whole' (*The Practice of Everyday Life*, translated by Steven Rendall (Berkeley: University of California Press, 1984), 88).
68. In my view, Brian Arkins neglects the unsettling effect of having the epitaph exist both within and without 'Under Ben Bulben'. In Arkins's Platonic interpretation, the text addresses 'the human aristocratic horseman of section VI, who mirrors, of course, the divine *daimones*, [and who] must pass Yeats' tomb regardless, as he seeks forever the Beauty of the Intelligible world through Eros' ('Yeats and Platonism', 283, in Anna Baldwin and Sarah Hutton (eds), *Platonism and the English Imagination* (Cambridge: Cambridge University Press, 1994)).

69. Jon Stallworthy's analysis does not dwell upon the epitaph's severance from the rest of the poem, but points out that the 'epitaph is addressed to a horseman who may be one of the Sidhe, or one of the "Hard-riding country gentlemen"; either the living or the dead – or both' (*Vision and Revision in Yeats' 'Last Poems'* (Oxford: Clarendon Press, 1969), 170).

70. For interpretations of the original, see Joachim Wolff's *Rilke's Grabschrift* (Heidelberg: Lothar Stiem Verlag, 1983). The translation is taken from the following edition: R. M. Rilke, *Selected Poems*, translated by A. E. Fleming (New York: Methuen, 1986), 225. Helen Vendler has pointed to the possible influence from two other sources: the epitaphs of Timon (in Shakespeare's *Timon of Athens*) and Coleridge (see Helen Vendler, 'Technique in the Earlier Poems of Yeats', 9–10, in *Yeats Annual*, 1991, no. 8).

71. Stallworthy, *Vision and Revision in Yeats' 'Last Poems'*, 162.

72. Dermot James, *The Gore-Booths of Lissadell* (Dublin: The Woodfield Press, 2004), 131.

73. Anne Marecco, *The Rebel Countess: The Life and Times of Countess Markiewicz* (London: Phoenix Press, 2000 (1967)), 75.

74. Eva Gore-Booth, *Poems* (London: Longmans, Green and Co., 1929), 509.

75. As only one of many examples of this tendency, see Elizabeth Butler Cullingford's claim that 'Markiewicz stands in for Gonne in "Easter 1916"' (*Gender and History in Yeats's Love Poetry* (New York: Syracuse University Press, 1996), 121). Terence Brown endorses this reading, citing the fact that the stone imagery of this poem involves an echo of Yeats's descriptions of Gonne. However, he does not dwell on the fact – mentioned earlier in his own study – that the image of a stone may (specifically in 'To a Friend Whose Work Has Come to Nothing') also be linked to autobiographical descriptions in Yeats's writings (cf. pages 231 and 203 of Brown, *The Life of W.B. Yeats: A Critical Biography* (Oxford: Blackwell, 2001)). Elsewhere, Brown shows scepticism regarding the identification of the female persona addressed in *The Wild Swans at Coole*: 'woman appears in these poems in various guises, more as the multiple figure of womanhood than as a particular person, though the biographers labour to establish specific identities' (ibid., 249).

76. Richard Ellmann, *Golden Codgers: Biographical Speculations* (New York: Oxford University Press, 1973), 107.

77. Yeats, *Autobiographies*, 321.

78. 'The Old Age of Queen Maeve', 30–33.

79. Yeats, *Autobiographies*, 212–213.

80. W. B. Yeats, *Memoirs*, edited by Denis Donoghue (New York: Macmillan, 1972), 78.

81. Cited in R. F. Foster, *W. B. Yeats: A Life. 1. The Apprentice Mage 1865–1914* (Oxford: Oxford University Press, 1998), 23.

82. William Butler Yeats, *The Plays*, edited by David R. Clark and Rosalind E. Clark (New York: Scribner, 2002), 544.

83. Ibid., 45.

84. Frawley, *Irish Pastoral*, 58.

85. Dames, *Amnesiac Selves*, 236.

4   Modernism, Tradition, and Organicism in T. S. Eliot and Heaney

1. Charles Baudelaire, 'The Painter of Modern Life', 142, in Lawrence Cahoone (ed.), *From Modernism to Postmodernism: An Anthology* (Oxford: Blackwell, 1996).
2. Ezra Pound, 'A Retrospect', 24, in W. N. Herbert and Matthew Hollis (eds), *Strong Words: Modern Poets on Modern Poetry* (Tarset: Bloodaxe, 2000).
3. Paul de Man, *Blindness and Insight: Essays in the Rhetoric of Contemporary Criticism*, second edition (London: Routledge, 1983), 161.
4. T. S. Eliot, *The Use of Criticism and the Use of Poetry: Studies in the Relation of Criticism to Poetry in England* (London: Faber and Faber, 1964), 108. All references to Eliot's poetry and drama will refer to the following edition: T. S. Eliot, *The Complete Poems and Plays* (London: Faber and Faber, 1969). References to 'Tradition and the Individual Talent' and other essays from *The Sacred Wood* made in the body of the text refer to T. S. Eliot, *The Sacred Wood* (London: Faber and Faber, 1997 (1960)).
5. In Maud Ellmann's account, Eliot's traditionalism here seems implicitly to constitute a failing of some sort: 'Eliot is attacking expressivism with its own weapons, and he reinstates the feeling subject at the centre of the process of creation at the same time that he attempts to circumscribe his will. While Mallarmé believed that language necessarily entails impersonality, since it is always borrowed from the tribe, Eliot avoids this issue' (*The Poetics of Impersonality: T. S. Eliot and Ezra Pound* (Brighton: The Harvester Press, 1987), 41).
6. Richard Shusterman, *T. S. Eliot and the Philosophy of Criticism* (London: Duckworth, 1988), 157. My disagreement with the readings of Shusterman and others finds some corroboration in a recent study by Gabrielle McIntire, which contends that '"Tradition and the Individual Talent" seems to have compelled generations of misreadings. It has been widely interpreted only in its narrowest sense, as valuing an outmoded and hierarchical value of "tradition"' (*Modernism, Memory, and Desire: T. S. Eliot and Virginia Woolf* (Cambridge: Cambridge University Press, 2008), 109).
7. Shusterman, *T. S. Eliot and the Philosophy of Criticism*, 157.
8. Ibid., 159.
9. Ibid.
10. Ibid.
11. I am of course not implying that the five figures singled out by my argument are the sole ones present in the text: I have made a pragmatically motivated selection.
12. Matthew Arnold, *Lectures and Essays in Criticism* (Ann Arbor: University of Michigan Press, 1963), 263.
13. T. S. Eliot, *The Varieties of Metaphysical Poetry*, edited by Ronald Schuchard (New York: Harcourt Brace, 1993), 138.
14. Ibid., 139.
15. Eliot, *The Use of Criticism and the Use of Poetry*, 51.
16. The same possibilities open themselves for the references, in 'Tradition and the Individual Talent', to the 'immortality' of dead poets (40) and the manner in which the historical sense 'is a sense of the timeless as well as of

the temporal and of the timeless and of the temporal together' (41). The historical bent of Eliot's criticism at the time makes one suspect that he is referring to a kind of transhistorical value – i.e., that which is within history, but constantly present in all historical times. Yet one cannot rule out that these might constitute a brief excursion into the viewpoint of eternity entertained in Eliot's later thought and verse.

17. Gerald L. Bruns, *Hermeneutics Ancient and Modern* (New Haven, CT: Yale University Press, 1992), 200.
18. Eliot, *The Use of Criticism and the Use of Poetry*, 85.
19. Douwe Draaisma, *Metaphors of Memory: A History of Ideas About the Mind*, translated by Paul Vincent (Cambridge: Cambridge University Press, 2000), 121. Draaisma's claim should, however, be tempered by the realization of how photography's reproductive facility actually undermines self-presence. According to Susan Sontag, 'All photographs are *memento mori*' (Susan Sontag, *On Photography* (London: Penguin, 1979), 15).
20. Henri Bergson, *Matter and Memory*, translated by N. M. Paul and W. S. Palmer (New York: Zone Books, 1991), 146. For a more comprehensive account of the link between Bergson and Eliot, see for instance Philip Le Brun, 'T. S. Eliot and Henri Bergson', in *Review of English Studies*, New Series 18, 1967.
21. Eliot, *The Varieties of Metaphysical Poetry*, 99.
22. Michael Levenson, 'The End of Tradition and the Beginning of History', 162, in Edward Lobb (ed.), *Words in Time: New Essays on Eliot's 'Four Quartets'* (London: Athlone, 1993).
23. T. S. Eliot, *Selected Essays*, third edition (London: Faber and Faber, 1951), 24–25, emphasis added.
24. A thorough discussion of *Phaedrus* 263b is provided by G. N. Giordano Orsini, *Organic Unity in Ancient and Later Poetics: The Philosophical Foundations of Literary Criticism* (Carbondale and Edwardsville: Southern Illinois University Press, 1975).
25. The inclusiveness of the imagination is the reason why Coleridge, in his famous definition in *Biographia Literaria*, claims that it 'struggles to idealize and unify' its elements into an organically structured whole (*Biographia Literaria*, volume I (*Collected Works*, volume 7:1), edited by James Engell and W. Jackson Bate (London: Routledge & Kegan Paul, 1983), 304).
26. Samuel Taylor Coleridge, *Biographia Literaria*, volume II (*Collected Works*, volume 7:2), edited by James Engell and W. Jackson Bate (London: Routledge & Kegan Paul, 1983), 72.
27. On this topic, see Sean Lucy, *T. S. Eliot and the Idea of Tradition* (London: Cohen and West, 1960), 17.
28. Shusterman, *T. S. Eliot and the Philosophy of Criticism*, 159.
29. Eliot, *Selected Essays*, 452.
30. T. S. Eliot, *Essays Ancient & Modern* (London: Faber and Faber, 1949), 38.
31. Ibid., 118.
32. Erik Svarny, *'The Men of 1914': T. S. Eliot and Early Modernism* (Milton Keynes and Philadelphia: Open University Press, 1988), 162.
33. Ibid., 166.
34. I'm referring to the footnote to line 218, beginning 'Tiresias, although a mere spectator and not indeed a "character", is yet the most important personage in the poem, uniting all the rest' (Eliot, *The Complete Poems and Plays*, 78).

35. Eliot, *The Use of Poetry and the Use of Criticism*, 146.
36. Terdiman, *Present Past*, 346.
37. Eliot, *The Varieties of Metaphysical Poetry*, 140.
38. Ibid., 147.
39. Ibid., 148.
40. Ibid., 155.
41. Ibid., 192.
42. Henry Adams, *The Education of Henry Adams*, cited in B. C. Southam, *A Guide to the Selected Poems of T. S. Eliot* (San Diego: Harcourt Brace & Company, 1996 (1968)), 75.
43. Jim McCue, 'Editing Eliot', 2, in *Essays in Criticism*, 2006, vol. lvi(1).
44. Donald Davie, *Modernist Essays: Yeats, Pound, Eliot*, edited by Clive Wilmer (Manchester: Carcanet, 2004), 23.
45. Eliot, *The Sacred Wood*, 87.
46. Ibid., 48.
47. See Lucy, *T. S. Eliot and the Idea of Tradition*, 8, 76, 95, and 109.
48. Helen Gardner, *The Art of T. S. Eliot* (London: Faber and Faber, 1949), 54.
49. Edward Lobb, 'Limitation and Transcendence in *"East Coker"*', 20, in Lobb (ed.), *Words in Time: New Essays on Eliot's 'Four Quartets'* (London: Athlone, 1993).
50. Jacques Derrida, 'Fors: The Anglish Words of Nicolas Abraham and Maria Torok', translated by Barbara Johnson, xiii, in Nicolas Abraham and Maria Torok, *The Wolf Man's Magic Word: A Cryptonymy*, translated by Nicholas Rand (Minneapolis: University of Minnesota Press, 1986). Compare this with the crypt of Gaston Bachelard: 'there exists for each one of us an oneiric house, a house of dream-memory, that is lost in the shadow of a beyond of the real past. I called this oneiric house the crypt of the house that we were born in' (*The Poetics of Space*, translated by Maria Jolas (Beacon Press: Boston, 1964), 15–16).
51. That does not imply that one might not undertake a Derridean unearthing of a crypt in *Four Quartets*; only that this is not my business here.
52. Derrida, 'Fors: The Anglish Words of Nicolas Abraham and Maria Torok', xvi–xvii.
53. Ibid., xvii.
54. Ibid., xiii.
55. See particularly 'Before the Law' and 'The Law of Genre', in Jacques Derrida, *Acts of Literature*, edited by Derek Attridge (London: Routledge, 1992), 181–252.
56. Eliot quoted in Helen Gardner, *The Composition of 'Four Quartets'* (London: Faber and Faber, 1978), 120.
57. Hugh Kenner, *The Invisible Poet: T. S. Eliot* (London: W. H. Allen, 1960), 262.
58. Eliot, in a letter to John Hayward, 5 August 1941, cited in Gardner, *The Composition of 'Four Quartets'*, 24.
59. Gardner, *The Composition of 'Four Quartets'*, 99.
60. See Lyndall Gordon, *Eliot's New Life* (Oxford: Oxford University Press, 1988), particularly 45–48 and 95–99.
61. Gardner, *The Art of T. S. Eliot*, 43.
62. de Certeau, *The Practice of Everyday Life*, 108.
63. See Lyndall Gordon, 'The American Eliot and "The Dry Salvages"', in Edward Lobb (ed.), *Words in Time: New Essays on Eliot's 'Four Quartets'*

(London: Athlone, 1993). For a more encompassing argument that claims Eliot sums up the temporalities of all the important American poets preceding him, see Georges Poulet, *Studies in Human Time*, translated by Elliott Coleman (Baltimore, MD: Johns Hopkins Press, 1956), 354–359.

64. See 'T. S. Eliot: The End of an Era', in Davie, *Modernist Essays*.
65. T. S. Eliot, *After Strange Gods: A Primer of Modern Heresy* (London: Faber and Faber, 1934), 57.
66. Ibid., 55.
67. Eliot, *The Use of Criticism and the Use of Poetry*, 108.
68. Ibid., 148.
69. Roland Barthes, *Camera Lucida*, translated by Richard Howard (London: Vintage, 2000), 102.
70. See 'Women's Time' in Julia Kristeva, *The Kristeva Reader*, edited by Toril Moi (Oxford: Blackwell, 1986).
71. Eliot, *Essays Ancient & Modern*, 187.
72. Ibid., 179 and 182.
73. Ibid., 187.
74. While the first part of Kant's *Critique of Judgement* concerns aesthetics, its second part – titled 'Critique of Teleological Judgement' – concerns the understanding and use of means–end relations. See Immanuel Kant, *The Critique of Judgement*, translated by James Creed Meredith (Oxford: Clarendon Press, 1952).
75. The latter quote is Eliot's, from *The Criterion* ix (1930), 184, cited in Christopher Ricks, *T. S. Eliot and Prejudice* (Berkeley: University of California Press, 1988), 272.
76. C. K. Stead, *The New Poetic: Yeats to Eliot* (Harmondsworth: Penguin, 1964), 185–186.
77. See Kenner, *The Invisible Poet*, 256–257. The same information is also provided in Gardner, *The Composition of 'Four Quartets'*, 86.
78. Kenner, *The Invisible Poet*, 257.
79. T. S. Eliot, *On Poetry and Poets* (London: Faber and Faber, 1957), 122–123.
80. Davie, *Modernist Essays*, 24.
81. Seamus Heaney, 'District and Circle', 34, in *District and Circle* (London: Faber and Faber, 2006).
82. 'District and Circle', 62–66, in ibid.
83. Seamus Heaney, *The Redress of Poetry: Oxford Lectures* (London: Faber and Faber, 1995), 48.
84. Christopher Ricks, 'Growing Up: Review of *Death of a Naturalist*', 23, in Michael Allen (ed.), *New Casebooks: Seamus Heaney* (Basingstoke: Macmillan, 1997).
85. 'Digging', line 28, in Seamus Heaney, *Death of a Naturalist* (London: Faber and Faber, 1991 (1966)), 2.
86. 'An Advancement of Learning', lines 28–36, in Heaney, *Death of a Naturalist*, 7.
87. 'Funeral Rites', line 65, in Seamus Heaney, *North* (London: Faber and Faber, 1996 (1975)), 8.
88. Seamus Heaney, *The Government of the Tongue: The 1986 T. S. Eliot Memorial Lectures and Other Critical Writings* (London: Faber and Faber, 1988), 41 and 44.
89. Ibid., 42.
90. Ibid., 115.

91. Arthur Rimbaud, *Complete Works*, translated by Paul Schmidt (London: Picador, 1988), 213.
92. A. Alvarez, 'A Fine Way with the Language', 17, in *The New York Review*, 6 March 1980.
93. Heaney, *The Government of the Tongue*, 116.
94. In his Nobel Prize lecture, though, a decade later, Heaney does make a couple of brief references to Celan. See Seamus Heaney, *Crediting Poetry* (Oldcastle: The Gallery Press, 1995), 19 and 28.
95. 'The First Flight', 22, in Seamus Heaney, *Station Island* (London: Faber and Faber, 1984).
96. Interpreting Heaney's poem 'Alphabets', Neil Corcoran refers to 'Heaney's version of the Russian formalists' *ostranenie* ("making strange", which is actually the title of a poem in [Heaney's volume entitled] *Station Island*)' (*Poets of Modern Ireland: Text, Context, Intertext* (Carbondale and Edwardsville: Southern Illinois University Press, 1999), 83).
97. See Helen Vendler, *Seamus Heaney* (London: Fontana Press, 1998), 152.
98. Heaney, *The Government of the Tongue*, 45.
99. Neil Corcoran, *The Poetry of Seamus Heaney: A Critical Study* (London: Faber and Faber, 1998), 165.
100. 'Station Island', xii, lines 29–30, in Heaney, *Station Island*, 93.
101. 'Markings', lines 16–18, in Seamus Heaney, *Seeing Things* (London: Faber and Faber, 1991), 8.
102. 'Wheels within Wheels', line 15, in Heaney, *Seeing Things*, 46.
103. Corcoran, *The Poetry of Seamus Heaney*, 176.
104. 'Fosterling', lines 12–14, in Heaney, *Seeing Things*, 50.
105. Patrick Crotty, 'All I Believe That Happened There Was Revision', 198, in Tony Curtis (ed.), *The Art of Seamus Heaney* (Dublin: Wolfhound Press, 2001).
106. 'I'm afraid I believe in the future, and that for the sake of the future I believe we must carry our possessions, we must do Aeneas's job and, you know, get Daddy on our back, and get the household materials together and carry them along' (Heaney in Rui Carvalho Homem, 'On Elegies, Eclogues, Translations, Transfusions: an Interview with Seamus Heaney', 29, in *The European English Messenger*, 2001, vol. X/2).
107. Hugo Friedrich, *The Structure of Modern Poetry: From the Mid-Nineteenth to the Mid-Twentieth Century*, translated by Joachim Neugroschel (Evanston, IL: Northwestern University Press, 1974).
108. Corcoran, *The Poetry of Seamus Heaney*, 192.
109. See Geoffrey Hartman, *Wordsworth's Poetry: 1787–1814* (New Haven, CT: Yale University Press, 1971), particularly the chapter entitled 'Synopsis: The Via Naturaliter Negativa'.
110. 'Squarings', no. xlviii, lines 1–2, in Heaney, *Seeing Things*, 108.
111. Ibid., line 4.
112. Heaney, *The Redress of Poetry*, 82.
113. On this theme, see Helen Vendler, *The Breaking of Style: Hopkins, Heaney, Graham* (Cambridge, MA: Harvard University Press, 1995).
114. Seamus Heaney and Karl Miller, *Seamus Heaney in Conversation with Karl Miller* (London: Between the Lines, 2000), 42.
115. On the angel of history, see Benjamin, *Illuminations*, 257–258.

116. 'Squarings', no. xvii, lines 10 and 12, in Heaney, *Seeing Things*, 73.
117. Heaney, *The Redress of Poetry*, 106–107.
118. Heaney, *Crediting Poetry*, 21.
119. *The Origin of the Work of Art*, 59, in Martin Heidegger, *Poetry, Language, Thought*, translated by Albert Hofstadter (New York: Harper & Row, 1971). On Heaney and Heidegger, see Irene Gilsenan Nordin, ' "A Way-Station Along a Way": Heaney and Heidegger and Wanderings and Home', in *Nordic Irish Studies*, 2002, vol. 1, 19–31.
120. Seamus Heaney, *Preoccupations: Selected Prose 1968–1978* (London: Faber and Faber, 1980), 47.
121. Ibid.
122. These are the two opening lines of the poem 'The Choice', included in Yeats's *The Winding Stair and Other Poems*.
123. Heaney, *The Government of the Tongue*, 151–152.
124. Seamus Heaney on *Electric Light* in Clare Brown and Don Paterson (eds), *Don't Ask Me What I Mean: Poets in Their Own Words* (London: Picador, 2003), 102–103.
125. Ibid., 103.
126. The organization of poetic sequences in terms of organic narrative is widespread in the twentieth century. See Rosenthal and Gall, *The Modern Poetic Sequence*.
127. Heaney in Homem, 'On Elegies, Eclogues, Translations, Transfusions', 24.
128. 'Out of the Bag', lines 51–52, in Seamus Heaney, *Electric Light* (London: Faber and Faber, 2001), 8.
129. Ibid., line 48.
130. Heaney's masculine bias has come under some scholarly fire. See for instance Patricia Coughlan, ' "Bog Queens": The Representation of Women in the Poetry of John Montague and Seamus Heaney', in Michael Allen (ed.), *New Casebooks: Seamus Heaney* (Basingstoke: Macmillan, 1997).
131. 'Out of the Bag', lines 56–67.
132. Ibid., line 36.
133. Cf. 'The Loose Box', in Heaney, *Electric Light*, 14.
134. Matthew Sweeney, 'A Haunting He Will Go', in *The Observer*, 15 April 2001.
135. Lines 32–33 of 'The Real Names', in Heaney, *Electric Light*, 46.
136. 'Perch', lines 9–10, in Heaney, *Electric Light*, 4.
137. See for instance Heaney, *The Redress of Poetry*, 82 and 113, for references to Mandelstam's phrase. For a conservative insistence upon building upon the past, see Heaney's 'Time and Again: Poetry and The Millennium', 23, in *The European English Messenger*, 2001, vol. X/2.
138. See for instance Heaney, *The Redress of Poetry*, 111–112. In addition to Frost, Ted Hughes is an important source for Heaney's frequent gestures towards this kind of poetic primitivism. Heaney also makes similar references to Eliot's notion of an auditory imagination: see particularly 'Learning from Eliot' in Seamus Heaney, *Finders Keepers: Selected Prose 1971–2001* (London: Faber and Faber, 2002), 26–38.
139. 'Two Lorries', lines 21–22, in Seamus Heaney, *The Spirit Level* (London: Faber and Faber, 1996), 13.
140. 'The Sharping Stone', lines 19–25, in Heaney, *The Spirit Level*, 59.

141. Heaney is also less sceptical than his contemporary, Eavan Boland. I will address the latter's use of memory in the next chapter.
142. Thomas Docherty, 'Ana-; or Postmodernism, Landscape, Seamus Heaney', 210, in Michael Allen (ed.), *New Casebooks: Seamus Heaney* (Basingstoke: Macmillan, 1997). I do not mean to endorse Docherty's definition here, but rather to employ it polemically to question what seems to me to be a too simplistic reading of both Heaney and historical development.
143. See Heaney's 'Introduction', vii, in William Wordsworth, *Poems Selected by Seamus Heaney* (London: Faber and Faber, 2001).
144. Heaney, *Preoccupations*, 41. The quoted lines are from *The Prelude*, XI, 337–338.
145. Heaney, 'Introduction', xi, in Wordsworth, *Poems Selected by Seamus Heaney*.
146. 'The Bookcase', line 30, in Heaney, *Electric Light*, 52.
147. Lines 5–6 of "57', a section of 'Bodies and Souls', in Heaney, *Electric Light*, 73.
148. Lines 13–16 of 'Mint', in Heaney, *The Spirit Level*, 6.
149. 'To Pablo Neruda in Tamlaghtduff', line 29, in Heaney, *District and Circle*, 65.
150. Quoted from the sixth of 'Ten Glosses', line 7, in Heaney, *Electric Light*, 55.

5 Other Times: Contemporary Poetry's Breaks with the Past

1. For a reading of memory's role in the autobiographical lyric of contemporary poetry, see chapter 5 in Peter Middleton and Tim Woods, *Literatures of Memory: History, Time and Space in Postwar Writing* (Manchester: Manchester University Press, 2000).
2. See Sean O'Brien, *The Deregulated Muse: Essays on Contemporary British and Irish Poetry* (Newcastle upon Tyne: Bloodaxe, 1998).
3. Eavan Boland, *Object Lessons: The Life of the Woman and the Poet in Our Time* (Manchester: Carcanet, 1995, xi). All further references to this source will be given in the body of the text. Unless otherwise is indicated, all references to Boland's poetry refer to the following edition: Eavan Boland, *New Collected Poems* (Manchester: Carcanet, 2005).
4. Eavan Boland, 'The Wrong Way', 217, in W. N. Herbert and Matthew Hollis (eds), *Strong Words: Modern Poets on Modern Poetry* (Tarset: Bloodaxe, 2000).
5. Cf. the reference to 'Befitting emblems of adversity', in 'Meditations in Time of Civil War', II, 30, in W. B. Yeats, *The Poems*, 248.
6. On the structure of the supplement, see 'That Dangerous Supplement ...,' in Derrida, *Acts of Literature*.
7. Boland is here echoing the title of Robert Frost's famous essay, 'The Figure a Poem Makes', included in W. N. Herbert and Matthew Hollis (eds), *Strong Words: Modern Poets on Modern Poetry* (Tarset: Bloodaxe, 2000), 44–46.
8. Guinn Batten, 'Boland, McGuckian, Ní Chuilleanáin and the Body of the Nation', 173, in Matthew Campbell (ed.), *The Cambridge Companion to Contemporary Irish Poetry* (Cambridge: Cambridge University Press, 2003).
9. Ibid., 175.
10. Ibid., 182 and 186.

11. Clair Wills, *Improprieties: Politics and Sexuality in Northern Irish Poetry* (Oxford: Clarendon Press, 1993), 59.
12. Boland in an interview with *Caffeine Destiny*, quoted in Jody Allen Randolph (ed.), *Eavan Boland: A Sourcebook. Poetry, Prose, Interviews, Reviews and Criticism* (Manchester: Carcanet, 2007), 130.
13. Ibid.
14. My decision to concentrate on 'Outside History' is primarily motivated by a desire to address Boland's feminism and use of memory in conjunction. If other concerns had been paramount (for instance a focus on postcolonial themes, which I unfortunately must neglect here), other texts would have been addressed.
15. For instructive readings that seek to address the fragility of voice and tenuousness of identity in Boland's poetry, see for instance Pilar Villar-Argáiz, 'Recording the Unpoetic: Eavan Boland's Silences', in *Irish University Review*, 2007, vol. 37(2), and Isabel Karremann, ' "I'd Rather Be a Cyborg Than a Goddess": Reading the Cyborg Poetics of Eavan Boland', in *Nordic Irish Studies*, 2004, vol. 3(1).
16. Frawley, *Irish Pastoral*, 151.
17. Ian Davidson, *Ideas of Space in Contemporary Poetry* (Basingstoke: Palgrave Macmillan, 2007), 104.
18. Ibid., 106.
19. Patricia L. Hagen and Thomas W. Zelman, ' "We Were Never on the Scene of the Crime" ', 446, in *Twentieth Century Literature*, 1991, vol. 37(4).
20. For an interesting reading of 'The Pomegranate' and related poems by Boland, that places them in the context of feminist revisions of myth, see Veronica House, ' "Words We Can Grow Old and Die In": Earth Mother and Ageing Mother in Eavan Boland's Poetry', in Irene Gilsenan Nordin (ed.), *The Body and Desire in Contemporary Irish Poetry* (Dublin and Portland: Irish Academic Press, 2006).
21. Eavan Boland, *Domestic Violence* (Manchester: Carcanet, 2007).
22. Eric Mottram, 'The British Poetry Revival, 1960–1975', in Robert Hampson and Peter Barry (eds), *New British Poetries: The Scope of the Possible* (Manchester and New York: Manchester University Press, 1993), 27.
23. Ibid., 36.
24. See for instance Fredric Jameson, *Postmodernism: Or, the Cultural Logic of Late Capitalism* (London: Verso, 1991), 154.
25. Davidson, *Ideas of Space in Contemporary Poetry*, 96.
26. Middleton and Woods, *Literatures of Memory*, 188.
27. N. H. Reeve and Richard Kerridge, *Nearly Too Much: The Poetry of J. H. Prynne* (Liverpool: Liverpool University Press, 1995), 1.
28. J. H. Prynne, *Field Notes: 'The Solitary Reaper' and Others* (Cambridge: 2007), 78.
29. For a reading of Prynne as a sceptical critic of utopias, see Andrew Duncan, *The Failure of Conservatism in Modern Poetry* (Cambridge: Salt, 2003), 118–127.
30. All references to Prynne's poetry giving the line numbers refer to the following edition: J. H. Prynne, *Poems*, second, enlarged edition (Fremantle, WA: Fremantle Arts Centre Press, Tarset (Northumbria, UK): Bloodaxe Books, 2005).

31. Line 88 of 'September 1, 1939', in W. H. Auden, *The English Auden: Poems, Essays and Dramatic Writings 1927–1939*, edited by Edward Mendelson (London: Faber and Faber, 1977), 246.
32. Prynne, *Field Notes*, 40–41.
33. Ken Edwards, *Futures* (London: Reality Street Editions, 1998).
34. J. H. Prynne, 'Response to *Futures* by Ken Edwards', in *Golden Handcuffs Review*, 2007–2008, vol. 1(9). Accessed on 15 August 2008, at http://www.goldenhandcuffsreview.com/gh9content/13.html.
35. For an early interpretation of the poem 'Of Movement Towards a Natural Place' and *Wound Response* in general, which brings up the issue of memory, see Douglas Oliver, 'J. H. Prynne's "Of Movement Towards a Natural Place"', in *Grosseteste Review*, 1979, vol. 12.
36. Reeve and Kerridge, *Nearly Too Much*, 151.
37. Kevin Nolan, 'Capital Calves: Undertaking an Overview', in *Jacket*, November 2003, no. 24. Accessed on 14 August 2008 at http://jacketmagazine.com/24/nolan.html.
38. For a detailed reading of how Prynne's snow imagery of this time relates to that of Paul Celan, see Anthony Mellors, *Late Modernist Poetics: From Pound to Prynne* (Manchester and New York: Manchester University Press, 2005), 191–194.
39. Lines 2–3 of 'The Love-Song of J. Alfred Prufrock', in Eliot, *The Complete Poems and Plays*, 13.
40. Edward D. Kosower, 'A Molecular Basis for Learning and Memory', in *Proceedings of the National Academy of Sciences of the United States of America*, 1972, vol. 69(11).
41. Ibid., 3295.
42. See for instance the defence of phenomenology against structuralist reductionism in J. H. Prynne, 'From a Letter to Douglas Oliver', in *Grosseteste Review*, 1973, vol. 6(1–4).
43. On this possibility, see Forrest Gander, 'The Right to Be Unidentified with This Work', in *Chicago Review*, 2007, vol. 53(1).
44. Kosower, 'A Molecular Basis for Learning and Memory', 3295.
45. The meaning of VRS is given in ibid., 3292.
46. Sigmund Freud, *A Difficulty in the Path of Psychoanalysis*, in *The Standard Edition*, vol. 16 (London: Hogarth, 1963 (1916)), 285.
47. Thomas Pfau cited in Prynne, *Field Notes*, 84.
48. Quoted from ibid., 21, 29, 39, and 94.
49. Wordsworth, 'The Solitary Reaper', 25–26, in Wordsworth, *The Poems*, I, 657.
50. Prynne, *Field Notes*, 87.
51. Ibid., 88.
52. Ibid., 87.
53. J. H. Prynne, 'China Figures', 368, in *New Songs from a Jade Terrace: An Anthology of Early Chinese Love Poetry*, translated with annotations and an introduction by Anne Birrell (London: Penguin, 1986).
54. Ibid.
55. J. H. Prynne, 'Jeremy Prynne lectures on *Maximus IV, V, VI*', part 1, transcribed by Tom McGauley and published in *Iron* (October 1971); reprinted in *Minutes of the Charles Olson Society*, no. 28 (April 1999), accessed on 21 August 2008 at http://charlesolson.ca/files/Prynnelecture1.htm.

56. Prynne, 'Jeremy Prynne lectures on *Maximus* IV, V, VI', part 1.
57. Ibid.
58. Prynne, 'China Figures', 368.
59. In 'China Figures', Prynne explicitly cites Culler's chapter on 'The Turns of Metaphor' in *The Pursuit of Signs: Semiotics, Literature, Deconstruction* (London and Henley: Routledge. 1981).
60. Prynne, 'Jeremy Prynne lectures on *Maximus* IV, V, VI', part 1.
61. J. H. Prynne, 'Jeremy Prynne lectures on *Maximus* IV, V, VI', part 2, transcribed by Tom McGauley and published in *Iron* (October 1971); reprinted in *Minutes of the Charles Olson Society*, no. 28 (April 1999), accessed on 21 August 2008 at http://charlesolson.ca/files/Prynnelecture2.htm.
62. Prynne, ' "Modernism" in German Poetry', cited in Mellors, *Late Modernist Poetics*, 195.
63. Paul Celan, *Collected Prose*, translated by Rosemarie Waldrop (Manchester: Carcanet, 2003), 55. The original wording is: 'etwas – wie die Sprache – Immaterielles, aber Irdisches, Terrestrisches, etwas Kreisförmiges, über beiden Pole in sich selbst Zurückkehrendes und dabei-heitererweise – sogar die Tropen Durchkreuzendes –: ich finde ... einen *Meridian*'. Paul Celan, *Gesammelte Werke*, dritter Band (Frankfurt am Main: Suhrkamp, 1986), 202.
64. On the hermeneutic circle, see for instance Hans-Georg Gadamer, *Truth and Method*, second edition, translation revised by Joel Weinsheimer and Donald G. Marshall (London: Sheed & Ward, 1989), 265–277.
65. See Christopher R. Miller, *The Invention of Evening. Perception and Time in Romantic Poetry* (Cambridge: Cambridge University Press, 2006).
66. Prynne, 'Jeremy Prynne lectures on *Maximus* IV, V, VI', part 1.
67. Beyond astrophysics, Prynne may also be alluding to Hölderlin here, and his claim that human life obeys an eccentric orbit: 'Wir durchlaufen alle eine exzentrische Bahn, und es ist kein anderer Weg möglich von der Kindheit zur Vollendung' (Friedrich Hölderlin, *Werke in einem Band* (Munich: Carl Hanser Verlag, 1990), 313).
68. Here there is a parallel to Seamus Heaney. Cf. Heaney, *Preoccupations*, 65.
69. Prynne, *Field Notes*, 92.
70. Roger Thompson, 'Emerson, Divinity, and Rhetoric in Transcendentalist Nature Writing and Twentieth-Century Ecopoetry', 36, in J. Scott Bryson (ed.), *Ecopoetry: A Critical Introduction* (Salt Lake City: University of Utah Press, 2002).
71. Jonathan Bate, *The Song of the Earth* (London: Picador, 2000), 42.
72. See 'Building, Dwelling, Thinking', in Heidegger, *Poetry, Language, Thought*.
73. Bate, *The Song of the Earth*, 258.
74. See Martin Heidegger, *The Essence of Truth: On Plato's Cave Allegory and Theaetetus*, translated by Ted Sadler (New York: Continuum, 2002).
75. The first edition of *The Thing in the Gap-Stone Stile* was published by Oxford University Press, but the book was subsequently reprinted by Faber and Faber eleven years later. All references will be made to these editions: Alice Oswald, *The Thing in the Gap-Stone Stile* (London: Faber and Faber, 2007); Alice Oswald, *Dart* (London: Faber and Faber, 2002); Alice Oswald, *Woods etc.* (London: Faber and Faber, 2005). In order to indicate the collections to which shorter, cited poems belong, I will use the abbreviations

Thing and *Woods* etc. In addition to the mentioned titles, Oswald has also published a volume of selected poems with an American publisher (titled *Spacecraft Voyager 1*), and edited *The Thunder Mutters: 101 Poems for the Planet*.

76. Alice Oswald, 'Wild Things', in *The Guardian*, 3 December 2005.
77. Bate, *The Song of the Earth*, 230.
78. Ibid., 231.
79. D. H. Lawrence, 'Preface to the American Edition of *New Poems*', 108, in Jon Cook (ed.), *Poetry in Theory: An Anthology 1900–2000* (Oxford: Blackwell, 2004). The desire for immediacy in literature goes back further than Lawrence, of course. See for instance Geoffrey H. Hartman, *The Unmediated Vision: An Interpretation of Wordsworth, Hopkins, Rilke, and Valéry* (New York: Harcourt, 1966 (1954)).
80. Oswald, 'Wild Things'.
81. Timothy Morton, *Ecology Without Nature: Rethinking Environmental Aesthetics* (Cambridge, MA, and London: Harvard University Press, 2007), 71.
82. John Keats, letter to John Hamilton Reynolds, 19 February 1818, in Harold Bloom and Lionel Trillings (eds), *Romantic Poetry and Prose* (Oxford: Oxford University Press, 1972), 772.
83. J. Scott Bryson, *The West Side of Any Mountain: Place, Space, and Ecopoetry* (Iowa: University of Iowa Press, 2005), 2.
84. Morton, *Ecology Without Nature*, 183.
85. Bate, *The Song of the Earth*, 281.
86. Ibid., 248.
87. See 'Différance' in Jacques Derrida, *Margins of Philosophy*, translated by Alan Bass (New York: Harvester Wheatsheaf, 1982).
88. Roland Barthes, *S/Z*, translated by Richard Miller (Oxford: Blackwell, 1990), 5.
89. Alice Oswald, comment on *The Thing in the Gap-Stone Stile*, 207, in Clare Brown and Don Paterson (eds), *Don't Ask Me What I Mean: Poets in their Own Words* (London: Picador, 2003).
90. Alice Oswald, 'Introduction', xiv, in Sir Thomas Wyatt, *Poems Selected by Alice Oswald* (London: Faber and Faber, 2008).
91. See 'Fragment of an Unfinished Morning', in Alice Oswald, *Spacecraft Voyager 1: New and Selected Poems* (Saint Paul: Graywolf Press, 2007), 142.
92. Morton, *Ecology Without Nature*, 21.
93. Oswald, *Dart*, 21. All subsequent quotations from *Dart*, given in the body of my text, will similarly be accompanied by page references (rather than line numbers).
94. Line 25 of 'That the Science of Cartography Is Limited' in Boland, *New Collected Poems*, 205.
95. See 'Map' in Elizabeth Bishop, *Complete Poems* (London: Chatto & Windus, 2004), 3.
96. Bate, *The Song of the Earth*, 280.
97. See ibid., 254–255. Bate refers to page 321 of 'The Question of Technology', in Martin Heidegger, *Basic Writings*, edited by David Farrell Krell (San Francisco: Harper, 1993 (1977)).
98. Bate, *The Song of the Earth*, 217.
99. Deryn Rees-Jones, *Consorting with Angels: Essays on Modern Women Poets* (Tarset: Bloodaxe, 2005), 234.

100. See for instance Maurice Blanchot, *The Step Not Beyond*, translated by Lycette Nelson (New York: State University of New York Press, 1992), 52.
101. Alice Oswald, comment on *Dart* in Clare Brown and Don Paterson (eds), *Don't Ask Me What I Mean: Poets in their Own Words* (London: Picador, 2003), 208.
102. Morton, *Ecology Without Nature*, 175.

6   Conclusion: Imperfect Hindsight

1. See Douwe Draaisma, *How Life Speeds Up As You Get Older: How Memory Shapes Our Past*, translated by Arnold and Erica Pomerans (Cambridge: Cambridge University Press, 2001), 1.
2. See Terdiman, *Present Past*.
3. Rylance, 'Twisting: Memory from Eliot to Eliot', 98.
4. For an outspoken expression of this view, see Glyn Maxwell, 'Make it Cohere', in *The Times Literary Supplement*, 5 July 2002.
5. Edward S. Casey, *The Fate of Place: A Philosophical History* (Berkeley: University of California Press, 1997), xii.

Bibliography

Ackroyd, Peter, *Albion: The Origins of the English Imagination* (London: Chatto & Windus, 2002).

Alvarez, A., 'A Fine Way with the Language', in *The New York Review*, 6 March 1980.

Ariès, Philippe, *The Hour of Our Death*, translated by Helen Weaver (Oxford: Oxford University Press, 1981).

Arkins, Brian, 'Yeats and Platonism', in Anna Baldwin and Sarah Hutton (eds), *Platonism and the English Imagination* (Cambridge: Cambridge University Press, 1994).

Armstrong, Isobel, *Victorian Poetry: Poetry, Poetics and Politics* (London and New York: Routledge, 1993).

Armstrong, Tim, *Haunted Hardy: Poetry, History, Memory* (Basingstoke: Palgrave Macmillan, 2000).

Arnold, Matthew, *Lectures and Essays in Criticism* (Ann Arbor: University of Michigan Press, 1963).

Auden, W. H., 'Introduction', in Alfred, Lord Tennyson, *Tennyson: A Selection and an Introduction*, edited by W. H. Auden (London: Phoenix House, 1946).

—— *The English Auden: Poems, Essays and Dramatic Writings 1927–1939*, edited by Edward Mendelson (London: Faber and Faber, 1977).

Augustine, Saint, *Confessions*, translated by R. S. Pine-Coffin (London: Penguin, 1961).

Austin, Linda M., *Nostalgia in Transition, 1780–1917* (Charlottesville and London: University of Virginia Press, 2007).

Bachelard, Gaston, *The Poetics of Space*, translated by Maria Jolas (Beacon Press: Boston, 1964).

Barthes, Roland, *S/Z*, translated by Richard Miller (Oxford: Blackwell, 1990).

—— *Camera Lucida*, translated by Richard Howard (London: Vintage, 2000).

Bate, Jonathan, *The Song of the Earth* (London: Picador, 2000).

Batten, Guinn, 'Boland, McGuckian, Ní Chuilleanáin and the Body of the Nation', in Matthew Campbell (ed.), *The Cambridge Companion to Contemporary Irish Poetry* (Cambridge: Cambridge University Press, 2003).

Baudelaire, Charles, 'The Painter of Modern Life', in Lawrence Cahoone (ed.), *From Modernism to Postmodernism: An Anthology* (Oxford: Blackwell, 1996).

Beer, Gillian, *Darwin's Plots: Evolutionary Narrative in Darwin, George Eliot and Nineteenth-Century Fiction* (London: Routledge & Kegan Paul, 1983).

Benjamin, Walter, *Illuminations: Essays and Reflections*, edited by Hannah Arendt, translated by Harry Zohn (New York: Schocken, 1968).

Bergson, Henri, *Matter and Memory*, translated by N. M. Paul and W. S. Palmer (New York: Zone Books, 1991).

Bishop, Elizabeth, *Complete Poems* (London: Chatto & Windus, 2004).

Blanchot, Maurice, *The Space of Literature*, translated by Ann Smock (Lincoln: University of Nebraska Press, 1982).

—— *The Step Not Beyond*, translated by Lycette Nelson (New York: State University of New York Press, 1992).

Bloom, Harold, *The Western Canon: The Books and School of the Ages* (London: Papermac, 1995).

Boland, Eavan, *New Collected Poems* (Manchester: Carcanet, 2005).

—— *Object Lessons: The Life of the Woman and the Poet in Our Time* (Manchester: Carcanet, 1995).

—— 'The Wrong Way', in W. N. Herbert and Matthew Hollis (eds), *Strong Words: Modern Poets on Modern Poetry* (Tarset: Bloodaxe, 2000).

—— '*Caffeine Destiny* Interview', in Jody Allen Randolph (ed.), *Eavan Boland: A Sourcebook. Poetry, Prose, Interviews, Reviews and Criticism* (Manchester: Carcanet, 2007).

—— *Domestic Violence* (Manchester: Carcanet, 2007).

Borges, Jorge Luis, *Labyrinths: Selected Stories and Other Writings*, edited by Donald A. Yates and James E. Irby (London: Penguin, 1970).

Bromwich, David, *Disowned by Memory: Wordsworth's Poetry of the 1790s* (Chicago: University of Chicago Press, 1998).

Brown, Terence, *The Life of W.B. Yeats: A Critical Biography* (Oxford: Blackwell, 2001).

Browning, Elizabeth Barrett, *Aurora Leigh*, edited by Kerry McSweeney (Oxford: Oxford University Press, 1993).

Bruns, Gerald L., *Hermeneutics Ancient and Modern* (New Haven, CT: Yale University Press, 1992).

Bryson, J. Scott, *The West Side of Any Mountain: Place, Space, and Ecopoetry* (Iowa: University of Iowa Press, 2005).

Campbell, Matthew, *Rhythm and Will in Victorian Poetry* (Cambridge: Cambridge University Press, 1999).

Casey, Edward S., *Remembering: A Phenomenological Study*, second edition (Bloomington: Indiana University Press, 2000 (1987)).

—— *The Fate of Place: A Philosophical History* (Berkeley: University of California Press, 1997).

Celan, Paul, *Gesammelte Werke*, volume three (Frankfurt am Main: Suhrkamp, 1986).

—— *Collected Prose*, translated by Rosemarie Waldrop (Manchester: Carcanet, 2003).

Chandler, James K., *Wordsworth's Second Nature: A Study of the Poetry and Politics* (Chicago: University of Chicago Press, 1984).

Coleridge, Samuel Taylor, *Biographia Literaria*, two volumes (*Collected Works*, volumes 7:1 and 7:2), edited by James Engell and W. Jackson Bate (London: Routledge & Kegan Paul, 1983).

Colley, Ann C., *Nostalgia and Recollection in Victorian Culture* (Basingstoke: Palgrave, 1998).

Corcoran, Neil, *The Poetry of Seamus Heaney: A Critical Study* (London: Faber and Faber, 1998).

—— *Poets of Modern Ireland: Text, Context, Intertext* (Carbondale and Edwardsville: Southern Illinois University Press, 1999).

Coughlan, Patricia, ' "Bog Queens": The Representation of Women in the Poetry of John Montague and Seamus Heaney', in Michael Allen (ed.), *New Casebooks: Seamus Heaney* (Basingstoke: Macmillan, 1997).

Crotty, Patrick, 'All I Believe That Happened There Was Revision', in Tony Curtis (ed.), *The Art of Seamus Heaney* (Dublin: Wolfhound Press, 2001).

Culler, Jonathan, *The Pursuit of Signs: Semiotics, Literature, Deconstruction* (London and Henley: Routledge, 1981).

Cullingford, Elizabeth Butler, *Gender and History in Yeats's Love Poetry* (New York: Syracuse University Press, 1996).

Curl, James Stevens, *The Victorian Celebration of Death* (Stroud: Sutton Publishing, 2000).

Dames, Nicholas, *Amnesiac Selves: Nostalgia, Forgetting, and British Fiction, 1810–1870* (Oxford: Oxford University Press, 2001).

Davidson, Ian, *Ideas of Space in Contemporary Poetry* (Basingstoke: Palgrave Macmillan, 2007).

Davie, Donald, 'Hardy's Virgilian Purples', in *Agenda*, 1972, vol. 10(2–3).

—— *Modernist Essays: Yeats, Pound, Eliot*, edited by Clive Wilmer (Manchester: Carcanet, 2004).

Davis, Philip, *Memory and Writing: From Wordsworth to Lawrence* (Liverpool: Liverpool University Press, 1983).

—— 'Memory through the Looking Glass: Ruskin Versus Hardy', in Matthew Campbell, Jacqueline M. Labbe, and Sally Shuttleworth (eds), *Memory and Memorials, 1789–1914: Literary and Cultural Perspectives* (London: Routledge, 2000).

De Certeau, Michel, *The Practice of Everyday Life*, translated by Steven Rendall (Berkeley: University of California Press, 1984).

De Man, Paul, *Blindness and Insight: Essays in the Rhetoric of Contemporary Criticism*, second edition (London: Routledge, 1983).

—— *The Rhetoric of Romanticism* (New York: Columbia University Press, 1984).

—— *The Resistance to Theory* (Minneapolis: University of Minnesota Press, 1986).

—— *Romanticism and Contemporary Criticism: The Gauss Seminar and Other Papers*, edited by E. S. Burt, Kevin Newmark, and Andrzej Warminski (Baltimore, MD: Johns Hopkins University Press, 1993).

Deleuze, Gilles, *Nietzsche and Philosophy*, translated by Janis A. Tomlinson and Hugh Tomlinson (New York: Columbia University Press, 1985).

Derrida, Jacques, *Margins of Philosophy*, translated by Alan Bass (New York: Harvester Wheatsheaf, 1982).

—— 'Fors: The Anglish Words of Nicolas Abraham and Maria Torok', translated by Barbara Johnson, in Nicolas Abraham and Maria Torok, *The Wolf Man's Magic Word: A Cryptonymy*, translated by Nicholas Rand (Minneapolis: University of Minnesota Press, 1986).

—— *Acts of Literature*, edited by Derek Attridge (London: Routledge, 1992).

Docherty, Thomas, 'Ana-; or Postmodernism, Landscape, Seamus Heaney', in Michael Allen (ed.), *New Casebooks: Seamus Heaney* (Basingstoke: Macmillan, 1997).

Douglas-Fairhurst, Robert, *Victorian Afterlives: The Shaping of Influence in Nineteenth-Century Literature* (Oxford: Oxford University Press, 2002).

Draaisma, Douwe, *Metaphors of Memory: A History of Ideas About the Mind*, translated by Paul Vincent (Cambridge: Cambridge University Press, 2000).

—— *How Life Speeds Up As You Get Older: How Memory Shapes Our Past*, translated by Arnold and Erica Pomerans (Cambridge: Cambridge University Press, 2001).

Duncan, Andrew, *The Failure of Conservatism in Modern Poetry* (Cambridge: Salt, 2003).

Edwards, Ken, *Futures* (London: Reality Street Editions, 1998).

Eliot, T. S., *After Strange Gods: A Primer of Modern Heresy* (London: Faber and Faber, 1934).

—— *Essays Ancient & Modern* (London: Faber and Faber, 1949).

—— *Selected Essays*, third edition (London: Faber and Faber, 1951).

—— *On Poetry and Poets* (London: Faber and Faber, 1957).

—— *The Sacred Wood* (London: Faber and Faber, 1997 (1960)).

—— *The Use of Poetry and the Use of Criticism: Studies in the Relation of Criticism to Poetry in England* (London: Faber and Faber, 1964).

—— *The Complete Poems and Plays* (London: Faber and Faber, 1969).

—— *The Varieties of Metaphysical Poetry*, edited by Ronald Schuchard (New York: Harcourt Brace, 1993).

Ellmann, Maud, *The Poetics of Impersonality: T. S. Eliot and Ezra Pound* (Brighton: The Harvester Press, 1987).

Ellmann, Richard, *Golden Codgers: Biographical Speculations* (New York: Oxford University Press, 1973).

Flowers, Betty S., 'Notes', in Christina Rossetti, *The Complete Poems*, text by R. W. Crump, notes and introduction by Betty S. Flowers (London: Penguin, 2001).

Foster, R. F., *W. B. Yeats: A Life. 1. The Apprentice Mage 1865–1914* (Oxford: Oxford University Press, 1998).

Frawley, Oona, *Irish Pastoral: Nostalgia and Twentieth-Century Irish Literature* (Dublin: Irish Academic Press, 2005).

Freud, Sigmund, *A Difficulty in the Path of Psychoanalysis*, in *The Standard Edition*, vol. 16 (London: Hogarth, 1963 (1916)).

—— *General Psychological Theory: Papers on Metapsychology*, edited by Philip Rieff (New York: Collier, 1963).

Friedman, Michael H., *The Makings of a Tory Humanist: William Wordsworth and the Idea of Community* (New York: Columbia University Press, 1979).

Friedrich, Hugo, *The Structure of Modern Poetry: From the Mid-Nineteenth to the Mid-Twentieth Century*, translated by Joachim Neugroschel (Evanston, IL: Northwestern University Press, 1974).

Frost, Robert, 'The Figure a Poem Makes', in W. N. Herbert and Matthew Hollis (eds), *Strong Words: Modern Poets on Modern Poetry* (Tarset: Bloodaxe, 2000).

Fussell, Paul, *The Great War and Modern Memory* (Oxford: Oxford University Press, 2000 (1975)).

Gadamer, Hans-Georg, *Truth and Method*, second edition, translation revised by Joel Weinsheimer and Donald G. Marshall (London: Sheed & Ward, 1989).

Gander, Forrest, 'The Right to Be Unidentified with This Work', in *Chicago Review*, 2007, vol. 53(1).

Gardner, Helen, *The Art of T. S. Eliot* (London: Faber and Faber, 1949).

—— *The Composition of 'Four Quartets'* (London: Faber and Faber, 1978).

Gilbert, Sandra M. and Susan Gubar, *The Madwoman in the Attic: The Woman Writer and the Nineteenth-Century Literary Imagination* (New Haven, CT, and London: Yale University Press, 1984).

Gilsenan Nordin, Irene, ' "A Way-Station Along a Way": Heaney and Heidegger and Wanderings and Home', in *Nordic Irish Studies*, 2002, vol. 1.

Girard, René, *Deceit, Desire and the Novel: Self and Other in Literary Structure*, translated by Yvonne Freccero (Baltimore, MD: Johns Hopkins University Press, 1966).

Gordon, Lyndall, *Eliot's New Life* (Oxford: Oxford University Press, 1988).

—— 'The American Eliot and "The Dry Salvages"', in Edward Lobb (ed.), *Words in Time: New Essays on Eliot's 'Four Quartets'* (London: Athlone, 1993).

Gore-Booth, Eva, *Poems* (London: Longmans, Green and Co., 1929).

Griffiths, Eric, 'The Disappointment of Christina G. Rossetti', in *Essays in Criticism*, 1997, vol. XLVII(2).

Hagen, Patricia L. and Thomas W. Zelman, ' "We Were Never on the Scene of the Crime" ', in *Twentieth Century Literature*, 1991, vol. 37(4).

Hardy, Thomas, *The Dynasts* and *the Famous Tragedy of the Queen of Cornwall* (London: Macmillan, 1931).

—— *Tess of the D'Urbervilles* (Oxford: Oxford University Press, 1983).

—— *The Complete Poems*, edited by James Gibson (Basingstoke: Palgrave, 2001).

—— *A Pair of Blue Eyes* (Oxford: Oxford University Press, 2005).

Hartman, Geoffrey, *The Unmediated Vision: An Interpretation of Wordsworth, Hopkins, Rilke, and Valéry* (New York: Harcourt, 1966 (1954)).

—— *Wordsworth's Poetry: 1787–1814* (New Haven, CT: Yale University Press, 1971).

—— *The Fate of Reading and Other Essays* (Chicago: University of Chicago Press, 1975).

—— *The Fateful Question of Culture* (New York: Columbia University Press, 1997).

Hassett, Constance W., *Christina Rossetti: The Patience of Style* (Charlottesville and London: University of Virginia Press, 2005).

Hazlitt, William, *The Complete Works*, volume I (London: J. M. Dent & Sons, 1930).

Heaney, Seamus, *Death of a Naturalist* (London: Faber and Faber, 1991 (1966)).

—— *North* (London: Faber and Faber, 1996 (1975)).

—— *Preoccupations: Selected Prose 1968–1978* (London: Faber and Faber, 1980).

—— *Station Island* (London: Faber and Faber, 1984).

—— *The Government of the Tongue: The 1986 T. S. Eliot Memorial Lectures and Other Critical Writings* (London: Faber and Faber, 1988).

—— *Seeing Things* (London: Faber and Faber, 1991).

—— *The Redress of Poetry: Oxford Lectures* (London: Faber and Faber, 1995).

—— *Crediting Poetry* (Oldcastle: The Gallery Press, 1995).

—— *The Spirit Level* (London: Faber and Faber, 1996).

—— 'Time and Again: Poetry and the Millennium', in *The European English Messenger*, 2001, vol. X/2.

—— 'Introduction', in William Wordsworth, *Poems Selected by Seamus Heaney* (London: Faber and Faber, 2001).

—— *Electric Light* (London: Faber and Faber, 2001).

—— *Finders Keepers: Selected Prose 1971–2001* (London: Faber and Faber, 2002).

—— Comments on *Electric Light* in Clare Brown and Don Paterson (eds), *Don't Ask Me What I Mean: Poets in Their Own Words* (London: Picador, 2003).

—— *District and Circle* (London: Faber and Faber, 2006).

Heaney, Seamus, and Karl Miller, *Seamus Heaney in Conversation with Karl Miller* (London: Between the Lines, 2000).

Heidegger, Martin, *Poetry, Language, Thought*, translated by Albert Hofstadter (New York: Harper & Row, 1971).

—— *Basic Writings*, edited by David Farrell Krell (San Francisco: Harper, 1993 (1977)).

—— *Being and Time: A Translation of 'Sein und Zeit'*, translated by Joan Stambaugh (New York: State University of New York Press, 1996).

—— *The Essence of Truth: On Plato's Cave Allegory and Theaetetus*, translated by Ted Sadler (New York: Continuum, 2002).

Hölderlin, Friedrich, *Werke in einem Band* (Munich: Carl Hanser Verlag, 1990).

Homem, Rui Carvalho, 'On Elegies, Eclogues, Translations, Transfusions: An Interview with Seamus Heaney', in *The European English Messenger*, 2001, vol. X/2.

House, Veronica, ' "Words We Can Grow Old and Die In": Earth Mother and Ageing Mother in Eavan Boland's Poetry', in Irene Gilsenan Nordin (ed.), *The Body and Desire in Contemporary Irish Poetry* (Dublin and Portland: Irish Academic Press, 2006).

Jacobus, Mary, 'Hardy's Magian Retrospect', in *Essays in Criticism*, 1982, vol. 32.

James, Dermot, *The Gore-Booths of Lissadell* (Dublin: The Woodfield Press, 2004).

Jameson, Fredric, *The Political Unconscious: Narrative as a Socially Symbolic Act* (London: Methuen, 1981).

—— *Postmodernism: Or, the Cultural Logic of Late Capitalism* (London: Verso, 1991).

Johnston, Kenneth R., *The Hidden Wordsworth: Poet, Lover, Rebel, Spy* (New York: W. W. Norton & Company, 1998).

Kant, Immanuel, *The Critique of Judgement*, translated by James Creed Meredith (Oxford: Clarendon Press, 1952).

Karremann, Isabel, ' "I'd Rather Be a Cyborg Than a Goddess": Reading the Cyborg Poetics of Eavan Boland', in *Nordic Irish Studies*, 2004, vol. 3(1).

Keats, John, letter to John Hamilton Reynolds, 19 February 1818, in Harold Bloom and Lionel Trillings (eds), *Romantic Poetry and Prose* (Oxford: Oxford University Press, 1972).

Kenner, Hugh, *The Invisible Poet: T. S. Eliot* (London: W. H. Allen, 1960).

Kosower, Edward D., 'A Molecular Basis for Learning and Memory', in *Proceedings of the National Academy of Sciences of the Unites States of America*, 1972, vol. 69(11).

Krell, David Farrell, *Of Memory, Reminiscence, and Writing: On the Verge* (Bloomington: Indiana University Press, 1990).

Kristeva, Julia, *The Kristeva Reader*, edited by Toril Moi (Oxford: Blackwell, 1986).

Lacan, Jacques, *Écrits: A Selection*, translated by Alan Sheridan (New York: Norton, 1977).

Lakoff, George, and Mark Johnson, *Metaphors We Live By* (Chicago: University of Chicago Press, 1980).

Langbaum, Robert, 'The Evolution of Soul in Wordsworth's Poetry', in W. J. Harvey and Richard Gravil (eds), *Wordsworth: The Prelude. A Casebook* (London: Macmillan, 1972).

Lanzano, Ellen Anne, *Hardy: The Temporal Poetics* (New York: Peter Lang, 1999).

Lawrence, D. H., 'Preface to the American Edition of *New Poems*', in Jon Cook (ed.), *Poetry in Theory: An Anthology 1900–2000* (Oxford: Blackwell, 2004).

Le Brun, Philip, 'T. S. Eliot and Henri Bergson', in *Review of English Studies*, New Series 18, 1967.

Leighton, Angela, '"When I Am Dead, My Dearest"': The Secret of Christina Rossetti', in *Modern Philology*, 1990, vol. 87(4).

—— 'Touching Forms: Tennyson and Aestheticism', in *The Tennyson Research Bulletin*, 2001, vol. 7(5).

Levenson, Michael, 'The End of Tradition and the Beginning of History', in Edward Lobb (ed.), *Words in Time: New Essays on Eliot's 'Four Quartets'* (London: Athlone, 1993).

Levinas, Emmanuel, *Time and the Other*, translated by Richard A. Cohen (Pittsburgh: Duquesne University Press, 1987).

Levinson, Marjorie, *Wordsworth's Great Period Poems: Four Essays* (Cambridge: Cambridge University Press, 1986).

Lipking, Lawrence, *Abandoned Women and Poetic Tradition* (Chicago: Chicago University Press, 1988).

Liu, Alan, *Wordsworth: The Sense of History* (Stanford: Stanford University Press, 1989).

Lobb, Edward, 'Limitation and Transcendence in *"East Coker"*', in Lobb (ed.), *Words in Time: New Essays on Eliot's 'Four Quartets'* (London: Athlone, 1993).

Locke, John, *An Essay Concerning Human Understanding*, volume I, edited by Alexander Campbell Fraser (New York: Dover, 1959).

Lucy, Sean, *T. S. Eliot and the Idea of Tradition* (London: Cohen and West, 1960).

Macfarlane, Robert, *Mountains of the Mind: A History of a Fascination* (London: Granta, 2003).

McCue, Jim, 'Editing Eliot', in *Essays in Criticism*, 2006, vol. lvi(1).

McGann, Jerome, *The Romantic Ideology: A Critical Investigation* (Chicago, University of Chicago Press, 1983).

—— 'Christina Rossetti's Poems', in Angela Leighton (ed.), *Victorian Women Poets: A Critical Reader* (Oxford: Blackwell, 1996).

McIntire, Gabrielle, *Modernism, Memory, and Desire: T. S. Eliot and Virginia Woolf* (Cambridge: Cambridge University Press, 2008).

Maddox, Brenda, *George's Ghosts: A New Life of W. B. Yeats* (London: Picador, 1999).

Malcolm, Norman, 'Memory and Representation', in *Noûs*, 1970, vol. 4(1).

Mallarmé, Stéphane, *A Tomb for Anatole*, translated by Paul Auster (San Francisco: North Point Press, 1983).

—— 'Tennyson, Seen from Here', translated by Mary Ann Caws, in *The Tennyson Research Bulletin*, 2001, vol. 7(7).

Marecco, Anne, *The Rebel Countess: The Life and Times of Countess Markiewicz* (London: Phoenix Press, 2000 (1967)).

Marsh, Jan, *Christina Rossetti: A Literary Biography* (London: Jonathan Cape, 1994).

Maxwell, Glyn, 'Make it Cohere', in *The Times Literary Supplement*, 5 July 2002.

Mellors, Anthony, *Late Modernist Poetics: From Pound to Prynne* (Manchester and New York: Manchester University Press, 2005).

Middleton, Peter, and Tim Woods, *Literatures of Memory: History, Time and Space in Postwar Writing* (Manchester: Manchester University Press, 2000).

Miller, Christopher R., *The Invention of Evening. Perception and Time in Romantic Poetry* (Cambridge: Cambridge University Press, 2006).

Miller, J. Hillis, *Thomas Hardy: Distance and Desire* (London: Oxford University Press, 1970).

—— *The Linguistic Moment: From Wordsworth to Stevens* (Princeton: Princeton University Press, 1985).

Morton, Timothy, *Ecology Without Nature: Rethinking Environmental Aesthetics* (Cambridge, MA, and London: Harvard University Press, 2007).

Mottram, Eric, 'The British Poetry Revival, 1960–1975', in Robert Hampson and Peter Barry (eds), *New British Poetries: The Scope of the Possible* (Manchester and New York: Manchester University Press, 1993).

Negri, Antonio, *Time for Revolution*, translated by Matteo Mandarini (New York: Continuum, 2003).

Nietzsche, Friedrich, *Also Sprach Zarathustra* in *Werke in drei Bänden*, volume 2, edited by Karl Schlechta (Darmstadt: Wissenschaftliche Buchgesellschaft, 1997 (1955)).

—— *Untimely Meditations*, edited by Daniel Breazeale, translated by R. J. Hollingdale (Cambridge: Cambridge University Press, 1997).

Nolan, Kevin, 'Capital Calves: Undertaking an Overview', in *Jacket*, 2003, 24. Accessed on 14 August 2008 at http://jacketmagazine.com/24/nolan.html.

Nora, Pierre, 'General Introduction: Between Memory and History', in Nora (ed.), *Realms of Memory: Rethinking the French Past*, volume I, edited by Lawrence D. Kritzman, translated by Arthur Goldhammer (New York: Columbia University Press, 1996).

O'Brien, Sean, *The Deregulated Muse: Essays on Contemporary British & Irish Poetry* (Newcastle upon Tyne: Bloodaxe, 1998).

Oliver, Douglas, 'J. H. Prynne's "Of Movement Towards a Natural Place"', in *Grosseteste Review*, 1979, vol. 12.

Orsini, G. N. Giordano, *Organic Unity in Ancient and Later Poetics: The Philosophical Foundations of Literary Criticism* (Carbondale and Edwardsville: Southern Illinois University Press, 1975).

Oswald, Alice, *Dart* (London: Faber and Faber, 2002).

—— Comment on *Dart* in Clare Brown and Don Paterson (eds), *Don't Ask Me What I Mean: Poets in their Own Words* (London: Picador, 2003).

—— Comment on *The Thing in the Gap-Stone Stile*, in Clare Brown and Don Paterson (eds), *Don't Ask Me What I Mean: Poets in their Own Words* (London: Picador, 2003).

—— *Woods etc.* (London: Faber and Faber, 2005).

—— 'Wild Things', in *The Guardian*, 3 December 2005.

—— *Spacecraft Voyager 1: New and Selected Poems* (Saint Paul: Graywolf Press, 2007).

—— *The Thing in the Gap-Stone Stile* (London: Faber and Faber, 2007).

—— 'Introduction', in Sir Thomas Wyatt, *Poems Selected by Alice Oswald* (London: Faber and Faber, 2008).

Paulin, Tom, *Thomas Hardy: The Poetry of Perception*, second edition (Basingstoke: Macmillan, 1986).

Peltason, Timothy, *Reading 'In Memoriam'* (Princeton: Princeton University Press, 1985).

Perry, Seamus, *Alfred Tennyson* (Tavistock: Northcote, 2005).

Poulet, Georges, *Studies in Human Time*, translated by Elliott Coleman (Baltimore, MD: Johns Hopkins Press, 1956).

Pound, Ezra, 'A Retrospect', in W. N. Herbert and Matthew Hollis (eds), *Strong Words: Modern Poets on Modern Poetry* (Tarset: Bloodaxe, 2000).

Prynne, 'Jeremy Prynne lectures on *Maximus* IV, V, VI', part 1, transcribed by Tom McGauley and published in *Iron* (October 1971); reprinted in *Minutes of the Charles Olson Society*, no. 28 (April 1999), accessed on 21 August 2008 at http://charlesolson.ca/files/Prynnelecture1.htm.

—— 'Jeremy Prynne lectures on *Maximus* IV, V, VI', part 2, transcribed by Tom McGauley and published in *Iron* (October 1971); reprinted in *Minutes of the Charles Olson Society*, no. 28 (April 1999), accessed on 21 August 2008 at http://charlesolson.ca/files/Prynnelecture2.htm.

—— 'From a Letter to Douglas Oliver', in *Grosseteste Review*, 1973, vol. 6(1–4).

—— 'China Figures', in *New Songs from a Jade Terrace: An Anthology of Early Chinese Love Poetry*, translated with annotations and an introduction by Anne Birrell (London: Penguin, 1986).

—— *Poems*, second, enlarged edition (Fremantle, WA: Fremantle Arts Centre Press, Tarset (Northumbria, UK): Bloodaxe Books, 2005).

—— *Field Notes: 'The Solitary Reaper' and Others* (Cambridge: 2007).

—— 'Response to *Futures* by Ken Edwards', in *Golden Handcuffs Review*, 2007–2008, vol. 1(9). Accessed on 15 August 2008, at http://www.goldenhandcuffsreview.com/gh9content/13.html.

Ramazani, Jahan, *Yeats and the Poetry of Death: Elegy, Self-Elegy, and the Sublime* (New Haven, CT: Yale University Press, 1990).

—— *Poetry of Mourning: The Modern Elegy from Hardy to Heaney* (Chicago and London: University of Chicago Press, 1994).

—— 'Is Yeats a Postcolonial Poet?' in David Pierce (ed.), *W. B. Yeats. Critical Assessments: Volume IV, Assessments: 1980–2000* (Mountfield: Helm Information, 2000).

Rees-Jones, Deryn, *Consorting with Angels: Essays on Modern Women Poets* (Tarset: Bloodaxe, 2005).

Reeve, N. H., and Richard Kerridge, *Nearly Too Much: The Poetry of J. H. Prynne* (Liverpool: Liverpool University Press, 1995).

Richards, I. A., *The Philosophy of Rhetoric* (Oxford: Oxford University Press, 1965 (1936)).

Ricks, Christopher, *T. S. Eliot and Prejudice* (Berkeley: University of California Press, 1988).

—— Editorial comments in *Tennyson: A Selected Edition*, edited by Christopher Ricks (Harlow: Longman, 1989 (1969)).

—— 'Growing Up: Review of *Death of a Naturalist*', in Michael Allen (ed.), *New Casebooks: Seamus Heaney* (Basingstoke: Macmillan, 1997).

Ricoeur, Paul, *Memory, History, Forgetting*, translated by Kathleen Blamey and David Pellauer (Chicago: University of Chicago Press, 2004).

Rilke, Rainer Maria, *Selected Poems*, translated by A. E. Fleming (New York: Methuen, 1986).

Rimbaud, Arthur, *Complete Works*, translated by Paul Schmidt (London: Picador, 1988).

Rosenthal, M. L., and Sally M. Gall, *The Modern Poetic Sequence: The Genius of Modern Poetry* (New York and Oxford: Oxford University Press, 1983).

Rossetti, Christina, *The Complete Poems*, with text by R. W. Crump, notes and introduction by Betty S. Flowers (London: Penguin, 2001).

Rylance, Rick, 'Twisting: Memory from Eliot to Eliot', in Matthew Campbell, Jacqueline M. Labbe, and Sally Shuttleworth (eds), *Memory and Memorials, 1789–1914: Literary and Cultural Perspectives* (London: Routledge, 2000).

Sacks, Peter M., *The English Elegy: Studies in the Genre from Spenser to Yeats* (Baltimore, MD: Johns Hopkins University Press, 1985).

Shusterman, Richard, *T. S. Eliot and the Philosophy of Criticism* (London: Duckworth, 1988).

Simpson, Roger, *Camelot Regained: The Arthurian Revival and Tennyson, 1800–1849* (Cambridge: D. S. Brewer, 1990).

Sontag, Susan, *On Photography* (London: Penguin, 1979).

Southam, B. C., *A Guide to the Selected Poems of T. S. Eliot* (San Diego: Harcourt Brace & Company, 1996 (1968)).

Stallworthy, Jon, *Vision and Revision in Yeats' 'Last Poems'* (Oxford: Clarendon Press, 1969).

Stead, C. K., *The New Poetic: Yeats to Eliot* (Harmondsworth: Penguin, 1964).

Svarny, Erik, *'The Men of 1914': T. S. Eliot and Early Modernism* (Milton Keynes and Philadelphia: Open University Press, 1988).

Sweeney, Matthew, 'A Haunting He Will Go', in *The Observer*, 15 April 2001.

Tennyson, Lord Alfred, *Tennyson: A Selected Edition*, edited by Christopher Ricks (Harlow: Longman, 1989 (1969)).

—— *In Memoriam*, edited by Susan Shatto and Marion Shaw (Oxford: Clarendon Press, 1982).

—— *Idylls of the King*, edited by J. M. Gray (London: Penguin, 1983).

Tennyson, Hallam T., *Alfred Lord Tennyson: A Memoir by His Son*, two volumes (Bridgewater: Baker & Taylor, 1989).

Terdiman, Richard, *Present Past: Modernity and the Memory Crisis* (Ithaca, NY, and London: Cornell University Press, 1993).

Thompson, Roger, 'Emerson, Divinity, and Rhetoric in Transcendentalist Nature Writing and Twentieth-Century Ecopoetry', in J. Scott Bryson (ed.), *Ecopoetry: A Critical Introduction* (Salt Lake City: University of Utah Press, 2002).

Tomalin, Claire, *Thomas Hardy: The Time-Torn Man* (London: Viking, 2006).

Vendler, Helen, 'Technique in the Earlier Poems of Yeats', 9–10, in *Yeats Annual*, 1991, no. 8.

—— *The Breaking of Style: Hopkins, Heaney, Graham* (Cambridge, MA: Harvard University Press, 1995).

—— *Seamus Heaney* (London: Fontana Press, 1998).

Villar-Argáiz, Pilar, 'Recording the Unpoetic: Eavan Boland's Silences', in *Irish University Review*, 2007, vol. 37(2).

Wills, Clair, *Improprieties: Politics and Sexuality in Northern Irish Poetry* (Oxford: Clarendon Press, 1993).

Wilson, A. N., *The Victorians* (London: Hutchinson, 2002).

Wolff, Joachim, *Rilke's Grabschrift* (Heidelberg: Lothar Stiem Verlag, 1983).

Wolfreys, Julian, *Victorian Hauntings: Spectrality, Gothic, the Uncanny and Literature* (Basingstoke: Palgrave Macmillan, 2002).

Wordsworth, William, *The Poems*, volume I, edited by John O. Hayden (Harmondsworth: Penguin, 1977).

—— *The Prelude: The Four Texts (1798, 1799, 1805, 1850)*, edited by Jonathan Wordsworth (London: Penguin, 1995).

Yeats, William Butler, *Memoirs*, edited by Denis Donoghue (New York: Macmillan, 1972).

—— *A Vision* (London: Papermac, 1981 (1937)).

—— *Mythologies* (London: Papermac, 1989 (1959)).

—— *Autobiographies*, edited by William H. O'Donnell and Douglas N. Archibald (New York: Scribner, 1999 (1965)).

—— *The Poems*, edited by Daniel Albright (London: J. M. Dent, 1990).

—— *Later Essays*, edited by William H. O'Donnell, with assistance from Elizabeth Bermann Loizeaux (New York: Scribner, 1994).

—— *The Plays*, edited by David R. Clark and Rosalind E. Clark (New York: Scribner, 2002).

Zietlow, Paul, *Moments of Vision: The Poetry of Thomas Hardy* (Cambridge, MA: Harvard University Press, 1974).

Index

Abraham, Nicholas, 119
Adams, Henry, 115
aestheticism, 41, 135, 140
Alvarez. A., 135
Anselm of Canterbury, 181
Ariès, Philippe, 209 n. 53
Aristotle, 40, 76, 105, 138, 139,
    209 n. 29
    On Memory and Reminiscence, 52
Arkins, Brian, 210 n. 68
Armstrong, Isobel, 33
Armstrong, Tim, 77, 208 n. 11,
    209 n. 31
Arnold, Matthew, 104
    Arnoldian touchstone, 45
Auden, W. H., 36, 135, 168
Augustine, Saint, 3, 168
Austin, Linda M., 51–2, 59, 96,
    205 n. 31
autonomy
    aesthetic, 34–5, 163–4
    of literature, 10, 49, 118, 137, 201
    of self, 17

Bachelard, Gaston, 214 n. 50
Barthes, Roland, 125, 190
Bate, Jonathan, 184–5, 187, 189,
    194, 195
Batten, Guinn, 156–7, 158, 159
Battle, Mary, 95
Baudelaire, Charles, 24, 98
Becket, Saint Thomas, 103
Beer, Gillian, 82–3
Benjamin, Walter, 43, 216 n. 115
Bergson, Henri, 5, 107–8, 213 n. 20
Bishop, Elizabeth, 193
Black Mountain poets, 176–7
Blanchot, Maurice, 42, 195
Bloom, Harold, 10, 23
Boland, Eavan, 7, 149–66, 192–3, 197,
    200–1
    'The Achill Woman,' 161

'Anna Liffey,' 162, 165
'The Art of Grief,' 160–1
'Distances,' 163
Domestic Violence, 165
'Falling Asleep to the Sound of
    Rain,' 165
'A False Spring,' 159–60
In a Time of Violence, 162
'Inheritance,' 165
'Is it It Still the Same,' 166
The Lost Land, 157
'The Making of an Irish
    Goddess,' 164
'Monotony,' 162
Object Lessons, 150–7, 163, 164, 197
'An Old Steel Engraving,' 158–9
'Outside History' (poem), 164–5
'Outside History' (sequence),
    158–60, 164–5, 219 n. 14
'The Pomegranate,' 164, 219 n. 20
'Suburban Woman,' 162
'That the Science of Cartography is
    Is Limited,' 192–3
'Unheroic,' 162
'We Are Always Too Late,' 160
'What We Lost,' 161
'White Hawthorn in the West of
    Ireland,' 161
Borges, Jorge Luis, 12
Bradley, F. H., 107, 110–11
Brecht, Bertolt, 135
Bromwich, David, 11, 20, 205 n. 26
Brown, Terence, 211 n. 75
Browning, Elizabeth Barrett, 24–5, 32
Browning, Robert, 98
Bruns, Gerald L., 106
Bryson, J. Scott, 188

Campbell, Matthew, 81
canon, 1–2, 23, 105–7, 150–1, 155, 197
    see also memory, aesthetic; tradition
Carlyle, Thomas, 67

235

everyday, the, 1, 44, 47, 77, 82, 127,
131, 137, 140, 153, 161,
164, 194

feminism, 7, 10, 26, 149, 150–1,
156–9, 161, 164, 197, 201
Ferrar, Nicholas, 121
fetishism, 10, 44, 47, 49
Fichte, Johann Gottlieb, 13
figurative language, 3–4, 6, 9, 17–20,
72, 86, 89, 99, 102–10, 115,
125–6, 148, 151–5, 165, 169–70,
175, 176, 177, 190, 192, 201–2
allegory, 35, 53, 61, 66, 159, 187
ambivalence of, 17–18, 67
catachresis, 72
cognitive theories of, 203 n. 5
connotation, 71, 73, 80, 179
displacement, 51–2, 73, 77, 81,
90–1, 94, 97, 207–8 n. 6
emblem, 7, 54–5, 57, 77, 94, 152–4,
157, 159–60, 165, 210 n. 56,
218 n. 5
instability of, 172
and intersection of time and
space, 5
meta-figures, 5, 177
metaphor, 3–5, 11, 13, 16, 19, 34,
71, 118, 120, 171–2,
176–7, 195
metonymy, 3, 4, 7, 26, 57, 91, 176,
178, 200, 202, 207–8 n. 6,
210 n. 67
symbol, 5, 89, 94, 125, 152
synecdoche, 90, 90–1
finitude, 6, 7, 10, 23, 40, 82–3, 87,
164–5, 195, 200
see also memory, and death
Flowers, Betty S., 28
forgetting, 1, 21–2, 34, 45–6, 54,
59–60, 64–5, 83, 98, 133–4, 140,
150–1, 169, 185
form, poetic, 118, 149
allusion, 81, 95, 188, 127, 176
experimental use of, 166–7
line, 177–83, 191–2
rebellion against traditional
uses of, 173
rhyme, 69–73, 80

rhythm, 25–7, 160
sequences, structure of, 44–5, 67–8,
142, 160–1, 192–3
stanza, 47–9, 179–82
style, 138
technique, 122, 139–40
typography, 167, 178
see also figurative language;
repetition
Foster, R. F., 211 n. 81
Frawley, Oona, 96, 162, 210 n. 66
French Revolution, 13, 20
Freud, Sigmund, 19, 37, 75, 101,
173–4, 207–8 n. 6
Friedman, Michael H., 17
Friedrich, Hugo, 137
Frost, Robert, 144, 200, 218 n. 7
Fussell, Paul, 209 n. 48
future, the, 1, 2, 8, 9, 16–17, 22–3, 24,
26–8, 67, 90, 97, 129, 134, 150,
168–70, 174–5, 183, 184, 197,
198, 200
openness of, 7, 27, 150, 169–70,
174–5, 183, 200
utopianism, 65–6, 168, 219 n. 29

Gadamer, Hans-Georg, 221 n. 64
Gall, Sally M., 68, 217 n. 126
Gander, Forrest, 220 n. 43
Gardner, Helen, 118, 122
Geoffrey of Monmouth, 61
George, Stefan, 33
Gilbert, Sandra M., 32
Gilsenan Nordin, Irene, 217 n. 119
Girard, René, 208 n. 10
Gonne, Maud, 94–6, 211 n. 75
Gordon, Lyndall, 122, 123
Gore-Booth, Constance, *see*
Markiewicz, Countess
Gore-Booth, Eva, 93
Gore-Booth, Sir Robert, 93
Gray, Thomas, 27
Gregory, Lady Augusta, 89, 93,
210 n. 65
Griffiths, Eric, 27
Gubar, Susan, 32
Guys, Constantin, 98

Hagen, Patricia L., 164